STUDY GUIDE FOR

The Last Dance

Encountering Death and Dying

SIXTH EDITION

Lynne Ann DeSpelder
Albert Lee Strickland

Boston   Burr Ridge, IL   Dubuque, IA   Madison, WI   New York
San Francisco   St. Louis   Bangkok   Bogotá   Caracas   Kuala Lumpur
Lisbon   London   Madrid   Mexico City   Milan   Montreal   New Delhi
Santiago   Seoul   Singapore   Sydney   Taipei   Toronto

McGraw-Hill Higher Education

*A Division of The **McGraw-Hill** Companies*

1 2 3 4 5 6 7 8 9 0 QPD / QPD 0 9 8 7 6 5 4 3 2 1

ISBN: 0-7674-2980-X

www.mhhe.com

Contents

CHAPTER 2

CHAPTER 3

CHAPTER 4

Health Care Systems: Patients, Staff, and Institutions   75

CHAPTER 5

Facing Death: Living with Life-Threatening Illness   89

CHAPTER 6

Medical Ethics: Dying in a Technological Age   105

CHAPTER 7

CHAPTER 8

CHAPTER 9

CHAPTER 12

Suicide

CHAPTER 13

Risks of Death in the Modern World

CHAPTER 14

Beyond Death/After Life

CHAPTER 15

PART III: RESOURCES FOR LEARNING AND WRITING ABOUT DEATH AND DYING

PART IV: APPENDIX

P R E F A C E

Using Your Study Guide

We have designed this Study Guide to help you achieve two important goals in learning about death and dying. First, it will make it easier for you to study, review, and comprehend the material from the sixth edition of *The Last Dance: Encountering Death and Dying*. Although it is true that each of us already has knowledge about death, dying, and bereavement, the amount of new information—as well as the number of terms and ideas presented in your class and textbook—may surprise you. Using this Study Guide will help you increase your success in learning, retaining, and integrating essential information.

Second, and of equal importance, this Study Guide will give you opportunities to think about death, dying, and bereavement in the context of your own life. You will find areas where theory, research, and practice apply to your experiences. Death studies is not just about death, dying, and bereavement. It is a subject that draws upon your psychological, cultural, and ethical makeup. Perhaps more that any other course that you will take in college, the ideas you will be learning about, the objective information that is presented, and the applications that are possible have the potential to affect your behavior and personal development. One student summed it up by saying: "We all will survive loss and one day each of us will be dead. This course tells me about how I want to live in the face of death."

To begin with, Part I, the **Introduction**, prepares you to think about your attitudes and values, as well as the resources you will draw upon to gain information about death studies. The section titled **Getting Acquainted with Your Text: A Self-Guided Tour** gives you an overview of *The Last Dance* and suggests ways to use each feature, sometimes directing you to perform a specific activity and then report on the results. The next section of the Introduction, **Death and Dying on the Web: Evaluating and Using Internet Resources**, suggests ways to understand the materials you find on the Internet, followed by an activity that applies what you have learned. The third section of the Introduction, **Examining Your Attitudes and Experiences**, gives you information and activities (marked with the symbol ➠) for examining your past experiences and attitudes, including further directions for applying the learnings from these exercises to help you write an essay. The fourth section of the Introduction, **Writing Your Own Deathography**, will lead you to reflect and learn more about your past experiences of loss through writing an autobiographical essay. Students say time and again that the information from this essay has provided relief, resolution, and understanding about current beliefs. We hope these explorations will help you as well.

Part II of your Study Guide contains materials for each of the fifteen chapters in *The Last Dance*. Each chapter begins with a narrative **Chapter Summary**. Read this summary *before* you begin reading the chapter in the text. It will help you get an idea of the focus of the chapter. Following the summary are the **Objectives**. You will likely find this listing of the concepts included in the chapter beneficial to read before the text chapter. **Key Terms and Concepts** are also listed. As you read the text, you will find many of these terms printed in italic the first time they are mentioned. Note the definitions. While some texts provide glossaries with terms defined, we have found that you are more likely to remember a term if you have seen the definition in context. Keep your list of key terms with you while you are reading a chapter in the text. Students find it helpful to check off each term in the Study Guide as they discover it in the text. Make notes in the margins of the Study Guide to remind you of any terms that seem difficult at first. The next section is titled **Questions for Guided Study and Review**. We suggest that you use these questions to reflect on the material you have read in the chapter and also as a guide for test review. Each chapter includes **Practice Test Questions** of multiple choice and true/false questions, as well as a matching question. Answers to the Practice Tests can be found in Part IV of this Study Guide. **Related Readings** give you additional resources and expand the information from Further Readings in the corresponding chapter of *The Last Dance*. In the Study Guide, readings are divided by topic; selections from *The Path Ahead: Readings in Death and Dying* are also included (indicated by the symbol 📖). This listing of resources is followed by a list of the **Major Points in This Chapter**. Use this section of your Study Guide to get a quick overview of the material in the chapter. You might want to look this section over both before and after reading the chapter in your text. **Observations and Reflections** gives you an opportunity to think about how this chapter's material might influence your attitudes and experiences. Finally, you will find **Activities** (marked with the symbol ⟶) designed to make the class content more relevant and meaningful. Some activities ask you to observe or evaluate information; others include exercises to analyze how the information in the chapter relates to your experiences, behavior, and opinions. Computer activities are indicated by the symbol 🖥.

Part III is composed of additional resources for your study of death, dying, and bereavement. Learning and writing about topics in death studies is aided by these tools. For example, take a look at the listing of **Organizations and Internet Resources**. There you will find that many of the listings provide information in a specific topic area.

Part IV, the Appendix, contains answers to the Practice Test Questions included in each chapter.

Every student in this course has a unique background and unique feelings about death, dying, and bereavement. We believe that your efforts in completing the activities in this Study Guide will give you new insights and, more importantly, encourage you to re-examine your attitudes and behaviors, as well as provide an understanding of the place of death in your life.

Over the years, many students and teachers have made helpful suggestions about the activities and information most useful for understanding death, dying, and bereavement. We thank all of those who have contributed to the resources included in this Study Guide.

L. A. D.

A. L. S.

⫸ *Getting Acquainted with Your Text: A Self-Guided Tour*

Over the next few months, you will be spending considerable time with the sixth edition of *The Last Dance: Encountering Death and Dying* and this Study Guide. Along with lectures, discussions, and other learning activities, your textbook will be an important tool. We have given a great deal of thought to how the various elements of this edition of *The Last Dance* fit together. Together, these elements form a whole that aims to further your understanding of death, dying, and bereavement.

The following questions provide you with a self-guided tour through your textbook. Write your responses to the following questions in the spaces provided. Your responses should be brief; a sentence or two will help you remember your full answers. (Note that this is an activity marked with the symbol ⫸ to alert you to the exercise.)

1. Take a few minutes to browse through *The Last Dance* to get a feel for it. What is your first impression of the book?

   _____

   _____

   _____

2. Read through the Table of Contents. These pages give you an overview of the material in the textbook. What is the title of the chapter that looks the most interesting to you?

   _____

   _____

   _____

- In which chapters do you have extensive information?

_____

_____

_____

- In which chapters would you like to have more information?

_____

_____

_____

3. Read the Preface. What purposes of the book are most interesting to you? Briefly list them.

_____

_____

_____

4. Read the Prologue. What is the message about death in this story by David Gordon?

_____

_____

_____

5. Each chapter begins with a photograph and throughout the chapter, there are additional photos, as well as boxed materials, tables, figures, and usually a cartoon. Each chapter concludes with a list of Further Readings, which are organized by topic in this Study Guide, along with readings from *The Path Ahead: Readings in Death and Dying*, eds. Lynne Ann DeSpelder and Albert Lee Strickland (Mountain View, C.A.: Mayfield, 1995). Skim through these elements in Chapter 1 of the textbook. List some of the most interesting elements and include the page numbers.

_____

_____

_____

6. In your textbook, information that relates to the numbered endnotes has been placed at the back of the book, beginning on page 559. This style of citation allows us to provide additional information that expands upon the basic source data associated with the note. For example, look in the endnotes for the full text of note 2 on page 42. What additional information did you find?

_____

_____

_____

7. Key terms are italicized in the text and defined in the context of the material you are reading. Look on page 10 of the text and write a brief definition of the term *epidemiologic transition*.

_____

_____

_____

Some students find it useful to prepare flash cards for Key Terms and Concepts to familiarize themselves with the language of death studies.

8. In your tour of the text, look at the end of a chapter for further readings. Which resource looks the most interesting to you?

_____

_____

_____

Check the same chapter in this Study Guide to see if the Related Readings section contains an additional resource that looks interesting. List it here.

_____

_____

_____

9. In your tour of *The Last Dance,* look through the photographs for each chapter. Don't read the captions just yet. Just pay attention to the images. As you think about how your own life history may relate to the photographs, respond to the following questions.

- Which images are the most provocative?

_____

_____

_____

- What thoughts and feelings are provoked?

_____

_____

_____

10. We have created a detailed index to help you find the information you are looking for in *The Last Dance.* Look up two or three topics in the index. Write down the topics and the page numbers.

_____

_____

_____

Turn to those pages in the text. Is the information where it should be? How does it help you to see it in the context of a chapter?

_____

_____

_____

11. Evaluate your tour of *The Last Dance.* Did we leave anything out that you think would be good for students to know before they start reading the book?

_____

_____

_____

Death and Dying on the Web: Evaluating and Using Internet Resources

While you are using this Study Guide, there will be opportunities for learning activities using the Internet. To provide better understanding of the web sites you access, here you will find a discussion of criteria for evaluating an Internet site, as well as an activity giving you the opportunity to evaluate several sites. When working with Internet-based research later in this Study Guide, you can refer back to this information.

Evaluating Internet Information

The Internet offers students, teachers, and researchers opportunities to gather information from around the world. It is important to recognize, however, that the Internet is unregulated. Thus, many Internet sites lack the "safety net" of peer review and the critical eye of a competent editor. To compensate for the scarcity of filters between you and the information you find on the Internet, you must carefully evaluate the quality of every Internet resource you use. Thinking critically about such information is vital in the absence of the peer-review process. Since excellent resources reside alongside dubious ones, it is necessary to develop skills to evaluate what you find. There are more issues concerning evaluating quality with respect to Internet sites than with traditional print resources. Along with the need to evaluate the objectivity and accuracy of the information available on the Internet, the technology itself introduces additional criteria that must be evaluated.[1] Keep the following questions in mind.

1. Can you access the site regularly? Is it well organized and easy to navigate?

2. Do the pages load quickly?

3. Do the links work, taking you to relevant material?

4. Can you print content easily and quickly?

5. Are the graphics on the site informative without being flashy or overpowering?

6. If the site has received awards, are they for design or for content? Can you confirm claims of award-winning quality?

Resources devoted to gathering information and developing skills for thinking critically about information are available online.[2] One of the best sites, developed by librarians Jan Alexander and Marsha Tate, includes criteria for evaluation, along with examples of information posted on the Internet designed to demonstrate principles of critical thinking.[3]

What follows is a brief discussion of some of the major criteria by which you can and should evaluate information presented on the Internet.[4]

AUTHORSHIP

Who is the author of the document or site? Is the author well known in the field? Is there a biography of the author stating his or her credentials? Is he or she even identified? Are there other Internet publications by this author that you trust? Does the author support his or her statements with other published work? Can you contact the author to request further information? Is the author's e-mail link "live" (that is, active), and does he or she respond to your questions?

PUBLISHING BODY

Can you tell if this is a personal home page established and maintained by the author? Is the name of any organization given on the page or in the document, or is a link to a sponsoring organization provided? Is this a recognized and respected organization in the field? Is it an appropriate organization for your topic? Are you able to determine what the relationship is between the author and the publishing body—assuming, of course, that it is not self-published?

POINT OF VIEW OR BIAS

Does the organization under which the author is publishing have a specific bias or stake in the issue? You might find clues in a web site's mission statement or purpose. Is this a corporate web site selling products? Is the information from the web site of an organization that has a political or philosophical agenda? Keep in mind the definition of bias and how such thinking might influence the form and content of the web page documents and links.

REFERRAL TO AND KNOWLEDGE OF THE LITERATURE

Does the document include a bibliography? Does the author appropriately reference the work of others, including citations and documentation? Does the author demonstrate knowledge of the field that is generally consistent with the theories, schools, and viewpoints prevalent within the field? Does the author discuss the limitations of his or her perspective, approach, and technique? If the subject is controversial, does the author acknowledge this fact?

ACCURACY OR VERIFIABILITY OF DETAILS

In the case of a research report, are the research methods described as well as the findings? Are the methods appropriate to the topic? Are traditional print resources cited in a bibliography? Are links provided to other Internet-based documents? Can all of these be checked for accuracy?

CURRENCY

Are dates provided for material on the page? Is the page itself dated? Does it include information on the most recent update? (To see the latest information about the date of latest revision, highlight the URL in the location bar and, on the drop-down menu, click "View Info," or click on view and select "Page Source.") If the page is updated on a regular basis, is there any indication of when this occurs? Is a copyright date included?

Understanding and Decoding URLs

Uniform Resource Locators (URLs) are the Internet addresses that you see on the location bars at the top or bottom of your web browser. URLs provide a standard format for the transmission and reception of a wide variety of information types. This is how they are constructed:

transfer protocol://servername.domain/directory/
subdirectory/filename.filetype

Every URL must have at least the first two elements shown above (the information directly before and after the //). Here is an example:

http://www.growthhouse.org/books/despeld.htm

In this example, "http" is the transfer protocol, "www.growthhouse" is the server name, and "org" is the domain. The directory is "books," the subdirectory is "despeld," and the file type is "htm."

Understanding the different elements that make up a URL will help you know what to expect before you click on a link. You will also be able to see what kind of organization or institution is providing the information.

As of the summer of 2001, the following classes of Internet domains are in use.

.edu: An educational institution (for example, msu.edu [Michigan State University, East Lansing, Michigan]).

.org: An organization that is typically part of the non-profit sector (for example, adec.org [Association for Death Education and Counseling]).

.com: A commercial enterprise, including commercial online services (for example, aol.com [America Online]).

.net: An Internet Service Provider (ISP); that is, an individual or group that provides access to the Internet (for example, earthlink.net).

.gov: A governmental body (for example, loc.gov [Library of Congress, Washington, D.C.]).

Notes

1. David R. Campbell and Mary V. Campbell, *The Student's Guide to Doing Research on the Internet* (Reading, Mass.: Addison-Wesley, 1995); John M. Grohol, *Insider's Guide to Mental Health Resources Online* (New York: Guilford Press, 1997); and Bernard Robin, Elissa Keeler and Robert Miller, *Educator's Guide to the Web* (New York: MIS Press, 1997), pp. 217-231.

2. Jan Alexander and Marsha Tate, "The Web as a Research Tool: Evaluation Techniques," 8 April 1998, <http://www.science.widener.edu/~withers/evalout.htm> (10 June 1998); Esther Grassian, "Thinking Critically about World Wide Web Resources," 5 May 1998, <http://www.library.ucla.edu/libraries/college/help/critical/index.htm> (26 April 2001); Robert Harris, "Evaluating Internet Research Sources," 17 November 1997, <http://www.virtualsalt.com/evalu8it.htm> (26 April 2001); Elizabeth E. Kirk, "Evaluating Information Found on the Internet," 5 March 1998, <http:// milton.mse.jhu.edu:8001 /research/education/net.htm> (10 June 1998); Ann Scholz, "Evaluating World Wide Web Information," 23 May 1996, <http://thorplus.lib.purdue.edu/library_info/instruction/gs175 /3gs175/evaluation.htm> (10 June 1998); and Hope N. Tillman, "Evaluating Quality on the Net," 30 May 2000, <http:// www.hopetillman.com/findqual.html> (26 April 2001).

3. Jan Alexander and Marsha Tate, "Evaluating Web Pages: Links to Examples of Various Concepts," 15 December 1999, <http://www2.widener.edu/Wolfgram-Memorial-Library/webevaulation/examples.htm> (26 April 2000).

4. Kathleen R. Gilbert, "Evaluating Internet Resources", 17 December 1997, <http://www.indiana.edu /~hperf656/spring98/evaluate.html> (26 April 2001).

🖥 *Evaluating Internet Resources*

Directions   *Read the section entitled "Evaluating and Using Internet Resources." For each of the web sites listed below, answer the questions about information and quality. Include any additional notes about the usefulness of each site.*

Bereavement Care Centre   <http://www.bereavementcare.com.au>

1. What is the URL? _____

2. What is the country of origin? _____

3. Can you access the site regularly? _____

4. Is it well organized and easy to navigate? _____

   _____

5. Do the links work? _____

6. Do they help you access relevant material? _____

   _____

7. Can you print content easily and quickly? _____

8. Are graphics informative without being flashy or overpowering? _____

9. Are advertisements embedded in the site? _____

10. Has the site received awards for design or content? _____

    _____

11. Can you authenticate these claims? _____

12. Who is(are) the author(s)? _____

    _____

13. Who is the publishing body? _____

    _____

14. Is a point of view or bias implied or specifically stated? If so, what is it?

    _____

15. Do the documents posted include authorship, bibliographies and information that are generally consistent with theories, schools and viewpoints within the field? Give examples. ____

    _____

    _____

16. What are the recent dates on information posted to the web site? _____

17. Describe the most interesting feature of this site. _____

    _____

    _____

    _____

    _____

    _____

    _____

The Centre for Grief Education   <http://www.grief.org.au>

1. What is the URL? _____

2. What is the country of origin? _____

3. Can you access the site regularly? _____

4. Is it well organized and easy to navigate? _____

    _____

    _____

5. Do the links work? _____

6. Do they help you access relevant material? _____

    _____

7. Can you print content easily and quickly? _____

8. Are graphics informative without being flashy or overpowering? _____

9. Are advertisements embedded in the site? _____

10. Has the site received awards for design or content? _____

_____

11. Can you authenticate these claims? _____

12. Who is(are) the author(s)? _____

_____

13. Who is the publishing body? _____

_____

14. Is a point of view or bias implied or specifically stated? If so, what is it? _____

_____

15. Do the documents posted include authorship, bibliographies and information that are generally consistent with theories, schools and viewpoints within the field? Give examples.

_____

_____

_____

16. What are the recent dates on information posted to the web site? _____

17. Describe the most interesting feature of this site.

_____

_____

_____

_____

_____

Site of your choice   Select a death, dying, or bereavement site that interests you and answer the following questions.

1. What is the URL? _____

2. What is the country of origin? _____

3. Can you access the site regularly? _____

4. Is it well organized and easy to navigate? _____

   _____

5. Do the links work? _____

6. Do they help you access relevant material? _____

   _____

7. Can you print content easily and quickly? _____

8. Are graphics informative without being flashy or overpowering? _____

9. Are advertisements embedded in the site? _____

10. Has the site received awards for design or content? _____

    _____

11. Can you authenticate these claims? _____

12. Who is(are) the author(s)? _____

    _____

13. Who is the publishing body? _____

    _____

14. Is a point of view or bias implied or specifically stated? If so, what is it? _____

    _____

15. Do the documents posted include authorship, bibliographies and information that are generally consistent with theories, schools and viewpoints within the field? Give examples. ____

_____

_____

16. What are the recent dates on information posted to the web site? _____

17. Describe the most interesting feature of this site.

_____

_____

_____

_____

_____

_____

Use the space provided below and on the following page to explain what you have learned about Internet research as a result of visiting and evaluating these three sites. Include notes about your ability to evaluate information found on the Internet. Review Jan Alexander and Marsha Tate's site: "Evaluating Web Pages: Links to Examples of Various Concepts," <http://www2.widener.edu/ Wolfgram-Memorial-Library/web evaluation/examples.htm>.

Examining Your Attitudes and Experiences

Though the goals and objectives of each death, dying, and bereavement course differ, one theme uniting all of them is the application of the information and concepts presented in class to your attitudes, beliefs, values, and behavior.

A variety of challenges may arise when you begin to examine your attitudes and experiences. For instance, you may have only incomplete memories of previous loss experiences. We suggest that you contact those adults who might be willing and able to fill in the gaps in your knowledge. Uncomfortable and sometimes painful feelings may result from reading, writing, and talking about certain experiences, perhaps for the first time. Students have reported that being in an environment where they are "not the only ones" exploring past experiences is helpful. Permission to "pass" in class discussions is an important safety valve. Give yourself that freedom. You can say something like, "I'd prefer not to get into that right now." Decisions about what you choose to address publicly during the course and in the following activities are yours. We suggest that you both prepare yourself to take some risks and protect yourself when you are feeling vulnerable.

Over the years of teaching about death, dying, and bereavement, we have found that exploring students' attitudes and subsequently writing a "Deathography" to be a valuable experience for many students. This essay will lead you to reflect on past experiences with loss.

The three activities that follow provide you with basic information about yourself. Begin with a survey of your attitudes. Continue by examining childhood losses. And finish with an overview of losses in your life to the present time. Completing these three activities will also give you the information needed for your "Deathography" essay, which is discussed more fully in the next section of this Introduction.

Time and again, students have been thankful for the opportunity to look closely at their attitudes and experiences and see, on paper, the various influences on their behavior. Insights about current beliefs and information about possible changes for the future are greatly valued.

⇒ *Questionnaire: You and Death*

Directions   *Begin by completing the ⇒ **Questionnaire: You and Death** located on the next several pages. Notice that a question may have several different answers, possibly even conflicting ones. Check all that apply. If your response is not listed, write it in. Use this activity to explore your attitudes and experiences. After you have completed the questionnaire, go back through it and code the questions using the following categories:*

PE	=	Answers based on personal experience
S	=	Answers about which you feel strongly
D	=	Question is difficult to answer
A	=	Answers about which you feel ambiguous
SB	=	Answers based on religious or spiritual beliefs

You may find that some questions seem to have no codes that you can apply to them. Other questions may have all five. This analysis will give you information about your experiences with particular areas of death studies. Finish this exercise by making notes about what you learned in the space below.

_____

_____

_____

_____

_____

_____

_____

_____

_____

_____

_____

➡ *Questionnaire: You and Death*

Answer the following questions by checking all the responses that apply. You may have more than one answer, or your answers may conflict. If you have a response that is not listed, write it in.

1. Who died in your first personal involvement with death?
a. Grandparent or great-grandparent
b. Parent
c. Brother or sister
d. Other family member
e. Friend or acquaintance
f. Stranger
g. Public figure
h. Animal

2. To the best of your memory, at what age were you first aware of death?
a. Under three
b. Three to five
c. Five to ten
d. Ten or older

3. When you were a child, how was death talked about in your family?
a. Openly
b. With some sense of discomfort
c. Only when necessary and then with an attempt to exclude the children
d. As though it were a taboo subject
e. Never recall any discussion

4. Which of the following best describes your childhood conceptions of death?
a. Heaven and hell concept
b. After-life
c. Death as sleep
d. Cessation of all physical and mental activity
e. Mysterious and unknowable
f. Something other than the above
g. No conception
h. Can't remember

5. Which of the following most influenced your present attitudes toward death?
a. Death of someone close
b. Specific reading
c. Religious upbringing
d. Introspection and meditation
e. Ritual (e.g., funerals)
f. TV, radio or motion pictures
g. Longevity of my family
h. My health or physical condition
i. Other (specify): _____

6. How much of a role has religion played in the development of your attitude toward death?
a. A very significant role
b. A rather significant role
c. Somewhat influential, but not a major role
d. A relatively minor role
e. No role at all

7. To what extent do you believe in a life after death?
a. Strongly believe in it
b. Tend to believe in it
c. Uncertain
d. Tend to doubt it
e. Convinced it does not exist

8. Regardless of your belief about life after death, what is your wish about it?
a. I strongly wish there were a life after death.
b. I am indifferent as to whether there is a life after death.
c. I definitely prefer that there not be a life after death.

9. To what extent do you believe in reincarnation?
a. Strongly believe it
b. Tend to believe it
c. Uncertain
d. Tend to doubt it
e. Convinced it cannot occur

10. How often do you think about your own death?
a. Very frequently (at least once a day)
b. Frequently
c. Occasionally
d. Rarely (no more than once a year)
e. Very rarely or never

11. If you could choose, when would you die?
a. In youth
b. In the middle prime of life
c. Just after the prime of life
d. In old age

12. When do you believe that, in fact, you will die?
a. In youth
b. In the middle prime of life
c. Just after the prime of life
d. In old age

13. Has there been a time in your life when you wanted to die?
a. Yes, mainly because of great physical pain.
b. Yes, mainly because of great emotional pain.
c. Yes, mainly to escape an intolerable social or interpersonal situation.
d. Yes, mainly because of great embarrassment.
e. Yes, for a reason other than above.
f. No.

14. What does death mean to you?
a. The end; the final process of life
b. The beginning of a life after death; a transition, a new beginning
c. A joining of the spirit with a universal cosmic consciousness
d. A kind of endless sleep; rest and peace
e. Termination of this life but with survival of the spirit
f. Don't know
g. Other (specify): _____

15. What aspect of your own death is the most distasteful to you?

a. I could no longer have any experience.

b. I am afraid of what might happen to my body after death.

c. I am uncertain as to what might happen to me if there is a life after death.

d. I could no longer provide for my family.

e. It would cause grief to my relatives and friends.

f. All my plans and projects would come to an end.

g. The process of dying might be painful.

h. Other (specify): _____

16. Based on your present feelings, what is the probability of your taking your own life in the near future?

a. Extremely high (I feel very much like killing myself)

b. Moderately high

c. Between high and low

d. Moderately low

e. Extremely low (very improbable that I would kill myself)

17. In your opinion, at what age are people most afraid of death?

a. Up to 12 years

b. Thirteen to 19 years

c. Twenty to 29 years

d. Thirty to 39 years

e. Forty to 49 years

f. Fifty to 59 years

g. Sixty to 69 years

h. Seventy years and over

18. What is your belief about the causes of most deaths?

a. Most deaths result directly from the conscious efforts of the person who dies.

b. Most deaths have strong components of conscious or unconscious participation by the persons who die (in their habits and use, misuse, nonuse, or abuse of drugs, alcohol, medicine, etc.).

c. Most deaths just happen; they are caused by events over which individuals have no control.

d. Other (specify): _____

19. To what extent do you believe that psychological factors can influence (or even cause) death?

a. I firmly believe that they can.

b. I tend to believe that they can.

c. I am undecided or don't know.

d. I doubt that they can.

20. When you think of your own death (or when circumstances make you realize your own mortality), how do you feel?

a. Fearful

b. Discouraged

c. Depressed

d. Purposeless

e. Resolved, in relation to life

f. Pleased, to be alive

g. Other (specify): _____

21. What is your present orientation to your own death?

a. Death-seeker

b. Death-hastener

c. Death-accepter

d. Death-welcomer

e. Death-postponer

f. Death-fearer

22. How often have you been in a situation in which you seriously thought you might die?

a. Many times

b. Several times

c. Once or twice

d. Never

23. To what extent are you interested in having your own death survive after your own death through your children, books, good works, etc.?

a. Very interested

b. Moderately interested

c. Somewhat interested

d. Not very interested

e. Totally uninterested

24. For whom or what might you be willing to sacrifice your life?

a. For a loved one

b. For an idea or a moral principle

c. In combat or a grave emergency where a life could be saved

d. Not for any reason

25. If you had a choice, what kind of death would you prefer?

a. Tragic, violent death

b. Sudden but not violent death

c. Quiet, dignified death

d. Death in line of duty

e. Death after a great achievement

f. Suicide

g. Homicidal victim

h. There is no "appropriate" kind

i. Other (specify): _____

26. If it were possible, would you want to know the exact date on which you are going to die?

a. Yes

b. No

27. If your physician knew that you had a terminal disease and a limited time to live, would you want him to tell you?

a. Yes

b. No

c. It would depend on the circumstances

28. If you were told that you had a terminal disease and a limited time to live, how would you want to spend your time until you died?

a. I would make a marked change in my life style and satisfy hedonistic needs, such as travel, sex, drugs, and other experiences.

b. I would become more withdrawn and spend my time reading, contemplating, or praying.

c. I would shift from my own needs to a concern for others, such as family and friends.

d. I would attempt to complete projects and tie up loose ends.
e. I would make little or no change in my life style.
f. I would try to do one very important thing.
g. I might consider committing suicide.
h. I would do none of these.

29. **How do you feel about having an autopsy done on your body?**
a. Approve
b. Don't care one way or the other
c. Disapprove
d. Strongly disapprove

30. **To what extent has the possibility of massive human destruction by nuclear war influenced your present attitudes toward death or life?**
a. Enormously
b. To a fairly large extent
c. Moderately
d. Somewhat
e. Very little
f. Not at all

31. **Which of the following has influenced your present attitudes toward your own death the most?**
a. Pollution of the environment
b. Domestic violence
c. Television
d. Wars
e. The possibility of nuclear war
f. Poverty
g. Existential philosophy
h. Changes in health conditions and mortality statistics
i. Other (specify): _____

32. **How often have you seriously contemplated committing suicide?**
a. Very often
b. Only once in a while
c. Very rarely
d. Never

33. **Have you ever actually attempted suicide?**
a. Yes, with an actual very high probability of death.
b. Yes, with an actual moderate probability of death.
c. Yes, with an actual low probability of death.
d. No.

34. **Whom have you known who has committed suicide?**
a. Member of immediate family
b. Other family member
c. Close friend
d. Acquaintance
e. No one
f. Other (specify): _____

35. **How do you estimate your lifetime probability of committing suicide?**
a. I plan to do it some day.
b. I hope that I do not, but I am afraid that I might.
c. In certain circumstances, I might very well do it.
d. I doubt that I would do it in any circumstances.
e. I am sure that I would never do it.

36. **Suppose that you were to commit suicide, what reason would most motivate you to do it?**
a. To get even or hurt someone
b. Fear of insanity
c. Physical illness or pain
d. Failure or disgrace
e. Loneliness or abandonment
f. Death or loss of a loved one
g. Family strife
h. Atomic war
i. Other (specify): _____

37. **Suppose you were to commit suicide, what method would you be most likely to use?**
a. Barbiturates or pills
b. Gunshot
c. Hanging
d. Drowning
e. Jumping
f. Cutting or stabbing
g. Carbon monoxide
h. Other (specify): _____

38. **Suppose you were ever to commit suicide, would you leave a suicide note?**
a. Yes
b. No

39. **To what extent do you believe that suicide should be prevented?**
a. In every case
b. In all but a few cases
c. In some cases, yes; in others, no
d. In no case; if a person wants to commit suicide, society has no right to stop him

40. **What efforts do you believe ought to be made to keep a seriously ill person alive?**
a. All possible efforts; transplantations, kidney dialysis, etc.
b. Efforts that are reasonable for that person's age, physical condition, mental condition, and pain.
c. After reasonable care has been given, a person ought to be permitted to die a natural death.
d. A senile person should not be kept alive by elaborate artificial means.

41. **If or when you are married, would you prefer to outlive your spouse?**
a. Yes; I would prefer to die second and outlive my spouse.
b. No; I would rather die first and have my spouse outlive me.
c. Undecided or don't know

42. **What is your primary reason for the answer that you gave for the question above?**
    a. To spare my spouse loneliness
    b. To avoid loneliness for myself
    c. To spare my spouse grief
    d. To avoid grief for myself
    e. Because the surviving spouse could cope better with grief or loneliness
    f. To live as long as possible
    g. None of the above
    h. Other (specify):_____

43. **How important do you believe mourning and grief ritual (such as wakes and funerals) are for the survivors?**
    a. Extremely important
    b. Somewhat important
    c. Undecided or don't know
    d. Not very important
    e. Not important at all

44. **If it were entirely up to you, how would you like to have your body disposed of after you have died?**
    a. Burial
    b. Cremation
    c. Donation to medical school or science
    d. I am indifferent

45. **Would you be willing to donate your heart for transplantation (after you die)?**
    a. Yes, to anyone
    b. Yes, but only to a relative or friend

    c. I have a strong feeling against it
    d. No

46. **What kind of a funeral would you prefer?**
    a. Formal, as large as possible
    b. Small, relatives and close friends only
    c. Whatever my survivors want
    d. None

47. **How do you feel about "lying in state" in an open casket at your funeral?**
    a. Approve
    b. Don't care one way or the other
    c. Disapprove
    d. Strongly disapprove

48. **What is your opinion about the costs of funerals in the U.S. today?**
    a. Very much overpriced
    b. No one has to pay for what he doesn't want
    c. In terms of costs and services rendered, prices are not unreasonable

49. **In your opinion, what would be a reasonable price for a funeral?**
    a. Under $500
    b. From $500 to $1500
    c. From $1500 to $3500
    d. From $3500 to $5000
    e. From $5000 to $6500
    f. More than $6500

50. **What are your thoughts about leaving a will?**
    a. I have already made one.
    b. I have not made a will, but intend to do so some day.
    c. I am uncertain or undecided.
    d. I probably will not make one.
    e. I definitely won't leave a will.

51. **To what extent do you believe in life insurance to benefit your survivors?**
    a. Strongly believe in it; have insurance
    b. Tend to believe in it; have or plan to get insurance
    c. Undecided
    d. Tend not to believe in it
    e. Definitely do not believe in it; do not have and do not plan to get insurance

52. **Who do you feel should be the one to tell you that you are dying?**
    a. Doctor
    b. Nurse
    c. Family member
    d. Close friend

53. **Which aspect of yourself would you take the most time with if you knew you would die soon? Rate 1–10 for urgency, 1 being most urgent**
    a. Physical
    b. Emotional
    c. Activities and plans
    d. Spiritual

    e. Relationships
    f. Playful
    g. Financial and practical
    h. Other (specify):_____

54. **List four things you would most like to learn, change, or do before you die. Number 1 through 4 in order of greatest to least priority.**

55. **If your parent, child, or close friend had a terminal illness, who would you want to tell them?**
    a. Doctor
    b. Nurse
    c. Myself
    d. Minister
    e. Other (specify):_____

56. **Which of the following rituals or activities do you feel may be helpful for survivors and their grief processes? Mark V =Very helpful, M = Moderately helpful, Q = Questionable, N=Not helpful, D = Detrimental**
    a. Embalming, open casket
    b. Viewing body, not embalmed
    c. Memorial service
    d. Getting rid of photos and belongings
    e. Taking trip later

f. Remembering the deceased on anniversary of their death, holidays
g. Talking about the deceased a lot
h. New social activities, dating
i. Wearing black
j. Taking a trip right away
k. Restricting social activities
l. Keeping belongings
m. Moving, selling house (when not necessary)
n. Joining widows' group
o. Grieving alone
p. Sharing grief with children
q. Other (specify): _____

57. Most often, how do you feel you probably will die?
a. Long illness
b. Stroke or heart attack
c. Auto accident
d. War
e. Violent encounter
f. Other (specify): _____

58. This new generation of adults has been called "hibakusha" or "explosion affected," like the survivors of Hiroshima and Nagasaki, due to growing up with the cold war, air-raid sirens, the atom bomb, and Vietnam. How much does this awareness affect you?
a. daily life
b. decisions for future
c. never think about it
d. no respect

59. What is your most vivid experience with death?
Age: _____
a. Dream
b. Experience with close person
c. Animal
d. Experience with stranger
e. Story
f. News story
If your answer was (a), (c), or (f), briefly describe: _____

60. How is death talked about in your family at this time?
a. Openly
b. Some discomfort
c. Only when necessary
d. Excludes children
e. Taboo
f. Never recall talking
g. Excludes dying person or survivor

61. Question #10 asked how often you think about death. What was your answer to #8? (a), (b), (c), (d), (e). Why do you think/not think about death with this frequency?
a. If I don't think about it, it won't happen
b. Figure I'll die suddenly
c. Preoccupied with death
d. Too much fear
e. Seems very real to me
f. Very unreal to me
g. Other (specify): _____

62. At what age have you experienced the most fear of death? _____
Do you know what was on your mind then? _____

63. If you knew you had only a limited time to live, would you want to know the exact date of your death?
a. Yes
b. No

64. If death was sudden, would you be willing to donate yours or a close relative's
a. needed organ.
b. heart.
c. retinas.
d. body for research.
Do you have a card for this?
a. Yes
b. No

65. Presuming a home death, how do you feel about friends and family viewing your body at home right after the death?
a. Good idea
b. Don't care
c. Up to family
d. Don't like the idea

66. If you had a terminal illness, who would you want to talk with about your "difficult" feelings? Number in preferential order, with 1 being the most preferred.
a. Spouse
b. Close family member
c. Doctor
d. Another patient
e. Friend
f. Nurse
g. Therapist
h. Clergy or spiritual friend
i. Understanding third party

67. If a doctor told you that an immediate family member was going to die, would you want them told?
a. Yes
b. No
c. Depends

68. If your close friend was dying, felt depressed, and wanted to talk, how would you feel?
a. Comfortable
b. Embarrassed
c. Distressed
d. Willing
e. Not sure
f. Would visit less

69. When thinking of dying, I fear the following (Rate H = High fear, M = Moderate fear, L = Low fear)

a. Being alone
b. Mentally disoriented
c. Pain
d. Disfigurement
e. Dependence on others
f. Loss of control over physical functions
g. What happens at/after death
h. Hospitalization & treatment
i. Other (specify): _____

70. When notified of a funeral not in immediate family I usually

a. decline.
b. hate to go.
c. happy to go.
d. attend if at all possible.
e. dread going.

71. The cause of death I'm most afraid of is

a. an accident.
b. xancer.
c. a bomb.
d. infection.
e. nerve disease.
f. heart failure.
g. kidney failure.
h. stroke.
i. violence.
j. Other (specify): _____

72. As of this date I _____ made out a will.

a. have
b. have not

73. When I die, the thing(s) I would like to happen to my body is (are) (check one or more of the following)

a. a funeral (body present).
b. a memorial service.
c. cremation.
d. embalming.
e. organ donation.
f. body donation.
g. cemetery burial.
h. above ground entombment.
i. burial at sea.
j. Cryonics (freezing of the body).
k. Other (specify): _____
l. I don't care what happens to my body after I die.

74. I _____ with the use of capital punishment for first degree murder.

a. strongly agree
b. agree
c. neither agree nor disagree
d. disagree
e. strongly disagree

75. I _____ with the use of abortion to terminate a pregnancy.

a. strongly agree
b. agree
c. neither agree nor disagree
d. disagree
e. strongly disagree

76. I _____ with the use of euthanasia to terminate the life of a dying person in a vegetative state is:

a. strongly agree
b. agree
c. neither agree nor disagree
d. disagree
e. strongly disagree

77. If I had a choice as to where I would die it would be

a. in a hospital.
b. while fighting for a good cause.
c. at home.
d. in an accident.
e. Other (specify): _____

78. Research findings of people who supposedly "died" on the operating table indicate that some of them reported floating out of their body, observing resuscitation efforts, moving through a dark tunnel to a "being" of light, reviewing life, etc. What is your opinion of this?

a. Definitely do not believe
b. Probably do not believe
c. Not sure
d. Probably do believe
e. Definitely do believe

Adapted from "You and Death: A Questionnaire" by Edwin S. Shneidman et al., published in *Psychology Today* (August 1970). Reprinted by permission of Edwin S. Shneidman.

This questionnaire was originally designed by Edwin Shneidman of the Center for Advanced Study in Behavioral Sciences in consultation with Edwin Parker and G. Ray Funkhouser of Stanford University. It is a modification of a questionnaire Shneidman developed at Harvard with the help of graduate assistants Chris Dowell, Ross Goldstein, Dan Goleman, and Bruce Smith.

Writing Your Deathography

A Deathography is an essay that details the death and loss events in your life, along with your present understanding of how each experience has influenced your attitudes and beliefs. Begin by recalling your past experiences with death and dying. Notice who in your life has influenced your attitudes toward death. Review your answers to the ➠ **Questionnaire: You and Death**, putting your finger on the ones that were difficult to answer.

Use the first activity in this section, ➠ **Childhood Loss Memories**, to focus on some of your earliest memories of loss and death.

After you have completed this exercise, turn to the next activity, ➠ **Questionnaire: Loss Inventory**, to brainstorm and record other death and loss events in your life. Think about your past experiences with loss. Remember that loss events include other losses in life, as well as those related to death. Some of the topics students have written about include the experience of the loss of health through a serious illness, the loss of a relationship through divorce, the loss of country through emigration, and the loss of the childbearing experience through infertility. Later, as you sit down to write your paper, you can select the important loss events in your life and make connections to your beliefs and behavior today.

The typewritten "Deathography" paper should be five to seven pages in length, although some students' essays may be longer. (For computer printouts, please use an easily readable serif typeface of 10 to 12 points.)

As an example of the "Deathography," read the following two excerpts about prior loss events and how these students connected them to their present beliefs and behaviors.

> "In examining my somewhat wishy-washy feelings about ground burial, I began to get an idea of where the conflicting notions came from in my experience. Pictures of my mother's response to digging up a long-buried goldfish join with the childhood rhyme, 'The worms crawl in, the worms crawl out, the worms play pinochle on his snout.' No wonder I am not centered about ground burial."

> "When my little sister died at birth, I was four. During the previous months I had been prepped to be a 'big brother.' My parents came home from the hospital and picked me up at my grandparents'. I asked, 'Where is my baby?' My parents responded, "She didn't live long enough to come home.' I never asked another question. For years I was sure that she didn't come home because I couldn't be a good enough big brother for her and really didn't

want the job anyway. While I was writing my paper, I called my mom and dad to ask them about my baby sister's death. They told me the details. When I asked them how I reacted, they said that I never talked about her. They thought that 'no questions meant no problems.' I can see now that my reluctance to ask questions of other survivors might have come from that childhood experience."

On your "Deathography," include your name, section number, and the date, along with your age. Consider creating a title that reflects your death experiences.

Use the space below to make notes about your "Deathography."

⇒ *Childhood Loss Memories*

Directions   *Reflect on your earliest memories of loss and death. Describe the "story" of your experience and respond to the following questions.*

What were your reactions?

_____

_____

_____

_____

_____

_____

_____

_____

What were the reactions of those around you?

_____

_____

_____

_____

_____

_____

_____

_____

_____

In what ways do you feel that you were supported or not supported at that time?

_____

_____

_____

_____

_____

_____

_____

_____

In what ways did this loss experience influence your reaction to subsequent losses in your life?

_____

_____

_____

_____

_____

_____

_____

_____

_____

Ⅲ➡ *Questionnaire: Loss Inventory*

Directions   Use this form to record the losses in your life. Place your age at the time of each loss in the space to the left and then briefly describe the event, including your beliefs about the impact of the loss.

_____   1. _____

_____

_____   2. _____

_____

_____   3. _____

_____

_____   4. _____

_____

_____   5. _____

_____

_____   6. _____

_____

_____   7. _____

_____

_____   8. _____

_____

_____   9. _____

_____

_____   10. _____

_____

_____ 11. _____

_____

_____ 12. _____

_____

_____ 13. _____

_____

_____ 14. _____

_____

_____ 15. _____

_____

_____ 16. _____

_____

_____ 17. _____

_____

_____ 18. _____

_____

_____ 19. _____

_____

_____ 20. _____

_____

_____ 21. _____

_____

_____ 22. _____

_____

➠ *Deathography Reading Assignment*

Directions   *In course sections where your instructor's preference and class size make it possible for you to read the "Deathographies" of other students, this assignment will guide those readings. At the reserve reading desk in the library, request the binder of "Deathographies" for your section. Each binder is marked with the section number and day of the week when your class meets. Read the "Deathographies" written by your classmates. As you are reading, make notes in the following areas by answering these questions.*

1. Which deaths seem like ones that might be particularly difficult for you to survive?

   _____

   _____

   _____

   _____

   _____

2. What kinds of similarities do you notice between the death experiences you have written about in your "Deathography" and those of your classmates?

   _____

   _____

   _____

   _____

   _____

3. Select at least two examples from the writings of your classmates that describe ways of thinking about a death or loss which seem particularly useful to you.

   _____

   _____

   _____

   _____

   _____

4. Note descriptions of understandings about loss that are helpful to you as a survivor.

_____

_____

_____

_____

_____

5. Identify what you believe to be a high-grief death from the experiences of your classmates.

_____

_____

_____

_____

_____

Come to class prepared with the answers to these questions, along with any other general or specific comments you have on the "Deathographies." It is helpful if you write down the student's name in conjunction with your answers. Use additional sheets of paper if necessary. Plan your reading time carefully. You will be able to read the "Deathographies" on reserve in the library on a time-limited checkout.

Begin this assignment well before it is due, since there is only one source for all the students in your section.

If you see a fellow student reading, it might be possible to share the "Deathographies." Make sure you return them to the same sequence in which they appeared. Some students will divide their time and read from front to back in the binder.

Attitudes Toward Death: A Climate of Change

Chapter Summary

Chapter 1 introduces the study of death and dying by focusing on individual and societal attitudes toward death. The perception that death is taboo, a subject not to be discussed, is contrasted with the goal of learning about dying and death as a means to enhance personal and social choices about these significant human experiences.

The experiences of death that most people bring to a class on death and dying, as persons living in a new millennium, are contrasted with those of Americans in earlier times. Our tendency to avoid discussion of death and dying is not necessarily so much a matter of individual choice as it is a result of social attitudes and shared practices concerning death. Our ancestors experienced death more frequently, and more often firsthand, than we do today. The typical funeral practices of the nineteenth and early twentieth centuries involved extensive participation by members of the dead person's family; today, the care of our dead is largely turned over to hired professionals. Our participation in rituals surrounding the dead is minimal.

The reasons for this change in the way we deal with dying and death involve a number of social and technological factors that have tended to lessen our familiarity with death. These factors include increased life expectancy, reduced mortality rates (especially among the young), geographical mobility, the displacement of death from the home to institutional settings, and advances in life-extending medical technologies.

Building on the awareness that attitudes and practices relative to death are not static but rather are subject to change, the chapter also introduces the wealth of cultural expressions by which we can discern both individual and social attitudes toward death. Examples are given of how euphemistic language may blur the reality of death or diminish its emotional impact, and of how humor is employed to defuse anxiety toward death or provide relief from painful situations. The role of the mass media in both reflecting and shaping attitudes toward death is examined, with examples cited from news reports about death as well as entertainment programs featuring death-related themes. Attention is paid to the issue of whether the images of death portrayed by the media accurately reflect the reality of death in human experience. Similarly, literature, the visual arts, and music are examined with respect to what they tell us about our own and other people's attitudes toward death.

The recent interest in formal education about death is traced to its foundation in the contributions made by such pioneers in the field as Herman Feifel, Elisabeth Kübler-Ross, Barney Glaser, Anselm Strauss, Cicely Saunders, Robert Fulton, Geoffrey Gorer, Jeanne Quint Benoliel, and others. The burgeoning of professional and scholarly literature about death in recent decades has been accompanied by the proliferation of courses dealing with death.

The interdisciplinary nature of death education is highlighted, as is its conjoining of both cognitive and affective content, the blending of objective facts and subjective concerns. For professionals who encounter dying and death in the course of their work—including nurses, fire fighters, police officers, and emergency medical personnel—death education is an important adjunct to training that imparts specific job-related skills.

The chapter concludes by noting that we are in an era when people are rethinking their assumptions about death. In a pluralistic society, there are many options for dealing with death. Education about dying and death is not simply academic or theoretical. It engages not only our intellect, but also our emotions. The experience of a loved one's death, or an encounter with our own mortality, makes our quest for a more meaningful understanding of death both practical and intimately relevant.

Objectives

- To identify historical antecedents of current attitudes toward death.
- To list and analyze the factors that have contributed to a lessened familiarity with death.
- To point out how attitudes toward death are expressed through language, humor, mass media, music, literature, and the visual arts.
- To evaluate the usefulness of expanding death awareness through death education.
- To examine assumptions about death.

Key Terms and Concepts

causes of death	*Dies Irae*
cultural lag	dirge
death awareness movement	elegy
death denial	epidemiologic transition
death education	euphemisms
death notices	gallows humor
"death talk"	geographical mobility
demographics	*hibakusha*

Holocaust literature

iconography of death

institutional denial

kanikau

life expectancy

life-extending technologies

"mean world" syndrome

mortality rates

mourning memorials

obituaries

personal death consultants

Postmodernism

revictimization

sites of memory

thanatology

vigilante literature

Questions for Guided Study and Review

1. Compare current customs and patterns of death and dying with those of the past.
2. Briefly describe the various factors that have had an impact on Americans' familiarity with death.
3. Distinguish between life expectancy and death rates.
4. How have death rates and causes of death changed over the past century?
5. Define the term *epidemiologic transition*.
6. What message is conveyed in the poem "Grandmother, When Your Child Died"?
7. How do language, humor, the mass media, music, literature, and the visual arts function as expressions of attitudes toward death?
8. What are some reasons for using euphemisms when speaking about death?
9. Explain how language and humor may be used to distance people from the reality of death.
10. How do sympathy cards reflect attitudes toward death?
11. What purposes does humor serve in situations related to death and dying?
12. How is death portrayed in the news and entertainment media?
13. Explain how the news media might be said to have an interest in the "pornography of death" ("If it bleeds, it leads")?
14. What is the difference between a death notice and an obituary?
15. How do the visual arts and music reflect modern issues related to death and dying?
16. What is a *dirge*?
17. Give examples of various death themes in popular music, rock, heavy metal, and blues.
18. How is death portrayed in cartoons?
19. Describe the relationship between nineteenth-century mourning customs and the Names Project AIDS Memorial Quilt.
20. How do modern memorials, such as the Vietnam Veterans Memorial and the AIDS Memorial Quilt, counter the social taboo against public mourning?
21. What is the definition of *thanatology*?
22. What were some of the achievements of significant pioneers in death studies?
23. What factors contributed to the rise of death education?
24. Why should we study death and dying?
25. Is there a social taboo against mentioning or talking openly about death?
26. Define the term *institutional denial*.
27. Assess the idea that "avoidance of death" has been replaced by "obsession with death" in American society.
28. What are some benefits of death education?

Practice Test Questions

MULTIPLE CHOICE

1. *Epidemiologic transition* is best defined as the
   a. trend toward more rapid and sudden death.
   b. contribution of Americans' highly mobile life styles to making death less immediate and intimate.
   c. shift in disease patterns characterized by a redistribution of deaths from the young to the old.
   d. change in cultural attitudes toward death as a significant determinant of how we live our lives.

2. What is meant by the phrase "medical technology that seems to one person a godsend, extending life, may seem to another a curse"?
   a. People do not believe in the technology.
   b. People do not know how to manipulate machinery.
   c. The effect of new technology involves personal and social consequences.
   d. The effect of new technology is unknown.

3. Which of the following is NOT cited in the text as a way in which humor functions relative to death?
   a. It can make us feel that death is always a threat.
   b. It provides an opportunity to rise above sadness.
   c. It provides distance for caregivers that come into frequent contact with death.
   d. It can raise our consciousness.

4. Cartoon character Bugs Bunny's being revived after a fatal incident is an example of
   a. reincarnation.
   b. sequencing.
   c. individuation.
   d. reversibility.

5. The major contribution of Elisabeth Kübler-Ross's book *On Death and Dying* was its focus on the
   a. social practices and customs related to death.
   b. care of dying patients.
   c. meaning of death.
   d. patterns associated with near-death experiences.

TRUE/FALSE

_____ 1. At the turn of the century, young children were often forbidden from attending burial rituals.

_____ 2. Death notices and obituaries differ in that death notices are brief, standardized, and printed in small type.

_____ 3. Popular music devotes little or no attention to death.

_____ 4. The Vietnam Veterans Memorial is an example of contemporary mourning art.

_____ 5. The initial reaction of people in the health care professions to books about death and dying was welcoming and enthusiastic.

MATCHING

For each of the following, place an "A" in the answer column if it is a characteristic of the nineteenth century. Place a "B" in the answer column if it is characteristic of the twentieth century.

_____ 1. People live comparatively shorter lives.

_____ 2. People prepare the bodies of loved ones for burial.

_____ 3. People typically die in hospitals.

_____ 4. People typically purchase, rather than construct, caskets.

_____ 5. People typically learn about death through intimate, hands-on experiences.

_____ 6. People tend to be observers rather than participants in funeral ceremonies.

_____ 7. People tend to use euphemisms, such as "succumbed," when referring to the act of dying.

❧ Answers to practice questions can be found in Part IV ❧

Related Readings

📖 Indicates selection from *The Path Ahead: Readings in Death and Dying*, eds. Lynne Ann DeSpelder and Albert Lee Strickland (Mountain View, Calif.: Mayfield, 1995).

CHANGING DEMOGRAPHICS OF DEATH

Patricia Anderson. *All of Us: Americans Talk About the Meaning of Death*. New York: Delacorte, 1996.

James K. Crissman. *Death and Dying in Central Appalachia: Changing Attitudes and Practices*. Urbana: University of Illinois Press, 1994.

📖 Charles E. Rosenberg, "What Is an Epidemic? AIDS in Historical Perspective," pp. 29–32.

Howard M. Spiro, Mary G. McCrea Curnen, and Lee Palmer Wandel, eds. *Facing Death: Where Culture, Religion, and Medicine Meet*. New Haven, C.N.: Yale University Press, 1996.

📖 Margaret Stroebe, Mary M. Gergen, Kenneth J. Gergen, and Wolfgang Stroebe, "Broken Hearts or Broken Bonds: Love and Death in Historical Perspective," pp. 231–241.

EXPRESSIONS OF DEATH ATTITUDES

📖 Allan B. Chinen, "The Mortal King," pp. 335–336.

Martha Cooper and Joseph Sciorra. *R.I.P.: Memorial Wall Art.* New York: Henry Holt, 1994.

📖 Mary N. Hall and Paula T. Rappe, "Humor and Critical Incident Stress," pp. 289–294.

James Kinsella. *Covering the Plague: AIDS and the American Media.* New Brunswick, N.J.: Rutgers University Press, 1990.

Lawrence L. Langer, ed. *Art from the Ashes: A Holocaust Anthology.* New York: Oxford University Press, 1995.

📖 Jack Lule, "News Strategies and the Death of Huey Newton," pp. 33–40.

Dan Nimmo and James E. Combs. *Nightly Horrors: Crisis Coverage by Television Network News.* Knoxville: University of Tennessee Press, 1985.

Robert F. Weir, ed. *Death in Literature.* New York: Columbia University Press, 1980.

DEATH EDUCATION

📖 Patrick Vernon Dean, "Is Death Education a Nasty Little Secret? A Call to Break the Alleged Silence," pp. 323–326.

📖 Herman Feifel, "Psychology and Death: Meaningful Rediscovery," pp. 19–28.

📖 Robert Kastenbaum, "Reconstructing Death in Postmodern Society," pp. 7–18.

📖 Hannelore Wass, "Visions in Death Education," pp. 327–334.

Tony Walter. *The Revival of Death.* New York: Routledge, 1994.

Major Points in This Chapter

- Our ancestors experienced death more frequently, and more often firsthand, than we do today. The reasons for this include changes in life expectancy and mortality rates, the causes of death, geographic mobility, displacement of death from the home to the hospital and other institutional settings, and advances in life-sustaining medical technologies.

- Attitudes toward death are expressed through language, humor, mass media, music, literature, and the visual arts.

- Since the 1960s, education about dying, death, and bereavement has achieved widespread acceptance.

- Although many people no longer consider death and dying as taboo topics, society as a whole continues to manifest features of death denial that hinder open discussion and acceptance.

Observations and Reflections

When you are reading through this chapter, you will likely become aware of thoughts and feelings about your own attitudes and experiences. We encourage you to notice your reactions to all the elements of the text. You may have strong reactions in response to particular photographs or boxed material. Throughout the text, you will probably discover that your strongest feelings result from *perceived similarity* (that is, a sense of identification with another person's characteristics or situation). This is an excellent opportunity to once again become aware of your own life history and experience with death. Use these insights to begin to understand yourself and others. You may be surprised—and comforted—to find that you share many essential similarities with classmates regarding your attitudes and behaviors.

Use the blank space below and on the following page to record your own observations and reactions about the elements of the text.

⇒ *Humor and Death: Cartoons*

Directions   *Search your comic sources for death-related cartoons. You may choose single panels (like the one on page 18 of the text) or cartoon strips (such as the "Peanuts" on page 345). Paste your choice(s) here and on additional sheets of paper. Be sure to identify the source, title, artist, and other information listed below for each cartoon selected.*

Source

Title: _____

Artist: _____

Date: _____

Cartoon Syndicate: _____

Humor and Death: Cartoons (continued)

⇒ *Humor and Death: Jokes*

Directions *Gather "death jokes" by questioning your friends, family members, coworkers, and acquaintances. Take note of the person's reaction to your request, "Heard any good death jokes lately?" Use this page and the next to record the text of each joke collected along with the verbal and nonverbal reactions to your request for "good death jokes." Place source data with each joke collected.*

Humor and Death: Jokes (continued)

⟶ *Music and Death*

Directions   *Review your music collection. Pay particular attention to your favorite musicians. Whatever the musical form (heavy metal, hip hop, grunge, rock and roll, oldies, country, gospel, etc.), choose the lyrics from one of your favorite groups or individual artists wherein the theme of the song has something to do with death. (See page 25 of the text for examples of songs.) Along with the lyrics and song title, identify the performing artist and composer.*

Lyrics:

Performer_____

Song _____

Theme _____

Music and Death (continued)

⟾ *Corporate Response to Death, Dying, and Bereavement: The Airlines*

Directions Airlines may provide discounted tickets for travel on family emergencies related to death, dying, and bereavement. For example, United Airlines has a fare that allows for travel on short notice at a discount from the regular economy fare. United's fare allows for flexible travel (no minimum or maximum stays required) for family emergencies as well as bereavement. In this activity, you are to call at least five airlines that operate from your local or regional airport. Initially speak to reservations and then to a supervisor to gather information about fare discounts for family emergencies and death. Below, indicate the airline, phone number, policy, and sample price differences for a selected route of your choice, as well as the situations that airlines cover under family emergency. Note the cost of a full fare ticket and the discounted one available in family emergencies along with any other information required by the airline. Divide your research between the major carriers and the regional ones in your area.

1. _____
   _____
   _____
   _____
   _____
   _____
   _____
   _____
   _____
   _____

2. _____
   _____
   _____
   _____
   _____
   _____
   _____
   _____
   _____
   _____
   _____

3. _____

_____

_____

_____

_____

_____

_____

_____

_____

4. _____

_____

_____

_____

_____

_____

_____

_____

_____

_____

5. _____

_____

_____

_____

_____

_____

_____

_____

_____

_____

Perspectives on Death: Cross-Cultural and Historical

Chapter Summary

Chapter 2 broadens our perspective by examining how people have dealt with death in cultural and historical settings other than our own. We begin by examining the functions of traditional mythologies, or beliefs about death. The relationship between beliefs and practices is apparent in the context of the view that many traditional societies hold concerning the "power of the dead." In addition, a society's attitude toward the dead is frequently evident in its naming practices, which can involve either avoiding or memorializing the name of the deceased. The explanations offered by traditional societies as to the causes of death and its ultimate origin offer yet another avenue toward understanding the central themes that still have currency in our efforts to understand death.

Attention is given to the death-related beliefs and practices that have prevailed at different times in the history of Western culture. Changes over the centuries in the manner of dying are discussed in the context of the dying person's anticipation of death and the scene around the deathbed. The attitude of survivors toward the dead is traced by examining changing fashions in burial customs, such as the contrast between anonymous burial in charnel houses and subsequent development of individual graves and memorialization of the dead. Changing attitudes about death are also revealed in the evolution of the *danse macabre*, or Dance of Death.

Our survey of historical perspectives on death and dying concludes with a discussion of "invisible death," a term that characterizes the way that death and dying have generally been dealt with by people living in modern, technological societies. It refers to the practice of delegating care of the dying and the dead to professionals and to the emphasis on delaying death by all means available, as well as to the comparative lack of social or cultural supports for placing death and dying within a meaningful context as an intrinsic part of human experience. Tracing the historical changes in death-related attitudes and customs heightens awareness of the possibility of further changes in our manner of dealing with death.

To expand our awareness of such possibilities, the chapter includes descriptions of four cultural traditions that provide contrasts with historically mainstream Euro-American traditions. Discussed are death-related attitudes and practices among native peoples of North America, as well as among various African societies, with a focus on funeral customs of the LoDagaa. Mexican traditions are discussed, with particular attention to the celebration of the Day of the Dead. Also examined are Asian traditions that emphasize respect for ancestors within Chinese and Japanese societies. The text encourages us to look for commonalities as well as differences in the ways human beings in different cultures relate to death.

The chapter concludes by noting that ultimate fulfillment, the sense of having lived one's life well, may be possible only within a community that acknowledges the significance of death. The examples of other cultures—more or less distant from our own in time or space—can offer us insights and inspiration for creating such a community.

Objectives

- To become acquainted with the diversity of death-related rituals and beliefs found in various cultures.
- To assess the correspondences among various cultures relative to death-related rituals and beliefs.
- To describe the historical changes in death-related beliefs and practices in the Western world.
- To analyze the impact of various beliefs and practices and to assess their value for survivors.

Key Terms and Concepts

All Souls' Day
anatomical theater
ancestor worship
Black Death
butsudan
charnel houses
ch'ing ming
cult of martyrs
danse macabre
death knell
death songs
deathbed scenes
el Día de los Muertos
effigy
fêng-shui

haka
invisible death
"living dead"
medicalization of death
mourning restraints
name avoidance
necromancy
o-bon
origin-of-death myths
power of the dead
reverence for the dead
rites of passage
ritual
shaman
tamed death

Questions for Guided Study and Review

1. How long have humans shown concern for the dead?
2. What are some characteristics of how death is viewed in traditional cultures?
3. What is the common theme in various myths of the origin of death?
4. How are illness and various causes of death viewed in traditional cultures?
5. What is meant by the phrase, "the power of the dead"?
6. What is name avoidance, and why is it practiced?
7. Identify the major changes that have taken place in Western attitudes toward death since the early Middle Ages (roughly A.D. 500). In framing your answer, consider the following historical periods: 500–1100, 1100–1500, 1500–1700, 1700–1900, and 1900–present.
8. What traditions illustrate these changing attitudes in Western culture? Consider, for example, deathbed scenes, burial customs, and memorialization.
9. Briefly describe the categories, "tamed death," "untamed death," and "invisible death," as used by Philippe Ariès.
10. What is the general viewpoint of Native American societies toward death?
11. What are some differences that can be noted about contrasting attitudes toward death among various Native American tribes?
12. Discuss differences in attitudes and funeral practices between the Cocopa and the Hopi.
13. Identify some practices among the Ohlone that illustrate beliefs related to the power of the dead.
14. What is a death song?
15. What is meant by the term *ancestor worship*?
16. How are treatment of the dead and the notion of the "living dead" related?
17. What are the four stages of LoDagaa mourning customs?
18. What are the two purposes served by the LoDagaa mourning rituals?
19. What meaning is given to the mourning restraints used by the LoDagaa?
20. What is the Day of the Dead?
21. What distinction is made between children and adults in customs relating to the Day of the Dead?
22. What awareness of death is reflected in Mexican death customs?
23. Using cross-cultural examples, support the theme that life and death may be perceived as a continuous process.
24. What is the role of ancestors in Asian cultures?
25. In the traditional Japanese view, what is special about the first forty-nine days after a death?
26. What is the purpose of the so-called "bone house" in Chinese mortuary practices?

Practice Test Questions

MULTIPLE CHOICE

1. A common theme in origin-of-death myths is that death
   a. comes as a teacher.
   b. comes from outside oneself.
   c. is the result of a transgression.
   d. is a punishment.

2. During the Romantic era, a "beautiful death" of a loved one elicited
   a. technology that reduced the pain of dying.
   b. family deathbed scenes to aid the dying in accepting the inevitability of death.
   c. feelings of melancholy and hopes for reunion.
   d. religious attitudes that emphasized the beauty of heaven and ignored the fires of hell.

3. The Dance of Death was influenced most significantly by the widespread fears of
   a. cholera.
   b. tuberculosis.
   c. epilepsy.
   d. plague.

4. The LoDagaa of Africa deal with death in the following manner.
   a. They tend to avoid the topic of death.
   b. They elect to withhold the topic of death from their youth until they reach adulthood.
   c. They use mourning restraints to show degrees of relationship to the deceased.
   d. They proceed with the funeral process as quickly as possible to allow the deceased to experience peace.

5. *El Día de los Muertos,* the Mexican Day of the Dead, blends Catholic, Spanish, and Indian rituals. This celebration exemplifies an attitude toward death that
   a. perceives death as the final chapter of a person's existence.
   b. views death in an open and often ironic manner.
   c. perceives death as an incomprehensible phenomenon.
   d. views death as the ultimate test.

TRUE/FALSE

____ 1. Most cultures deal with death and dying in a similar manner.

____ 2. In Western culture, attitudes toward death have changed significantly during the past one hundred years.

____ 3. Historically, the deathbed scene has focused on allowing the dying person to prepare for death.

____ 4. The Lakota battle cry, "It is a good day to die," expresses the belief that death is a natural process.

____ 5. The way a generation within a culture copes with death is entirely created by that generation.

Study Guide
The Last Dance: Encountering Death and Dying, 6th ed.

50   Chapter 2

MATCHING

Match each of the items on the left with the appropriate tradition on the right.

____ 1. Compose "death songs" to express confrontation with death

____ 2. Ongoing community of the "living dead"

____ 3. A celebration begins at midday on October 31st

____ 4. Memorial services for the deceased are held at periodic intervals

a. African Tradition

b. Asian Tradition

c. Native American Tradition

d. Mexican Tradition

❧ Answers to practice questions can be found in Part IV ❧

Related Readings

📖 Indicates selection from *The Path Ahead: Readings in Death and Dying*, eds. Lynne Ann DeSpelder and Albert Lee Strickland (Mountain View, Calif.: Mayfield, 1995).

HISTORICAL STUDIES

Philippe Ariès. *The Hour of Our Death*. New York: Alfred A. Knopf, 1981.

Paul Binsky. *Medieval Death: Ritual and Representation*. London: British Museum Press, 1996.

Patrick J. Geary. *Living with the Dead in the Middle Ages*. Ithaca, N.Y.: Cornell University Press, 1994.

Patricia Jalland, *Death in the Victorian Family*. New York: Oxford University Press, 1996.

Colin Platt. *King Death: The Black Death and Its Aftermath in Late-Medieval England*. London: University College of London Press, 1996.

📖 Charles E. Rosenberg, "What Is an Epidemic? AIDS in Historical Perspective," pp. 29–32.

📖 Margaret Stroebe, Mary M. Gergen, Kenneth J. Gergen, and Wolfgang Stroebe, "Broken Hearts or Broken Bonds: Love and Death in Historical Perspective," pp. 231-241.

CROSS-CULTURAL PERSPECTIVES

📖 Ronald K. Barrett, "Contemporary African-American Funeral Rites and Traditions," pp. 80–92.

John Greenleigh and Rosalind Rosoff Beimler. *The Days of the Dead: Mexico's Festival of Communion with the Departed*. San Francisco: HarperCollins, 1991.

Yoel Hoffman. *Japanese Death Poems*. Rutland, V.T.: Charles E. Tuttle, 1986.

Åke Hultkrantz. *Shamanic Healing and Ritual Drama: Health and Medicine in Native North American Religious Tradition*. New York: Crossroad, 1992.

Thomas A. Kselman. *Death and the Afterlife in Modern France*. Princeton, N.J.: Princeton University Press, 1993.

John S. Mbiti. *Introduction to African Religion*, 2nd ed. Oxford: Heinemann, 1991.

📖 Nancy Scheper-Hughes, "Death Without Weeping: The Violence of Everyday Life in Brazil," pp. 41–58.

James L. Watson and Evelyn S. Rawski, eds. *Death Ritual in Late Imperial and Modern China*. Berkeley: University of California Press, 1988.

Major Points in This Chapter

- Studying death in early and traditional cultures provides information about origin-of-death myths, ways of assessing the causes of death, and practices associated with the use of a deceased person's name.

- The history of attitudes toward death in Western European culture includes such phenomena as the Dance of Death (*danse macabre*) and the charnel house, as well as changes in the deathbed scene, burial customs, and practices for memorializing the dead.

- Tracing the historical changes in death-related attitudes and customs increases awareness of the possibility of further changes in our own lifetimes.

- Native American attitudes and customs relative to death vary widely among the different tribal groups, although they share a belief in the cyclic nature of life and death.

- African attitudes and customs relative to death are based on a cyclical view of birth and death whereby deceased ancestors remain part of their survivors' lives.

- LoDagaa mourning customs exemplify complex rituals that include specific ceremonies and practices to be enacted by mourners.

- The Mexican tradition of *el Día de Los Muertos* blends indigenous death rituals with the Catholic Church's commemoration of All Souls' Day to produce a unique fiesta; death is confronted by Mexican artists and writers with an attitude of humorous sarcasm.

- Respect for ancestors occupies a central place in Asian cultures. As honored members of a household, ancestors continue to be important to the lives of family members.

- During the Chinese celebration known as *ch'ing ming*, families visit graves and burn paper replicas of money, clothes, jewelry, and even modern necessities such as video cameras as a way of showing regard and care for deceased relatives.

- During the midsummer *o-bon* festival, the Japanese celebrate the return of ancestral spirits to their families. Japanese death rituals are distinctive not only because of their duration but also because of the strong association between the ancestor's spirit and ongoing benefits to the family.

Observations and Reflections

A primary goal of this chapter is to help you recognize the validity of diverse cultural responses to the basic human experience of death and dying. Understanding that each culture has its own way of responding to death, you can learn to suspend judgment and recognize the value of various practices in terms of how they benefit survivors. For example, although name avoidance might at first seem to be a rather exotic practice, you may have seen the correlation between this practice as it exists in other cultures and the reluctance to mention the deceased's name to recently bereaved people in your own culture. Note, however, that the beliefs behind these two practices may differ.

You can learn to recognize that your own beliefs and practices may seem no less bizarre than the beliefs and practices of other people. This understanding allows you to evaluate the degree to which your own beliefs and practices benefit you. Reflect on the practices and beliefs that come from your own "culture."

Use the blank space below and on the following page to record some of your own beliefs and practices regarding death.

➠ *Death Customs*

Directions *Use the space below to develop a list of death customs that you have participated in or heard about. Compare and contrast these customs with those of the cultures described in* The Last Dance. *Discuss the functions served by the customs you list and the beliefs associated with each of them.*

1. Death customs I have participated in or heard about:

_____

_____

_____

_____

_____

_____

_____

_____

_____

_____

_____

_____

_____

2. Similarities and differences between what I know about death customs and those mentioned in the text:

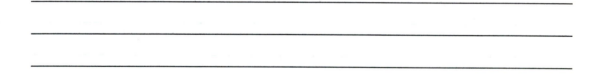

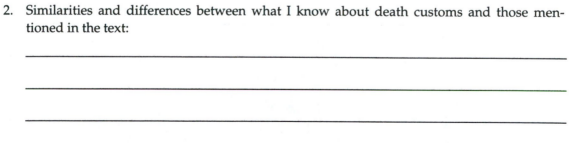

_____

_____

_____

_____

_____

_____

_____

_____

_____

_____

_____

_____

_____

3. Functions served by the customs and the beliefs associated with each. For example, the chapter opening photograph shows a cultural belief that manifests in a burial custom. A belief in a return of the body's elements to the "natural world" is accomplished by platform burial.

_____

_____

_____

_____

_____

_____

_____

_____

_____

_____

_____

_____

_____

💻 Cultural Diversity: Internet Exercise

Directions   *Visit at least three web sites that have information about cultural diversity. Apply the criteria for evaluating a web site explained in the Introduction of this Study Guide. Rate each website 1–5 (with 1 being the best and 5 the poorest). Here are several from which you may choose, or you can find others.*

http://dying.about.com/health/dying/mbody.htm

http://www.trinity.edu/~mkearl/death-1.html

http://www.azcentral.com/rep/deadl

http://www.geocities.com/Athens/1044/

1. List the web sites you visited. Rate each one.

_____

_____

_____

_____

_____

_____

_____

_____

_____

_____

_____

_____

2. What kinds of cultural information did you find?

_____

_____

_____

_____

_____

_____

_____

_____

_____

_____

3. Pick one aspect of each site and describe its value.

_____

_____

_____

_____

_____

_____

_____

_____

_____

4. What did you learn from visiting the three sites?

_____

_____

_____

_____

_____

_____

_____

_____

_____

_____

Learning About Death:
The Influence of Sociocultural Forces

Chapter Summary

Chapter 3 deals with the way that individuals in a given society learn about death. This process of learning about death is one of continuous adjustment and refinement as new experiences cause individuals to reexamine their values and responses. During their formative years, children eventually arrive at what is known as a mature concept of death—that is, an understanding of death shared by the majority of adults in a particular culture. Within modern societies, a mature concept of death includes four basic components.

1. Death is universal. All living things eventually die, and death is inevitable and unavoidable.

2. Death is irreversible. Organisms that die cannot be made alive again.

3. Death involves nonfunctionality; that is, it is the cessation of all physiological functioning, or signs of life.

4. Death involves causality. In other words, there are biological reasons for the occurrence of death.

It is important to note, however, that individuals may also hold *nonempirical* ideas about death—that is, ideas that are not subject to scientific proof. Such ideas deal mainly with the notion that human beings may survive in some form after the death of the physical body. These beliefs are usually of a religious or spiritual nature.

In comprehending the various sociocultural influences on how we learn about and gain an understanding about death, the chapter provides discussion of three helpful theoretical perspectives which are structural-functionalism, symbolic interactionism, and the social learning approach. We find that our understanding of death is greatly influenced by various "agents of socialization." These agents include family, school and peers, the mass media, and religion.

Parental messages, general cultural influences, and particular life experiences all play important roles in influencing a person's understanding of death and attitude toward it. Sometimes these influences are communicated subtly or unconsciously, as when the suggestion is made that a dead pet can be replaced without acknowledging the grief resulting from the loss. Children's literature and television programs also communicate cultural expressions and attitudes relevant to how we understand death. Deaths that are widely reported by the media—such as the death of President John F. Kennedy and the deaths of the Challenger astronauts—also set into motion processes of socialization about death. Life experiences, especially those involving an encounter with a significant loss or death, can powerfully affect our beliefs and attitudes.

In contemporary multicultural societies, which are composed of a number of social groups with distinctive customs and life styles, we typically find a variety of attitudes and practices related to death. Hawaii is cited in the text as an example of cultural diversity that reflects such sociological concepts as "local identity," as well as the dynamics of assimilation and accommodation among groups. Broadening our perspectives to embrace other cultural contexts provides an antidote to ethnocentrism, or the fallacy of making judgments about others solely in terms of one's own assumptions and biases.

The process of socialization is complex and ongoing. Our understanding of death evolves throughout life. Even though we may be identified with a particular social group or culture, we are also individuals who sometimes do things our own way. As we experience loss in our lives, we may modify previously held beliefs, exchanging them for new ones that provide a better fit with our developing understanding of death and its meaning in our lives.

Objectives

- To identify the components of a mature concept of death.
- To name the factors that influence a child's understanding of and attitude toward death.
- To explain how agents of socialization influence the understanding of death.
- To describe how early experiences with death can influence one's later conceptions of death.
- To appraise the impact of life experiences and environment on a child's understanding of death.
- To analyze teachable moments as an aspect of socialization about death.
- To describe the way a society responds to death by using three theoretical perspectives: structural-functionalism, symbolic interactionism, and social
- To assess the contributions of a variety of subcultures in understanding contemporary death customs and attitudes, with particular attention paid to the cultural diversity found in Hawaii.

Key Terms and Concepts

accommodation

assimilation

cultural diversity

culture

death system

ethnocentrism

"fuzzy" concepts of death

local identity

mature concept of death

noncorporeal continuity

norms

parental messages

pidgin

pluralism

religiosity

replaceability

resocialization

social construction of reality

social learning

social structure

socialization

society

structural-functionalism

subcultures

symbolic interactionism

tactical socialization

Taoist traditions

teachable moments

values

Questions for Guided Study and Review

1. What are the four major characteristics of a mature concept of death?
2. What are *nonempirical* ideas about death?
3. Contrast the definitions of *society* and *culture*.
4. Identify and define three theoretical perspectives on socialization and discuss how they apply to learning about death.
5. What are the major components of what Robert Kastenbaum terms the "death system," and how do they function in society?
6. How do cultural norms influence the expression of grief?
7. Identify at least four of the major agents of socialization and describe their impact on learning about death.
8. Distinguish between *socialization* and *resocialization*.
9. What is the role of early childhood experiences with death in relation to processes of socialization?
10. What different meanings are found in the Western version of *Little Red Riding Hood* and the Chinese tale of *Lon Po Po* (Granny Wolf)?
11. What are some of the messages or themes communicated in lullabies?
12. What is the function of religion in societies?
13. How does religiosity differ from religious affiliation?
14. What are teachable moments?
15. What is the meaning of "cultural diversity"?
16. What are some characteristics of subcultures in relation to the larger society?
17. Why is sensitivity to other cultural groups important?

18. How might cultural diversity tend to increase anxiety about death-related attitudes and behaviors?
19. How do the concepts of *assimilation* and *accommodation* apply to the various cultural groups living in Hawaii?
20. What is "local identity"?
21. How are "fuzzy" concepts related to a mature understanding of death?

Practice Test Questions

MULTIPLE CHOICE

1. The statement "Death involves causality" means that
   a. the grieving process is caused by death.
   b. organisms are unable to return to life after they die.
   c. there are biological reasons for death.
   d. the growing world population is the basis of people dying of starvation.

2. Which of the following tends NOT to be an important influence on the development of children's attitudes toward death?
   a. children's stories
   b. parents
   c. rising funeral costs
   d. television programs

3. The story of *Little Red Riding Hood* in Chinese tradition differs from the Western version in which of the following ways?
   a. There is no wolf in the Chinese version.
   b. The three children in the Chinese version work together to kill the wolf.
   c. The wolf does not die in the Chinese version.
   d. The wolf eats the children in the Chinese version.

4. Children who have had firsthand experience with death tend to
   a. shy away from any mention of it.
   b. still believe in reversible death.
   c. develop a more mature outlook on death.
   d. deny its existence.

5. Childhood experiences with death are most likely to
   a. affect a person's attitudes toward death only if the experiences are negative.
   b. be forgotten by the time adulthood is reached.
   c. have little effect on a person's attitudes toward death.
   d. affect a person's attitudes toward death throughout his or her lifetime.

TRUE/FALSE

_____ 1. Following the assassination of President Kennedy, younger children were more concerned than older children about the appearance of the president's body.

_____ 2. A child with a good self-concept is generally less fearful of death.

_____ 3. Teachable moments are ideal vehicles for learning because they occur naturally.

_____ 4. In modern society, signs that death is pushed aside and avoided reveal that the social practices for dealing with death are uniform.

_____ 5. According to the social learning theory, we learn by attaching meanings to actions and things.

MATCHING

Match each of the following terms on the left with the appropriate definition on the right. There is one answer for each.

_____ 1. Irreversibility

_____ 2. Symbolic interactionism

_____ 3. Structural-functionalism

_____ 4. Nonfunctionality

_____ 5. Social learning approach

a. parts working together to maintain society as a whole

b. cessation of all physiological functioning

c. behavior is shaped by consequences and imitation

d. organisms that die cannot be made alive again

e. socialization is a two-way process

⌁ Answers to practice questions can be found in Part IV ⌁

Related Readings

📖 Indicates selection from *The Path Ahead: Readings in Death and Dying*, eds. Lynne Ann DeSpelder and Albert Lee Strickland (Mountain View, Calif.: Mayfield, 1995).

GENERAL CULTURAL STUDIES

Nigel Barley. *Grave Matters: A Lively History of Death Around the World*. New York: Henry Holt, 1997.

David Clark, ed. *The Sociology of Death: Theory, Culture, Practice*. Cambridge, Mass.: Blackwell, 1993.

David R. Counts and Dorothy A. Counts, eds. *Coping with the Final Tragedy: Cultural Variation in Dying and Grieving*. Amityville, N.Y.: Baywood, 1991.

Robert Fulton and Robert Bendiksen, eds. *Death and Identity*, 3d ed. Philadelphia: The Charles Press, 1994.

Geri-Ann Galanti. *Caring for Patients from Different Cultures: Case Studies from American Hospitals*, 2d ed. Philadelphia: University of Pennsylvania Press, 1997.

James Garbarino, "Challenges We Face in Understanding Children and War: A Personal Essay," pp. 169–174.

James Garbarino, Nancy Dubrow, Kathleen Kostelny, and Carole Pardo. *Children in Danger: Coping with the Consequences of Community Violence*. San Francisco: Jossey-Bass, 1992.

Donald P. Irish, Kathleen F. Lundquist, and Vivian Jenkins Nelsen, eds. *Ethnic Variation in Dying, Death, and Grief*. Washington, D.C.: Taylor and Francis, 1993.

Colin Murray Parkes, Pittu Laungani, and Bill Young, eds. *Death and Bereavement Across Cultures*. New York: Routledge, 1997.

STUDIES OF SPECIFIC CULTURES

Ronald K. Barrett, "Contemporary African-American Funeral Rites and Traditions," pp. 80–92.

Kevin E. Early and Ronald L. Akers, "It's a White Thing: An Exploration of Beliefs About Suicide in the African-American Community," pp. 198–210.

Zlata Filipovic, "Zlata's Diary: A Child's Life in Sarajevo," pp. 175-178.

Christopher L. Hayes and Richard A. Kalish, "Death-Related Experiences and Funerary Practices of the Hmong Refugee in the United States," pp. 75–79.

Ice T, "The Killing Fields," pp. 178–181.

Joseph M. Kaufert and John D. O'Neil, "Cultural Mediation of Dying and Grieving Among Native Canadian Patients in Urban Hospitals," pp. 59–74.

Nancy Scheper-Hughes, "Death Without Weeping: The Violence of Everyday Life in Brazil," pp. 41–58.

Unni Wikan. "Bereavement and Loss in Two Muslim Communities: Egypt and Bali Compared." *Social Science and Medicine* 17, no. 5 (1988): 451–460.

Major Points in This Chapter

- As children get older they gradually reach a mature understanding of death. This means that the child understands that death is universal, is irreversible, renders the person non-functional, and is caused by biological reasons.

- Agents of socialization regarding death include family, school and peers, mass media, religion, and early experiences with death.

- Life experiences—particularly those that involve an encounter with significant loss or death—are powerful in shaping attitudes and beliefs.

- Teachable moments in death education involve adults who take advantage of a spontaneous or planned event by teaching a child something about death.

- Three sociological theoretical perspectives are useful in helping us understand how social and cultural factors influence our attitudes and behaviors relative to death. They are structural-functionalism, symbolic interactionism, and social learning.

- By recognizing the richness of cultural diversity in the United States, we can also appreciate the vast array of subcultural death rituals, beliefs, and attitudes.

- Hawaii is a unique example of cultural diversity in death customs and practices.

Observations and Reflections

What are your early childhood memories concerning death and dying? Are you able to apply the examples in this chapter to your own attitudes toward death? Can you appreciate the contributions from your cultural heritage? What about those children who are growing up in different cultures? Do you understand more about cultural diversity?

The information and activities in this chapter bring with them ethical concerns involving interviews with children. Before you interview a child (other than your own) about death-related subjects, make sure that you obtain permission from the child's parents. You can ask if the parent(s) would like to be informed about the topics that will be discussed. If so, you can provide a list of applicable topics before interviewing the child. One way to make the interaction non-threatening is to engage the child's interest in "teaching" a grown-up.

As you explore your childhood experiences, notice the messages about death that have come from your family, peers, school, and community, as well as from the books you've read and movies you've seen. Especially reflect on the ideas and understandings that you have about death that come from your experiences.

Use the blank space below and on the following page to record some of your own childhood experiences.

⇒ *Questionnaire: You and death*

Directions   *Your answers to the following questions will provide a review of some of the issues related to death and dying.*

1. How openly is death spoken about in your family, your circle of friends, and your work environment? What do you believe accounts for the ease (or lack of ease) about discussing death in each of these environments?

   _____

   _____

   _____

   _____

   _____

   _____

2. Are you afraid of death? What particular aspects of death elicit fear or anxiety in you?

   _____

   _____

   _____

   _____

   _____

   _____

3. Do you have written plans for carrying out your wishes at and after death? What are they?

   _____

   _____

   _____

   _____

   _____

   _____

4. Are there legal or consumer matters that you need to complete before your death? What are they?

_____

_____

_____

_____

_____

_____

5. What important interpersonal or unfinished business would you like to complete before your death?

_____

_____

_____

_____

_____

_____

6. Do you believe that you would make changes in your life style (relationships, home, work, travel, education, etc.) if you discovered that you had a terminal illness? What would those changes include?

_____

_____

_____

_____

_____

_____

➠ *A Mature Concept of Death*

Directions *Interview two children, one between the ages of four and seven, and another between the ages of eight and eleven (Make sure parental permission is obtained.) Ask the two children the following questions related to the mature concept of death.*

Child 1: Age_____

Child 2: Age_____

1. Will all the people in the world die someday, or do some people never die?

Child 1: _____

_____

_____

_____

_____

_____

Child 2: _____

_____

_____

_____

_____

_____

2. When a person dies, can they eat? Can they breathe? Can they move?

Child 1: _____

_____

_____

_____

_____

_____

Child 2: _____

_____

_____

_____

_____

3. When a person dies, can they ever come back to life again?

Child 1: _____

_____

_____

_____

_____

Child 2: _____

_____

_____

_____

_____

➠ *Television as Teacher*

Directions *Watch two or three television programs directed toward children or adolescents in which death is likely to be depicted. Provide a summary of the plot and provide answers to the following questions for each program viewed. Use additional paper as necessary to answer the questions for additional programs.*

1. What was the title of the program?

   _____

2. What was the plot or story?

   _____

   _____

   _____

   _____

3. Which character(s) died?

   _____

   _____

   _____

   _____

4. How did the character(s) die?

   _____

   _____

   _____

   _____

5. How was death determined?

_____

_____

_____

_____

6. What were the survivors' reactions (grief or otherwise) to death?

_____

_____

_____

_____

7. Was there a funeral ritual or commemoration of the death?

_____

_____

_____

_____

8. If children were depicted in the story, how were they told about the death and what were their reactions?

_____

_____

_____

_____

9. What portion of the program content included issues of cultural diversity in dying, death, or grief?

_____

_____

_____

_____

10. Were the characters who died mentioned again? In what manner or context?

_____

_____

_____

_____

11. What did this program teach children about death?

_____

_____

_____

_____

12. How could the presentation of death-related actions or topics have been improved?

_____

_____

_____

_____

Health Care Systems: Patients, Staff, and Institutions

Chapter Summary

Chapter 4 examines the American health care system as it relates to care of persons with life-threatening and terminal illnesses. The chapter begins with an introduction to modern health care, including issues concerning health care financing and the various pressures to ration scarce resources. These issues raise questions about the limits of medical progress and how best to achieve a balance between extension of life and quality of life.

Modern health care embodies a tripartite relationship among patient, institution, and staff. Each of the parties to this relationship contributes to the overall shape and quality of health care. Excessive bureaucratization can create situations wherein care of the dying becomes impersonal, thereby undermining the "subjecthood" of the patient. In such cases, biological death may be preceded by social death. Alternatives to such depersonalization and abstraction require that both caregivers and patients break the illusion of immortality and recognize that all lives have an end.

Although hospitals remain the primary setting for care of terminally ill patients, other options have become more available. The emphasis of hospice and palliative care, for example, is oriented specifically toward the needs of the dying patient and his or her family. Home care is also increasingly recognized as an appropriate alternative for some patients and their families. Even within conventional hospital settings, there is a greater emphasis on providing appropriate care for dying patients—that is, care intended to alleviate pain and other symptoms, as opposed to measures intended to extend life. Most terminally ill patients use a combination of all these forms of care, depending on the stage of illness and their particular situation. Organized support groups that focus on specific interests and needs of patients have also become important in the total health care system.

Emergency care for life-threatening injury and trauma is another area related to the study of death and dying. Nearly 55 percent of trauma deaths occur instantly after injury. For those who survive with injuries, speed of care is crucial. Many of the advances in emergency medicine have resulted from a focus on the critical "golden hour" following injury. The use of the helicopter air ambulance and the triage system for evacuating casualties have increased the chances of surviving many types of injury, as has the development of specialized trauma centers, where surgery and other medical interventions can be provided expeditiously. Even more lives could be saved if funding were available to provide such emergency services on a broader scale.

Compassionate care of patients with life-threatening conditions requires sensitivity to issues of communication between caregivers and patients. Good communication between caregiver and patient helps to motivate the patient's own healing system, creating the potential for a positive outcome regardless of the ultimate prognosis. Total care encompasses attention to the patient's physical, mental, emotional, and spiritual needs.

Helping professionals who work in environments where death occurs frequently are subject to high levels of stress. Decisions involving life or death may have to be made under extreme time pressures. Caregivers may face the task of delivering bad news to relatives and handling their reactions. Medical and nursing professionals need to work within a supportive environment that allows death to be discussed openly among those involved in patients' care. They must also be confident that the care they provide is appropriate, beneficial, and in patients' best interests.

People may feel uncomfortable in the presence of a someone who has been diagnosed with a life-threatening illness or who is dying. Being with someone who is dying involves a confrontation with one's own mortality. An antidote to discomfort and uncertainty in such situations is to remember that the essence of caregiving and companionship is to leave your own agenda at the door and attend to the needs of the other person. In such circumstances, we learn that we cannot expect ourselves to have all the answers. Being with someone who is dying can help us recognize just how precious life is, and how uncertain.

Objectives

- To list the three components of a health care system and to explain how their interrelationship influences the effectiveness of patient care.
- To summarize the various types of health care for terminally ill patients and to differentiate between their functions and purposes.
- To describe the characteristics of an optimal patient-caregiver relationship.
- To evaluate modes of communication that facilitate being with someone who is dying.
- To explain the factors influencing the onset of stress among health professionals who care for dying patients and to point out ways of alleviating such stress.
- To identify psychosocial factors influencing one's relationship with a loved one who is dying.

Key Terms and Concepts

acute care

bureaucratization of death

burnout

caregiver stress

chronic illness

classic and ideal caring situations

communications chasm

covenantal relationship

depersonalization

diagnosis-related groups (DRGs)

health care rationing

home care

hospice care

hospital

life review

medical paternalism

nursing home

palliative care

primary caregiver

quality-adjusted life years (QALYs)

skilled nursing facility

support groups

total care

trauma/emergency care

triage

Questions for Guided Study and Review

1. What are the differences between hospitals, nursing homes, and hospices?
2. What are the components of the "health care triangle"?
3. How do written and unwritten rules affect patient care?
4. How do depersonalization and abstraction affect human medical care and quality of life?
5. How is the cost of health care related to financial and technological innovations?
6. What is the definition of rationing, and when does it occur?
7. How might bureaucratic attitudes and organizational structure affect interactions among patients, family members, and health care professionals?
8. What five strategies for responding to a dying patient's communication are discussed in the text?
9. Discuss the contrast between "cure" and "care" orientations of medical care.
10. What are the main goals of palliative care?
11. Describe the settings in which palliative care is provided to patients.
12. What is the historical background of hospice care?
13. What are the goals of hospice care?
14. In what ways does St. Christopher's embody the goals and characteristics of hospice care?
15. What challenges face hospices and hospice care?
16. Summarize the Medicare guidelines for hospice care.
17. What is a primary caregiver?
18. What are the potential advantages and disadvantages to home care?
19. What is the Zen Hospice Project, and how does it work?
20. What are the central aims of social support programs for dying patients and their families?
21. What is the historical background of modern-day trauma care?
22. What is the "golden hour"?
23. What category of medical problem has been termed the "principal public health problem in America"?
24. What is medical *paternalism*?
25. What important characteristics should be considered in disclosing a life-threatening diagnosis?

26. How do *iconics* affect staff-patient communication in medical settings?
27. What sources of stress may be present in caring for the dying?
28. How might caregivers deal constructively with stress related to caring for patients?
29. How is *life review* a useful counseling tool with dying people?
30. How might an individual counteract feelings of discomfort and uncertainty when in the presence of someone who is seriously ill or dying?

Practice Test Questions

MULTIPLE CHOICE

1. Hospital health care focuses primarily on the _____ aspect of the patient's well-being.
   a. emotional
   b. mental
   c. physical
   d. spiritual

2. A staff member says to a terminally ill patient, "Oh, you'll live to be a hundred," to
   a. mock the patient.
   b. cheat the patient.
   c. help the patient realize that everybody has to die sometime.
   d. avoid discussion of death with the patient.

3. Hospice care is distinguished by its orientation toward
   a. the needs of cancer patients.
   b. working only with lay people.
   c. the needs of dying patients.
   d. eliminating nursing homes.

4. Most people diagnosed with a life-threatening illness
   a. do not want their families to be told.
   b. would rather suspect it without being told directly.
   c. would rather not know.
   d. want to be told.

5. The emphasis on cure among medical professionals can cause death to be
   a. seen as a natural event.
   b. viewed as a medical failure.
   c. seen as an oddity.
   d. discussed objectively and openly.

TRUE/FALSE

_____ 1. Rather than be subjected to futile treatments at the end of life, people may express their preferences by means of advance directives.

_____ 2. Historically, hospices were built on a military model of efficiency.

_____ 3. A covenantal relationship implies an absence of giving and receiving between caregivers and patients.

_____ 4. Home care is unsupervised medical care that is provided in the patient's home.

_____ 5. Because of their frequent exposure to death, health care professionals find it less stressful than other people do.

MATCHING

Match each of the following characteristics with the most appropriate medical care institution or organization.

_____ 1. Provides care for chronically ill patients   a. hospital

_____ 2. Encourages the use of peer counseling   b. nursing home

_____ 3. Meets the needs of dying patients   c. hospice care

_____ 4. Intense pressure and little or no feedback from the patient   d. emergency room

_____ 5. Provides short-term acute care   e. Shanti Project

⨎ Answers to practice questions can be found in Part IV ⨎

Related Readings

📖 Indicates selection from *The Path Ahead: Readings in Death and Dying*, eds. Lynne Ann DeSpelder and Albert Lee Strickland (Mountain View, Calif.: Mayfield, 1995).

MODERN HEALTH CARE

Daniel Callahan. *What Kind of Life: The Limits of Medical Progress.* New York: Simon & Schuster, 1990.

📖 Daniel Callahan, "The Limits of Medical Progress: A Principle of Symmetry," pp. 103—05.

Mickey Eisenberg. *Life in the Balance: Emergency Medicine and the Quest to Reverse Sudden Death.* New York: Oxford University Press, 1997.

John D. Lantos. *Do We Still Need Doctors?* New York: Routledge, 1997.

Carolyn L. Wiener and Anselm L. Strauss, eds. *Where Medicine Fails*, 5th ed. New Brunswick, N.J. Transaction, 1997.

CARE OF THE DYING

📖 William G. Bartholome, "Care of the Dying Child: The Demands of Ethics," pp. 133–143.

Ira Byock. *Dying Well: The Prospect for Growth at the End of Life*. New York: Riverhead Books, 1997.

Stephen R. Connor. *Hospice: Practice, Pitfalls, Promise*. Washington, D.C.: Taylor & Francis, 1997.

Marilyn J. Field and Christine K. Cassel, eds. *Approaching Death: Improving Care at the End of Life*. Washington, D.C.: National Academy Press, 1997.

📖 Joseph M. Kaufert and John D. O'Neil, "Cultural Mediation of Dying and Grieving Among Native Canadian Patients in Urban Hospitals," pp. 59–74.

📖 William M. Lamers, Jr., "Hospice: Enhancing the Quality of Life," pp. 116–124.

Marcia Lattanzi-Licht, John J. Mahoney, and Galen W. Miller. *The Hospice Choice: In Pursuit of a Peaceful Death*. New York: Fireside, 1998.

Rodger McFarlane and Philip Bashe. *The Complete Bedside Companion: No-Nonsense Advice on Caring for the Seriously Ill*. New York: Simon & Schuster, 1998.

📖 Balfour M. Mount, "Keeping the Mission," pp. 125–132.

📖 Richard S. Sandor, "On Death and Coding," pp. 144–147.

Cecily Saunders and Robert Kastenbaum. *Hospice Care on the International Scene*. New York: Springer, 1997.

Virginia F. Sendor and Patrice M. O'Connor. *Hospice & Palliative Care: Questions and Answers*. Lanham, M.D.: Scarecrow Press, 1997.

📖 Janmarie Silvera, "Crossing the Border," pp. 301–302.

THE PATIENT-CAREGIVER RELATIONSHIP

Merrill Collett. *Stay Close and Do Nothing: A Spiritual and Practical Guide to Caring for the Dying at Home*. Kansas City, Mo.: Andrews McMeel, 1997.

Dale G. Larson. *The Helper's Journey: Working with People Facing Grief, Loss, and Life-Threatening Illness*. Champaign, Ill.: Research Press, 1993.

📖 Stanley Joel Reiser, "The Era of the Patient: Using the Experience of Illness in Shaping the Missions of Health Care," pp. 106–115.

Howard Spiro, Mary G. McCrea Curnen, Enid Peschel, and Deborah St. James, eds. *Empathy and the Practice of Medicine: Beyond Pills and the Scalpel*. New Haven, Conn.: Yale University Press, 1993.

Major Points in This Chapter

- The kind and quality of modern health care depends on the relationships among the patient, the medical/nursing staff, and the institution.

- Individual and social choices about financing health care exert an influence on the options available for care of the seriously ill and dying.

- Hospice care for the dying results from concerns about care of the terminally ill as well as about costs of health care at the end-stage of life.

- Health care institutions are increasingly oriented toward providing "total" or "whole-person" care (physical, emotional, and spiritual) and social support.

- In the context of health care, a covenantal relationship implies a mutuality of interest between health care providers and patients; it encourages clear communication and promotes sharing of decision making.
- Palliative care involves active total care of patients whose disease is not responsive to curative treatment.
- Hospice care is specialized palliative care of patients with terminal illness.
- Emergency personnel and other caregivers are exposed to stress related to the helping role.
- Being with someone who is dying involves a confrontation with one's own mortality.

Observations and Reflections

It is important to recognize that there is nothing inherently bad or good about any particular health care system. What makes a setting good or bad are the values, beliefs, and practices of the people involved. Consequently, through education, any health care system can become more responsive to the needs of dying patients.

Use the blank space below and on the following page to brainstorm some ways that health care systems can become more responsive to the needs of dying patients and their families.

Study Guide
The Last Dance: Encountering Death and Dying, 6th ed.

Chapter 4 ⌒ 81

⇒ *Health Care Dramas: Television and the Terminally Ill*

Directions   *Watch three different medical programs on television, paying attention to how terminally ill patients, their doctors, nurses, other caregivers, family, and friends are portrayed. Then answer the following questions and bring the responses to class.*

What was the patient's age, sex, and socioeconomic level?

Program 1 _____

Program 2 _____

Program 3 _____

Describe his or her personality.

Program 1 _____

Program 2 _____

Program 3 _____

How was he or she treated by family members and medical personnel?

Program 1 _____

Program 2 _____

Program 3 _____

Was the death presented in a realistic context?

Program 1 _____

Program 2 _____

Program 3 _____

What was the cause of death?

Program 1 _____

Program 2 _____

Program 3 _____

In what ways was the death similar or different from your own experience with death?

Program 1 _____

Program 2 _____

Program 3 _____

Was the death portrayed realistically?

Program 1 _____

Program 2 _____

Program 3 _____

What life values were expressed in the death?

Program 1 _____

Program 2 _____

Program 3 _____

What suggestions would you make to the program writers?

Program 1 _____

Program 2 _____

Program 3 _____

⇒ *Home Care*

Directions *Imagine that your closest relative has become terminally ill and is a candidate for home care. Answer the following questions about your ability to be a caretaker.*

Given your present schedule, how much time per day (or week) would you be able to devote to caring for your relative?

_____

_____

_____

What training or preparation have you had to be a caretaker?

_____

_____

_____

If your relative's nurse needed assistance in carrying out the following duties, which of them do you think you could do?

- ❏ Provide a listening ear.
- ❏ Push wheelchair on outings for shopping or medical visits.
- ❏ Spend the night.
- ❏ Evaluate hospice care in your area.
- ❏ Coordinate home health care.
- ❏ Administer medication orally.
- ❏ Administer medication rectally.
- ❏ Administer an injection.
- ❏ Clean and maintain a catheter.
- ❏ Turn your relative in bed every hour to prevent bedsores.
- ❏ Clean up a bowel movement.
- ❏ Clean up vomit.
- ❏ Be with your relative as he or she dies.

Use this page to describe what you have learned by doing this exercise in combination with your readings about caregivers from *The Last Dance*.

_____

_____

_____

_____

_____

_____

_____

_____

_____

_____

_____

_____

_____

_____

_____

_____

_____

_____

_____

_____

_____

⇒ *Creating a Hospice*

Directions   *Imagine you are on the advisory board for the creation of a new free-standing hospice in the community. The National Hospice and Palliative Care Organization (NHPCO) [www.nhpco.org] has descriptions of hospice care along with qualities to consider in selecting a hospice. Read about hospice care and answer the following questions:*

What characteristics would you require of the medical staff (medical and non-medical) hired to care for dying patients?

_____

_____

_____

What would your facility look like?

_____

_____

_____

What visiting hours would you permit?

_____

_____

_____

Would you permit animals? If so, how would you accommodate patients who prefer not to be around animals?

_____

_____

_____

What would you do to reduce staff burnout?

_____

_____

_____

What other ideas would you want to implement?

_____

_____

_____

_____

_____

_____

_____

Summarize what you have learned from this activity.

_____

_____

_____

_____

_____

_____

_____

88   Chapter 4

Study Guide
The Last Dance: Encountering Death and Dying, 6th ed.

Facing Death:
Living with Life-Threatening Illness

Chapter Summary

Chapter 5 focuses on the experience of living with life-threatening illness, including its personal and social meanings. The chapter opens with an anecdotal presentation that describes a typical pattern associated with coping with life-threatening illness. This presentation takes the reader from initial discovery of symptoms through diagnosis and treatment, the ups and downs of changing circumstances, and finally confrontation with death.

Potentially fatal diseases are often accompanied by an unjustified social stigma. Life-threatening illness may be perceived as somehow taboo. The patient may assume responsibility for the illness through the medium of magical thinking or similar self-questioning. The reality is that life-threatening illnesses affect people in all walks of life.

The personal and social costs of life-threatening illness include not only direct financial costs attributable to the disease, but also the burden of disrupted lives, distorted self-concept, and anxiety about the future. Positive approaches to dealing with life-threatening illness include education, counseling, and social support. These techniques help promote understanding that places the crisis in a more affirmative context, thus restoring a sense of personal control over a confusing situation.

The adaptive response to losses associated with life-threatening illness changes as circumstances change. The ways in which individuals cope with such illness is described in terms of Elisabeth Kübler-Ross's pioneering work with dying patients, as well as in terms of more recent task-based and pattern-oriented approaches. Considered as a whole, these various descriptive and theoretical approaches provide a solid foundation for understanding how people cope with serious and life-threatening illness.

Awareness of a serious or life-threatening illness is likely to be reflected in one of four patterns of communication and interaction: closed, suspected, mutual pretense, or open. The awareness context may change as the severity of the prognosis or problems related to care and treatment change during the course of illness.

Even though certain general patterns can be distinguished, however, it is important to recognize that different individuals cope with life-threatening illness differently. Also, the way we might imagine the course of events leading to eventual death is not necessarily an accurate reflection of how those events will be experienced by a particular person. It is often the case that idealized versions of dying tend to leave out pain, nausea, constipation, bedsores, and insomnia, as well as loneliness, anxiety, and fear—all of which typicaly accompany the dying trajectory.

The options available for treating serious illness vary not only according to the particular disease and the medical technologies available for treating it, but also because of decisions made by society as a whole. It is obviously not possible for all diseases and interventions to occupy the place of highest priority. Focusing primarily on cancer as the prototypic life-threatening illness, the discussion of treatment options centers on the main therapies employed against the disease—surgery, radiation therapy, and chemotherapy. Also discussed is the role of alternative, or complementary, and adjunctive therapies. "Symbolic healing," for example, may be an adjunct to conventional therapies in terms of its value in helping to mobilize a patient's inner resources and will to live. Regardless of the therapeutic modality employed to treat life-threatening illness, pain management becomes increasingly important when a disease continues to progress and as patients near death. Pain is the most common symptom of terminally ill patients; managing it effectively is a chief goal of palliative care. The perception of pain differs among individuals as well as cultures. The phenomenon of pain is increasingly being addressed by interdisciplinary approaches that relate to a patient's "total pain" which includes physical, psychological, social, and spiritual pain.

Until about the middle of the twentieth century, a social role for the dying person was more or less fixed by custom and circumstance. Since then, however, pervasive social and technological changes have tended to eliminate the traditional role of the dying without offering a new role to replace it. It may be that, as people become more willing to face the issues of dying and death squarely, and as hospice and palliative care become more widely available, we will see the creation of a new social role for the dying that is appropriate for our own time. Such a role would not not require a terminally ill or dying patient to maintain false hope or an appearance of expecting to live forever. On the contrary, it would acknowledge the prospect of death while emphasizing an appropriate sense of empowerment whereby farewells are communicated and attention is given to the special physical, psychological, social, and spiritual needs that pertain to the end of life. The perception of a dying person's "fading away" might be accompanied by a task of redefinition, during which family members and friends begin to deal with the burden of letting go before picking up the new.

Objectives

- To list the personal and social costs of life-threatening illness.
- To design a personal strategy for health care (both physical and psychological) should one be faced with a life-threatening illness.
- To describe and assess patterns of coping with life-threatening illness.
- To identify and assess treatment strategies for individuals with life-threatening illness.
- To assess the benefits and risks of alternative therapies.
- To summarize the essential strategies for pain management.
- To distinguish among the various dying trajectories.
- To explain the factors influencing the social role of the dying patient and to create an ideal model.

Key Terms and Concepts

adjunctive treatment
active dying
awareness contexts
biopsy
cancer
chemotherapy
complementary therapy
coping mechanisms
curanderismo
diagnosis
dying trajectory
ethnomedicine
immunotherapy
infection
life-threatening illness

malignancy
metastasis
magical thinking
oncologist
pain management
prognosis
radiation therapy
relapse
remission
social death
social role of dying person
symbolic healing
tumor
unorthodox treatment
visualization

Questions for Guided Study and Review

1. How might a person's concerns and fears change during the course of a life-threatening illness?
2. In what way is the diagnosis of life-threatening illness sometimes treated as something "taboo"?
3. What is "social death," and how might it be manifested?
4. What is "magical thinking" as it applies to coping with life-threatening illness?
5. How does the phrase, "adapting to living/dying" relate to life-threatening illness?
6. What are the "five stages" of coping with life-threatening illness as described by Elisabeth Kübler-Ross?
7. How do "task-based" different models differ from "stage-based" models of coping with serious illness and dying?
8. In reviewing the different models of coping behavior put forward by Charles Corr, Avery Weisman, Therese Rando, and Ken Doka, what common elements or patterns do you notice?

9. Accoding to Barney Glaser and Anselm Strauss, what are the four awareness contexts that may be observed in communicational interactions with the dying?
10. What does it mean to "maintain coping potency"?
11. How did Presidents John Adams and Thomas Jefferson illustrate the "will to live" that may be observed in dying persons?
12. What is the definition of *metastasis*?
13. What are the advantages and disadvantages of the three main conventional cancer therapies?
14. Why are alternative and complementary therapies becoming increasingly important in health care?
15. What is *ethnomedicine*?
16. Are *adjunctive* therapies different from *alternative* or *complementary* therapies?
17. What are "unorthodox treatments"?
18. What is the most common symptom of terminally ill patients?
19. What are the two main types of pain?
20. How is pain generally managed?
21. What drug is most commonly used to relieve severe cancer pain?
22. What factors hamper adequate pain management?
23. Is "pain" a single, well-defined entity?
24. What is a "dying trajectory"?
25. How does a "lingering" trajectory differ from an "expected quick" trajectory?
26. In the last phase of a fatal illness, what are the signs of "active dying"?
27. How does the "sick role" differ from the social role of the dying patient?
28. What are three important spiritual needs of the dying?

Practice Test Questions

MULTIPLE CHOICE

1. The way in which an individual copes with dying
    a. depends mostly on the length of the illness.
    b. usually contrasts with other coping patterns.
    c. usually resembles lifelong coping patterns.
    d. depends on his or her doctors' attitudes.

2. According to the text, which of the following is NOT one of the four types of family interaction when a family member is diagnosed with a life-threatening illness?
    a. closed awareness
    b. open awareness
    c. suspected pretense
    d. mutual pretense

3. According to the concept of open awareness, when in the presence of someone who is dying, a person should
   a. continually offer reassurance about regaining health.
   b. admit feelings of uncertainty.
   c. display a confident attitude.
   d. avoid contact if uncomfortable.

4. An oncologist is a specialist in
   a. the study of avian cancer.
   b. creating cancer medicines.
   c. surgical methods of treating cancer.
   d. non-surgical methods of treating cancer.

5. Metastasis is
   a. the correcting of a contagious disease.
   b. fear of dying.
   c. research done on various types of cancerous tumors.
   d. the spreading of cancer to various body parts.

TRUE/FALSE

_____ 1. Bargaining is NOT a response that may occur in facing a life-threatening illness.

_____ 2. In cases of life-threatening disease, the hope that there will be a cure always remains with the patient right up until the time of death.

_____ 3. The term *cancer* refers to various types of malignant, potentially lethal growth which may occur in different parts of the body.

_____ 4. Some cancers develop resistance to chemotherapy.

_____ 5. The growing interest in so-called alternative therapies is due to the ability of mainstream medicine to address the whole person.

Matching

Below are facts regarding particular treatments for cancer and other diseases. Match the description on the left with the appropriate therapy on the right. Each choice may be used only once.

____	1. The greatest percentage of cancer cures is due to this treatment	a. surgery
____	2. In this treatment toxic drugs are used to kill cancer cells	b. symbolic healing
____	3. What we believe to be meaningful potentially affects the functioning of our bodies	c. chemotherapy
____	4. The patient imagines diseased parts of the body becoming well again	d. visualization

❧ Answers to practice questions can be found in Part IV ❦

Related Readings

📖 Indicates selection from *The Path Ahead: Readings in Death and Dying*, eds. Lynne Ann DeSpelder and Albert Lee Strickland (Mountain View, Calif.: Mayfield, 1995).

COPING WITH LIFE-THREATENING ILLNESS

Mitch Albom. *Tuesdays with Morrie: An Old Man, a Young Man, and Life's Greatest Lesson*. New York: Doubleday, 1997.

📖 Thomas Attig, "Coping with Mortality: An Essay on Self-Mourning," pp. 337–341.

📖 Sandra L. Bertman, "Bearing the Unbearable: From Loss, the Gain," pp. 348–354.

📖 Harold Brodkey, "To My Readers," pp. 295–300.

Maggie Callanan and Patricia Kelley. *Final Gifts: Understanding the Special Awareness, Needs, and Communications of the Dying*. New York: Bantam, 1997.

📖 Allan B. Chinen, "The Mortal King," pp. 335–336.

📖 Charles A. Corr, "A Task-Based Approach to Coping with Dying," pp. 303–311.

Betty Davies, Joanne Cherkryn Reimer, Pamela Brown, and Nola Martens. *Fading Away: The Experience of Transition in Families with Terminal Illness*. Amityville, N.Y.: Baywood, 1996.

Kenneth J. Doka. *Living with Life-Threatening Illness: A Guide for Patients, Their Families, and Caregivers*. New York: Lexington, 1993.

📖 Herman Feifel, "Psychology and Death: Meaningful Rediscovery," pp. 19–28.

Jerome Groopman. *The Measure of Our Days: New Beginnings at Life's End*. New York: Viking, 1997.

Marie de Hennezel. *Intimate Death: How the Dying Teach Us To Live*. New York: Alfred A. Knopf, 1997.

📖 Robert Kastenbaum, "Reconstructing Death in Postmodern Society," pp. 7–18.

📖 Joseph M. Kaufert and John D. O'Neil, "Cultural Mediation of Dying and Grieving Among Native Canadian Patients in Urban Hospitals," pp. 59–74.

📖 Alfred G. Killilea, "The Politics of Being Mortal," pp. 342–347.

📖 Janmarie Silvera, "Crossing the Border," pp. 301–302.

TREATMENT OPTIONS AND ISSUES

Geoffrey M. Cooper. *The Cancer Book: A Guide to Understanding the Causes, Prevention, and Treatment of Cancer*. Boston: Jones and Bartlett, 1993.

Ilana Löwy. *Between Bench and Bedside: Science, Healing, and Interleukin 2 in a Cancer Ward*. Cambridge, Mass.: Harvard University Press, 1996.

David B. Morris. *The Culture of Pain*. Berkeley: University of California Press, 1991.

Sherwin B. Nuland. *How We Die: Reflections on Life's Final Chapter*. New York: Alfred A. Knopf, 1994.

📖 Stanley Joel Reiser, "The Era of the Patient: Using the Experience of Illness in Shaping the Missions of Health Care," pp. 106–115.

Barry D. Schoub. *AIDS & HIV in Perspective: A Guide to Understanding the Virus and Its Consequences*. New York: Cambridge University Press, 1994.

Arthur Selzer. *Understanding Heart Disease*. Berkeley: University of California Press, 1992.

"What You Need to Know About Cancer" (Special Issue). *Scientific American* 275, no. 3 (September 1996).

Major Points in This Chapter

- When life-threatening illness is made to seem taboo, it creates difficulties in communication and hampers social support.
- Life-threatening illness is costly, personally as well as socially and spiritually.
- The adaptive response to losses associated with life-threatening illness changes as circumstances change.
- The awareness contexts relative to dying patients, families, and caregivers include closed awareness, suspected awareness, mutual pretense, and open awareness.
- The manner in which individuals cope with life-threatening illness is described in terms of Elisabeth Kübler-Ross's pioneering stage-based approach as well as more recent task-, phase-, and pattern-oriented approaches.
- Maintaining coping potency in the face of life-threatening illness requires access to both inner and external resources.
- The options for treatment of serious illness vary according to the illness and ongoing developments in medical knowledge; withholding or discontinuing treatment may also be an option.
- Alternative therapies encompass adjunctive or complementary therapies, as well asunorthodox therapies.
- Pain management is an essential component of a comprehensive treatment plan.

- Studies of the dying trajectory distinguish two main types: (1) a lingering trajectory whereby death takes place gradually and over an extended period of time, and (2) a quick trajectory whereby death is the outcome of an acute medical crisis.
- The social role of a dying patient differs between cultural groups and among individuals and families.

Observations and Reflections

This chapter emphasizes the importance of patient choice based on an individual's need to achieve a sense of self-control and empowerment. Notice if you find yourself judging too quickly or harshly the care options and dying styles chosen by someone who is terminally ill. Even though a patient's choices may seem wrong or odd to you for any number of reasons, it is important to acknowledge that a crucial aspect of such choices is that they not be made solely by health care providers or family members.

➠ *Death Fears*

Directions *Respond to each of the following statements with "yes," "no," or "maybe" in the blank spaces. After completing the questionnaire, use the following page to write about your experience of completing this activity.*

_____ 1. I am afraid of nothingness—the end of everything.

_____ 2. I am afraid of abandoning the people who depend on me.

_____ 3. I am afraid of making those who love me unhappy.

_____ 4. I am afraid of not having time to make amends for all my sins of commission and omission.

_____ 5. I am afraid that death will be the end of feeling and thinking.

_____ 6. I am afraid of losing control over what is being done to my body.

_____ 7. I am afraid of pain and dying.

_____ 8. I am afraid of punishment after death.

_____ 9. I am afraid of losing those I care about.

_____ 10. I am afraid of being helpless and having to depend completely on others.

_____ 11. I am afraid of dying because I don't know what happens after death.

_____ 12. I am afraid of dying before I am ready to go.

_____ 13. I am afraid of taking a long time to die.

_____ 14. I am afraid of dying suddenly and violently.

_____ 15. I am afraid of dying alone.

Use the space below to write about the experience of completing the Death Fears questionnaire on the previous page.

_____

_____

_____

_____

_____

_____

_____

_____

_____

_____

_____

_____

_____

_____

_____

_____

_____

➠ *Questionnaire: Life-Threatening Illness*

Directions *Respond to each of the statements below by indicating one of the following.*

SA	=	strongly agree
A	=	agree
U	=	undecided
D	=	disagree
SD	=	strongly disagree

_____ 1. A physician's decision to inform a patient about his or her terminal illness should be made on a case-by-case basis.

_____ 2. A close family member should be the one to inform the patient about his or her life-threatening illness.

_____ 3. A patient who is prematurely informed about his or her terminal illness will lose the will to live.

_____ 4. A child with a life-threatening illness should not be told about the possibility of his or her death.

_____ 5. I would not want the responsibility of informing a member of my family about the nature of his or her life-threatening illness.

_____ 6. If I had a life-threatening illness, I definitely would want to be informed by my physician.

_____ 7. A person can make important changes in his or her life when given knowledge of impending death.

_____ 8. Knowledge of impending death gives both the patient and his or her family an opportunity to communicate about important matters.

_____ 9. Sudden death is much easier for an individual and his or her family than death resulting from a lingering degenerative illness.

_____ 10. Overwhelming and unrelenting physical pain would be the worst aspect of coping with a life-threatening illness.

⟩ *Signs and Symptoms Near Death*

Directions   Read the following description of the physical, emotional, spiritual, and mental signs and symptoms of impending death and complete the questions that follow. They are designed to help you understand the natural changes that may occur during the dying process and how to best respond. All of these signs and symptoms will not occur with everyone, nor will they occur in this particular sequence. Each person is unique and needs to do things in his or her own way. In general, however, the body prepares itself for the final days of life in the following ways.

DECREASING FLUID AND FOOD CONSUMPTION

There is usually little interest in eating and drinking. Allow the person to eat and drink whatever is appetizing. Nourishment should be taken slowly and in small amounts. Let the person decide how much and when to eat and drink. Reflexes needed to swallow may be sluggish. Do not force fluids if the person coughs soon after. Small chips of ice, frozen juices, or popsicles may be refreshing.

The body lets a person know when it no longer desires and cannot tolerate food or liquids. The loss of this desire is a signal that the person is preparing to die. This is not a painful process. Dehydration no longer makes them uncomfortable. Glycerin swabs may help keep the mouth and lips moist and comfortable. A cool, moist washcloth on the forehead may also be welcome.

DECREASING SOCIALIZATION

The person may want to be alone with just one person or with just a few people. Speech is often slow or difficult or the person may not have the ability to speak at all. It is natural to feel like not socializing when feeling weak and fatigued. It may be disturbing to the dying person to have more than a few people in the room. Consider taking shifts in order for different people to be with the person. Keep the environment quiet and calm. Reassure the person that it is okay to sleep.

SLEEPING

The person may spend an increasing amount of time sleeping and become uncommunicative, unresponsive, and difficult to arouse at times. This normal change is due partly to changes in the metabolism of the body. Sit with the patient. Hold his or her hand gently. Speak softly and naturally. At this point *being with* is more important than *doing for*. Do not assume that the person cannot hear. Hearing is said to be the last of the five senses to be lost. Hearing may still remain very acute even when the person may seem asleep. Therefore do not say anything you would not say when the person is awake.

RESTLESSNESS

The person may make restless and repetitive motions, such as pulling at sheets or clothing, or have visions of people or things that do not exist. These symptoms may result from a decrease in oxygen circulation to the brain or a change in the body's metabolism. Do not be alarmed or try to restrain such motions. Talk calmly and reassuringly with the person so as not to startle or frighten him or her further. Lightly massage the hands, feet, or forehead. Reading to the person or playing soft music can also have a calming effect.

DISORIENTATION

The person may seem confused about time, place, and the identity of people in the room, including close and familiar people. Identify yourself by name rather than asking the person to guess who you are. In conscious moments, the person may speak or claim to have spoken to people who have already died or to see places not presently accessible or visible to you. This is not necessarily a hallucination or a reaction to medication. It signifies a person beginning the normal detachment from this life.

Accept this transitional time. There is no need to contradict, explain away, belittle, or argue about what the person claims to see or hear. Respectfully listen to whatever the person has to say. Allow free expression of feelings and offer comfort through touching and talking reassuringly and calmly.

INCONTINENCE

The person may lose control of urine or bowels as the muscles begin to relax. Diapers or disposable pads can help protect the bed and assist in keeping the person clean and comfortable.

URINE DECREASE

Urine output normally decreases, becomes more concentrated, and may become the color of tea. This is due to decreased fluid intake and to a lessening of circulation through the kidneys.

BREATHING

The person's usual breathing patterns may change. Breathing can become abnormal, shallow, irregular, fast, or slow. A common pattern consists of breathing irregularly with shallow respiration or periods of no breaths for 5 to 30 seconds, followed by a deep breath. The person may also have periods of rapid and shallow panting. Sometimes there is a moaning-like sound on exhalation. This does not indicate distress, but rather the sound of air passing over relaxed vocal chords. Changed breathing patterns are very common for a person nearing death. They indicate decreased circulation in the internal organs and buildup of body waste products. Elevating the head and turning the patient onto his or her side may help to increase comfort.

CONGESTION

Oral secretions may become more profuse and collect in the back of the throat. The person may develop gurgling sounds coming from the chest. These sounds can become loud and may be distressing to hear. These normal changes come from fluid imbalance and an inability to cough up normal secretions. It is helpful to raise the head of the bed or use pillows to raise the person's head so that the secretions pool lower and do not stimulate the gag reflex. Turn the person's head to the side and allow gravity to drain the congestion. You can also gently wipe the person's mouth with a moist cloth.

Color Changes

Due to changes in circulation, the person's arms and legs may become cold, hot, or discolored. This may be especially noticeable in the extremities (arms or legs) where the color may change to a darker, bluish hue. This is a normal indication that the circulation is conserving energy to the core of the body to support the most vital organs.

Irregular temperatures can be the result of the brain sending unclear messages. Keep the person warm if they appear cold, but do not use an electric blanket. If the person continually removes the covers, use just a light sheet. Sweating may occur, and there may be an odor resulting from the many physiological changes taking place in the body. The heartbeat and pulses may become slower, weaker, and irregular.

Permission to Go

When someone enters the last days of dying, the body begins the process of shutting down, a process which ends when all the physical systems stop functioning. This is usually an orderly and non-dramatic series of physical changes. They are not medical emergencies and do not require invasive interventions. These physical changes are a normal, natural way in which the body prepares itself for death. This release may accompany the resolution of unfinished business. It may include seeking or receiving permission from family members to "let go."

A dying person may try to hold on, even though it brings discomfort, in order to be assured that those left behind will be all right. A family's ability to reassure and release the dying person from this concern is the greatest gift of love that can be given at this time.

Saying Goodbye

When the person is ready to die and the family is able to let go, this is the time to say goodbye in personal ways. It may be helpful to just lie in bed with the person, hold his or her hand, and say anything you need to say. Tears are a normal and natural part of saying goodbye and do not need hiding or apology. Tears express your love and help you to let go.

At the Time of Death

It may be helpful for family members to discuss ahead of time what to do when the final moments arrive. At the time of death breathing ceases, heartbeat ceases, the person cannot be aroused, the eyelids may be partially open with the eyes in a fixed stare, and the mouth may fall open as the jaw relaxes. There is sometimes a release of bowel and bladder contents as the body relaxes.

The death of someone you are caring for, although an anxious event for family and friends, is not an acute medical emergency. It is not necessary to immediately call the medical examiner, the police, or 911. After the death has occurred, take the time needed to call a supportive person or adjust to the situation. There is no rush. Taking care of yourself is more important.

The physical, emotional, spiritual, and mental signs and symptoms of impending death described here are intended to help you understand what may happen as a person's body completes the natural process of shutting down and the person completes the natural process of dying. Ideally, these processes happen in a way that is appropriate and unique to the values, beliefs, and lifestyle of the individual and his or her family.

After reading this information answer the following questions.

1. With which of the signs and symptoms of dying would you feel most comfortable observing and providing assistance?

   _____

   _____

   _____

   _____

   _____

2. Which of the signs and symptoms causes you anxiety or fear?

   _____

   _____

   _____

   _____

   _____

3. How comfortable are you responding to a dying person's version of reality? (For example, seeing people in the room or asking, "Have you got the tickets for my trip?")

   _____

   _____

   _____

   _____

   _____

4. Describe the most important information you have gained from reading this article.

_____

_____

_____

_____

_____

_____

Adapted from *On Our Own Terms: Moyers on Dying Discussion Guide* (New York: Educational Broadcasting Corporation and Public Affairs Television, Inc., 2000). Original Copyright © 2000 Metropolitan Hospice of Greater New York. Reprinted by permission.

Medical Ethics: Dying in a Technological Age

Chapter Summary

Chapter 6 deals with central issues in medical ethics, which have become more prominent with advances in biomedical technology. Modern techniques of cardiopulmonary resuscitation (CPR) and organ transplantation, for example, make possible life-sustaining interventions that were not available just a few decades ago. Yet such technological advances present us with difficult questions about how they should be used. Sophisticated medical technologies can dramatically alter the course of dying and thereby challenge the traditional definition of death. The long-standing Hippocratic obligation to keep people alive can lead to confusing consequences in the modern era. Coming to terms with these consequences and finding a satisfactory guide to behavior requires grappling with fundamental ethical principles such as autonomy, beneficence, and justice.

Although moral philosophers have discussed these principles for hundreds if not thousands of years, their application in medical practice has varied, reflecting changes in public attitudes and social situations. For example, studies done in the 1960s showed that most physicians tended to withhold information about a terminal prognosis. Telling the unadulterated truth was viewed as possibly harmful to a patient's best interest. Instead, patients with incurable cancer were told that they had a "lesion" or "mass." Adjectives such as "suspicious" or "degenerated" were used to temper the impact of a disturbing diagnosis. Within a period of about twenty years, however, a very different climate of truth telling emerged. Physicians became much more likely to reveal the true nature of a terminal diagnosis.

In tracing the reasons for this change, we can discern the influence of consumer attitudes as well as improvements in the medical outlook for patients with life-threatening disease. As consumers began to demand a greater voice in decisions affecting their welfare, medical practitioners were increasingly being held accountable for the services provided to patients. Medical paternalism, wherein doctors assume responsibility for making decisions about patient care, opens the door to allegations of malpractice when outcomes differ from expectations. Furthermore, newer therapies tend to require more knowledgeable cooperation from patients in successfully following treatment regimes.

Informed consent is based on three principles. First, the patient must be competent to give consent. Second, consent must be given voluntarily. Third, consent must be based on an adequate understanding of the proposed treatment program. Because individual and cultural attitudes toward autonomy or self-determination as applied to medical care differ, the process of giving information and obtaining consent to a treatment plan must be flexible. Although forced, coercive treatment is rare, caregivers may exert undue influence on patients by means of subtle or overt manipulation. Thus, shared decision-making places special emphasis on the process of communication between caregivers and patients. Not simply a laundry list of risks to be recited in an effort to avoid potential complaints or legal problems, informed consent actually can be a mechanism for facilitating communication between patient and physician, leading to greater cooperation toward the common goal of optimal health care.

In recent years, the most emotionally charged issues in medical ethics have been those concerning euthanasia, or intentionally and actively bringing about the death of a terminally ill person, and forgoing life-sustaining treatment, either by withholding or withdrawing treatment. Debates about a "right to die" have been prominent since the landmark case involving Karen Ann Quinlan during the mid-1970s. What is the proper balance between sustaining life and preventing suffering in cases where further treatment is likely to be futile? What is the effect of life-sustaining medical technologies on the quality of patients' lives?

Advocates of the notion that human beings have an inherent "right to die" and that it should be permissible for physicians to assist terminal patients in voluntarily ending their lives have received support in many quarters. Yet critics of euthanasia and physician-assisted suicide express concerns that a legally sanctioned "right" to die could become an "obligation" to die, because of subtle pressures to lessen the burden on loved ones or lessen the economic impact of terminal care on society as a whole. Where would one draw the line, they ask, once the "slippery slope" of physician-assisted suicide has been embarked upon? Critics also say that requests for physician-assisted suicide or euthanasia tend to evaporate when pain and depression are adequately treated.

In contrast to the ongoing debate about euthanasia and physician-assisted suicide, the practice of withholding or withdrawing treatment that is considered medically useless has become increasingly well-established and accepted. For virtually any life-threatening condition, some medical intervention is capable of delaying the moment of death (or, as some would say, prolonging dying). Although there is general agreement among medical practitioners as well as the general public that extraordinary interventions are not required when a patient is hopelessly ill, gray areas remain. One such area involves the meaning of the term "extraordinary." For example, is artificial provision of nutrition and hydration an extraordinary intervention or ordinary care? Discussions about such issues often revolve around conceptual ambiguities—in this case, those involving the artificial delivery of food and fluids. The symbolic significance of providing nutrition and the specter of "starving a person to death" are deeply rooted in the human psyche.

In the summer of 1990, the U.S. Supreme Court ruled on a petition to end the artificial feeding of Nancy Beth Cruzan, a Missouri woman who had been in a persistent vegetative state resulting from an automobile accident since 1983. The Court said that a competent person has a right to refuse life-sustaining medical treatment, but also ruled that states (in this case, Missouri) had the right to establish procedural requirements for "clear and convincing evidence" about an incompetent patient's wishes. Since Nancy Cruzan had not formally made her wishes known by executing an advance directive (such as a living will or health care proxy, discussed in Chapter 9), the case was referred back to the Missouri courts where, after further consideration and new testimony from three of Nancy's friends, it was ruled that the "clear and convincing" standard had been met. Permission was then granted to remove the tube supplying food and water. The Cruzan case points up not only the diversity of opinions about what constitutes extraordinary treatment, but also the sort of confusing legal situations that occur in the context of medical ethics. The burden of such uncertainty weighs heavily on families when patients cannot express their own choices, either because they have lost that capacity (as with individuals who are in a coma), or because they have not yet achieved power to exercise autonomy (as with newborns who are seriously ill).

Organ donation and transplantation, yet another area of interest to the student of death and dying, involves both ethical issues and the impact of governmental regulation and standardized procedures. The Uniform Anatomical Gift Act, which has been enacted in some form in all fifty states, provides for the donation of the body or specific body parts upon the death of the donor. The Act was revised in 1987 to simplify organ donation by removing requirements that the document be witnessed and that next of kin give consent. Organ donation can be accomplished easily by completing a brief donor card (available from the Motor Vehicle department of most states). It should be noted, however, that even though consent by next of kin is not legally required to effect organ donation, it is nonetheless prudent to discuss one's plans for donation with relatives to ensure that such wishes are carried out. A central office, known as the United Network for Organ Sharing (UNOS), to help match donated organs with potential recipients was established as part of the National Organ Transplant Act (1984).

Another area of medical ethics wherein modern medical technology has had an important impact is that of creating new guidelines for defining death. The conventional signs of death—most notably, absence of heartbeat and lack of respiration—are rendered inadequate when vital processes are maintained artificially. In many cases, bodily organs destined for transplantation are harvested from donors who are "brain dead" but whose heartbeat and respiration are maintained by a machine. When a patient is placed on a device that artificially sustains his or her vital functions, it opens the possibility of ethical questions over how death should be defined.

Most efforts to expand the criteria for determining death beyond the conventional signs have focused on loss of the capacity for bodily integration. This is popularly known as "brain" death, which is essentially defined as an irreversible coma confirmed by a flat electroencephalogram (EEG), and unresponsiveness to all external stimuli. The crucial factor is the presence or absence of the capacity for bodily integration. For example, a person whose vital processes are sustained artificially during surgery is not dead. But a person who has lost the capacity for bodily integration, even though the body's vital processes are maintained artificially, is dead.

Ethical issues in medicine have increasingly come to the forefront due to rapid and innovative advances in medical technologies. Such advances have, in many instances, revolutionized medical practice. At the same time, they have contributed to a "booming business" for ethicists and others—both professionals and laypeople—who recognize the need to find answers (at least tentative ones) to difficult questions. As Leon Kass observes, however, theorizing has its place, but the "morality of ordinary practice" is where the rubber meets the road. When it comes to ethical issues, our choices result not only from the unique blend of our own personal values, but also from values present within our particular cultural group and community. It is important to reflect on the reality that decisions about medical ethics have an impact not only on some vague realm of public policy "out there," but also, often poignantly, on the lives of individuals and families.

Objectives

- To explain how the fundamental ethical principles of autonomy, beneficence, and justice apply to medical ethics.
- To describe the factors affecting truth telling in cases involving terminal illness.
- To assess patients' rights with respect to self-determination and informed consent.
- To identify the consequences of withholding the truth from the point of view of both patient and physician.
- To evaluate the ethical issues involved in euthanasia.
- To explain how issues regarding competency affect decisions to withhold treatment from infants or comatose patients.
- To describe the stipulations contained in the Uniform Anatomical Gift Act and to assess its pertinence to you.
- To describe the emotional, physical, and ethical components of organ transplantation.
- To name four approaches to the definition of death and to evaluate the usefulness of each.
- To give an example of a practical definition of death and its application to making a determination of death.

Key Terms and Concepts

artificial nutrition and hydration
autonomy
beneficence
brain death
cellular death
clinical death
CMO (comfort measures only)
comatose
CPR (cardiopulmonary resuscitation)
definition of death
DNR (do not resuscitate)
ethics
etiology
euthanasia
extraordinary measures
Harvard criteria
higher-brain theory

Hippocratic oath
informed consent
justice
life-sustaining treatment
National Organ Transplant Act
neonatal intensive care
organ donation
organ transplanation
persistent vegetative state
physician-assisted suicide (PAS)
placebo
right to die
rigor mortis
soul
Uniform Anatomical Gift Act
vital signs
xenotransplantation

Questions for Guided Study and Review

1. How might the impact of medical technology tend to prolong the dying process as opposed to extending the living process?
2. What is the relationship among the fundamental ethical principles of autonomy, beneficience, and justice?
3. What are some reasons for limiting the ethical principle of autonomy?
4. What is "informed consent," and what three legal principles are involved?
5. How do today's attitudes among physicians toward disclosing a terminal diagnosis differ from attitudes prevalent in the 1950s?
6. What personal and social factors should be considered in the context of informing patients about a terminal prognosis?
7. Why is the case of Karen Ann Quinlan important in medical ethics?
8. What three options have medical ethicists outlined when a patient is hopelessly ill?
9. What is the difference between withholding and withdrawing treatment?
10. What is the distinction between allowing to die and helping to die?
11. What is "terminal sedation"?
12. What is the principle of "double effect"?
13. What criteria have been established in the Netherlands concerning euthanasia and physician-assisted suicide?
14. What is the "wedge" or "slippery slope" argument?
15. What is the difference between *ordinary care* and *extraordinary measures*?
16. What "conceptual ambiguity" is evoked in ethical issues involving artificial nutrition?
17. Why is the case of Nancy Beth Cruzan important in medical ethics?
18. With respect to forgoing life-sustaining treatment, what factors were emphasized by the President's Commission as important?
19. What are the major provisions of the Uniform Anatomical Gift Act?
20. How was the Uniform Anatomical Gift Act revised in 1987?
21. What does *required request* mean in terms of organ donation?
22. What are some areas of current controversy about organ donations?
23. What is the purpose of the National Organ Transplant Act?
24. What is the function of the United Network for Organ Sharing?
25. How do physicians and other medical personnel function as "gatekeepers" in cases of organ transplantation?
26. In what way does the "coffin bell-pull device" demonstrate concern about defining death?
27. What five steps are involved in the process of making decisions about the death of a human being?
28. What are the traditional "signs of death"?
29. What is the distinction between *clinical death* and *cellular death*?
30. What is a *persistent vegetative state*?
31. What are the four approaches to defining and determining death outlined by Robert Veatch?
32. What is "brain death"?
33. What are the criteria for determining brain death developed by the Harvard Medical School Ad Hoc Committee?
34. What is the distinction between the "higher-brain theory" and the "whole-brain" theory?
35. What issue does Leon Kass address in speaking about "the morality of ordinary practice"?

Practice Test Questions

MULTIPLE CHOICE

1. Informed consent is based on all of the following principles EXCEPT
    a. the patient must be competent to provide consent.
    b. the patient must freely and voluntarily give consent.
    c. consent must result from a detailed recitation of the risks of a treatment.
    d. consent must result from adequate understanding of the circumstances and alternatives.

2. The notion of keeping a patient alive at all costs
    a. is mandatory by law.
    b. was more prevalent in the 1940s.
    c. is fostered by the Hippocratic Oath.
    d. is a relatively recent development.

3. In the Nancy Beth Cruzan case, the United States Supreme Court ruled that
    a. artificial means of sustaining life could not be arbitrarily removed by doctors or family.
    b. the Cruzans had the right to remove Nancy's feeding tube.
    c. Missouri had the right to enact laws regarding treatment issues.
    d. comatose patients do not have the same rights as competent individuals.

4. An accurate definition of clinical death is necessary to
    a. improve record keeping and documentation.
    b. clarify legal questions related to the use of respirators and forced feedings.
    c. better ascertain when life-sustaining procedures are needed.
    d. identify when organs can be legally removed for transplantation.

5. The Uniform Anatomical Gift Act is concerned with
    a. bone marrow transplantation.
    b. blood donation.
    c. organ transplantation.
    d. organ donation.

TRUE/FALSE

_____   1. Physicians today are less apt to inform a patient of the terminal nature of a disease than they were in the 1950s.

_____   2. The New Jersey Supreme Court allowed Karen Ann Quinlan's parents to discontinue her artificial respiration.

_____   3. Passive euthanasia is the bringing about of death through the administration of lethal injection.

_____   4. Parents are the sole decision makers in determining the type of treatment their newborn receives.

5. Due to advances in medical technology, the question of when a person actually dies has become easier to answer.

MATCHING

Match each of the definitions on the left with the appropriate term from on the right.

_____	1. cessation of vital signs	a. informed consent
_____	2. care of the terminally ill	b. passive euthanasia
_____	3. death caused by the withholding of treatment	c. active euthanasia
_____	4. doctor-patient decision making	d. hospice
_____	5. death through lethal injection	e. clinical death

❧ Answers to practice questions can be found in Part IV ☙

Related Readings

📖 Indicates selection from *The Path Ahead: Readings in Death and Dying*, eds. Lynne Ann DeSpelder and Albert Lee Strickland (Mountain View, Calif.: Mayfield, 1995).

ETHICAL PRINCIPLES

📖 Daniel Callahan, "The Limits of Medical Progress: A Principle of Symmetry," pp. 103–105.

Mickey S. Eisenberg. *Life in the Balance: Emergency Medicine and the Quest to Reverse Sudden Death.* New York: Oxford University Press, 1997.

Albert R. Jonsen. *The New Medicine and the Old Ethics.* Cambridge, Mass.: Harvard University Press, 1990.

📖 Robert Kastenbaum, "Reconstructing Death in Postmodern Society," pp. 7–18.

Bert Keizer. *Dancing with Mister D: Notes on Life and Death.* New York: Doubleday, 1997.

Edmund D. Pellegrino and David C. Thomasma. *The Virtues in Medical Practice.* New York: Oxford University Press, 1993.

📖 Stanley Joel Reiser, "The Era of the Patient: Using the Experience of Illness in Shaping the Missions of Health Care," pp. 106–115.

Robert M. Veatch. *Cross Cultural Perspectives in Medical Ethics.* Boston: Jones and Bartlett, 1989.

Robert M. Veatch, ed. *Medical Ethics.* 2nd ed. Boston: Jones and Bartlett, 1997.

INFORMED CONSENT

📖 William Bartholome, "Care of the Dying Child: The Demands of Ethics," pp. 133–143.

📖 Margot L. White and John C. Fletcher, "The Story of Mr. and Mrs. Doe: 'You Can't Tell My Husband He's Dying; It Will Kill Him,'" pp. 148–153.

Euthanasia, Physician-Assisted Suicide, and Allowing Death

Renee Anspach. *Deciding Who Lives: Fateful Choices in the Intensive Care Nursery.* Berkeley: University of California Press, 1993.

Lisa Belkin. *First, Do No Harm.* New York: Simon & Schuster, 1993.

📖 Charles J. Dougherty, "The Common Good, Terminal Illness, and Euthanasia," pp. 154–164.

Herbert Hendin. *Seduced by Death: Doctors, Patients, and the Dutch Cure.* New York: Norton, 1996.

Fiona Randall and R. S. Downie. *Palliative Care Ethics: A Good Companion.* New York: Oxford University Press, 1996.

📖 Richard S. Sandor, "On Death and Coding," pp. 144–147.

Marilyn Webb. *The Good Death: The New American Search to Reshape the End of Life.* New York: Bantam, 1997.

Robert F. Weir, ed. *Physician-Assisted Suicide.* Bloomington: Indiana University Press, 1997.

Organ Donation and Transplantation

George J. Annas. *The Rights of Patients: The Basic ACLU Guide to Patient Rights*, 2nd ed. Clifton, N.J.: Humana Press, 1991.

Stuart J. Youngner, Renée C. Fox, and Laurence J. O'Connell, eds. *Organ Transplantation: Meanings and Realities.* Madison: University of Wisconsin Press, 1996.

Major Points in This Chapter

- As medical technologies evolve, assuming greater importance in health care, individuals are confronted by situations that involve difficult ethical issues.

- Autonomy, beneficence, and justice are ethical principles that apply to decision making in health care.

- Informed consent requires that the patient is competent, understands the treatment options, and freely and voluntarily makes choices.

- Euthanasia (a "good" or gentle and painless death) encompasses a range of medical decisions. It includes choosing to withhold a particular treatment; withdrawing artificial life support or nutrition and hydration; administering high doses of pain medication that have the "double effect" of hastening death; providing a terminally ill person with the means to end his or her own life; and actively assisting in causing death (as in the case of a lethal injection administered by a physician).

- Right-to-die advocates view euthanasia as a basic human right, an alternative to needless suffering. Opponents argue that it is often difficult or impossible to obtain a patient's clear consent to euthanasia, that there is always a risk of faulty diagnosis, that a timely cure may be found, that palliative care can ease pain and discomfort, and that opening the door to euthanasia will inevitably lead down a "slippery slope" toward inhumane and unethical practices.

- The high-profile cases of Karen Ann Quinlan and Nancy Cruzan have provoked public debate about dying in an era of sophisticated medical technology.
- Neonatal intensive care frequently involves painful decisions with respect to life-sustaining medical interventions.
- Organ donation is voluntary; however, because there is a shortage of transplantable organs, most states have enacted "required request" laws that obligate hospitals to institute policies encouraging organ and tissue donations.
- Organ transplantation involves issues of rationing that require medical personnel to act as gatekeepers in determining prospective recipients.
- As medical technology has advanced to the point that machines can sustain bodily functions, the definition of death has become more complex and new methods of determining death have been instituted.

Observations and Reflections

The discussion and consideration of ethical issues may bring up past experiences that determine your present stands. Take a moment to relate your experiences to your beliefs.

Use the blank space below and on the following page to record your thoughts about ethical issues in medicine and health care.

⇒ *End-of Life-Issues: Withdrawing Life Support*

Directions   *Read the following scenario and complete the assignment.*

Your closest relative is in a hospital, hooked up to life-sustaining machinery. First, in the space to the right of the numbers, make a list of all of the factors you would need to consider before you formed an opinion about his or her care, or decided on your stance about turning off the machines.

<u>Ranking</u>   <u>Factors to consider</u>

_____   1. _____

_____   2. _____

_____   3. _____

_____   4. _____

_____   5. _____

_____   6. _____

_____   7. _____

_____   8. _____

_____   9. _____

_____   10. _____

_____   11. _____

_____   12. _____

Now, in the space to the left of the numbers, rate each of these factors on a scale of 1–5 (from 1 as very important to 5 as not important at all).

After completing this portion of the activity, continue by responding to the questions on the following page:

If it were totally your decision and the doctors said that there was no hope of recovery, what would you do?

_____

_____

_____

_____

_____

_____

_____

_____

Explain your decision.

_____

_____

_____

_____

_____

_____

_____

_____

_____

_____

_____

⇒ *Final Wishes*

Directions   *Fill out the following information.*

- I have signed an advance directive (also known as a living will or durable power of attorney for health care). _____ It is located at_____

  _____

- The individuals to be contacted regarding this document are _____

  _____

  I would most like to die at _____

  And I would like (who) _____

  _____ there.

- If this isn't possible, I would like to die _____

  _____

- To prepare before my death, I would like (clergy, close friend, special reading, service, or . . .)

  _____

- My family (or loved one) may need extra support. Please contact (agency or individual) ____

  _____

- I have a donor card. I would like to donate _____

  _____

- If given a choice, I would (approve/not approve) of an autopsy _____

  _____

- Immediately after my death, please notify _____

  _____

- As soon as possible, please notify _____

  _____

- Later, please notify _____

  _____

- For my children, I have requested (who) to be their guardian. _____
_____

- My important papers (vital statistics, veteran's papers, life insurance and other benefits, financial records, will, safe deposit box key) are located at

_____

- Other important information is _____

_____

_____

_____

_____

_____

_____

_____

_____

_____

_____

_____

_____

_____

_____

_____

DATE: _____   SIGNED: _____

118   Chapter 6

Study Guide
The Last Dance: Encountering Death and Dying, 6th ed.

Survivors:
Understanding the Experience of Loss

Chapter Summary

Chapter 7 provides a comprehensive inquiry into the human experience of loss. We are all survivors of loss, whether of "little deaths," exemplified by endings and changes that occur throughout the normal course of life, or of more significant losses related to the deaths of loved ones. Although the terms are often used more or less interchangeably, it can be helpful to define *bereavement* as the objective event of loss, *grief* as the response engendered by a loss, and *mourning* as the process by which a survivor incorporates an experience of loss into his or her ongoing life.

Various models have been proposed to explain patterns of grief and mourning. Such models are useful in providing an overview, or "snapshot," of a living process, but they may also tend to oversimplify and even distort the reality experienced by the bereaved. The well-known "five stages" model, described by Elisabeth Kübler-Ross, has become almost a modern mythology of how grieving should be done. The concept of "working through" a loss has been an important part of the standard theoretical formulations on grief. As usually understood, the main message of the "grief work" model is that the bereaved person must break his or her ties with the deceased by "letting go" of the attachment and forming a new identity in which the deceased is absent. Such models can indeed be useful, and they are part of any comprehensive understanding of grief. However, problems arise when the implication is that "one size fits all," that everyone must cope with grief in just the same way for successful "recovery" from loss.

Learning about other models of grief and bereavement expands understanding and brings us closer to an accurate representation of the different and various ways human beings actually cope with loss. Task-oriented models, such as those proposed by William Worden and Therese Rando, are valuable in this regard. The emphasis on "letting go" that formed a central part of the "grief work" model has been balanced in recent years by an appreciation of the fact that healthy grievers can also find ways to maintain bonds with the deceased. The contributions of Dennis Klass, Phyllis Silverman, Margaret Stroebe, and other researchers and clinicians have been very important in broadening our perspectives on grief.

Indeed, grief can be usefully examined from a number of viewpoints. The various physical, emotional, and behavioral reactions associated with grief can be observed, leading to recognition of the great variability in such manifestations among individuals and circumstances. We can look at how the experience of grief changes over time. We can examine the potential effects of grief on the bereaved's physical and psychological functioning. We can investigate situations that make the bereaved more prone to complicated grief. Each of these approaches adds detail to the portrait of grief.

Many variables must be considered in developing an adequate understanding of grief. These variables include the survivor's model of the world (personality, social roles, perceived importance of the deceased, and value structure), mode of death (natural, accidental, homicide, or suicide), circumstances of the death (whether it occurred suddenly or was anticipated), perceptions (whether the death is seen as having been preventable or unavoidable), the relationship of the survivor to the deceased (central or peripheral), the presence of unfinished business between the deceased and the survivor, any conflict between intellectual and emotional responses to the death, and the amount of social support available to the bereaved. Funerals and other leave-taking rituals serve as a framework within which survivors can receive social support. Support groups offer the bereaved another avenue for sharing concerns and empathy with others.

Bereavement usually creates significant change in many aspects of a person's life. The family unit is different, social realities have changed, and legal and financial matters require attention. In all of these areas, survivors are challenged. In the midst of a burden of loss and grief, it may be difficult to recognize that bereavement can be an opportunity for growth. In coping with a loss, creative energy is generated. The tragic event of loss can become a stepping stone to new opportunities. This does not mean that the impact of the loss or resulting pain is diminished or dismissed. Still, many bereaved people describe themselves as stronger, more competent, more mature, more independent, and better able to face other crises in life because of their journey through grief. For these survivors, grief becomes a unifying rather than alienating experience. The lost relationship is viewed as changed, but not ended. By making space in one's life to accommodate loss, grief is seen as part of the warp and weft of human experience.

Objectives

- To define *bereavement, grief,* and *mourning.*
- To describe the experience of grief.
- To list the somatic, perceptual, and emotional manifestations of grief and to assess its impact on morbidity and mortality.
- To evaluate the concept of complicated mourning.
- To describe and evaluate different models of grief.
- To explain the variables that influence grief.
- To list various coping mechanisms and assess the value of each.
- To draw conclusions regarding bereavement support.
- To assess how bereavement may provide an opportunity for growth.

Key Terms and Concepts

acute grief

affectional bonds

anniversary reaction

anticipatory mourning

bereavement

bereavement burnout

central vs. peripheral relationship

complicated mourning

course of grief

deathbed promises

directive mourning therapy

disenfranchised grief

dual-process model of grief

grief

"grief work"

high grief vs. low grief

intuitive vs. instrumental grieving

"little deaths"

loss-oriented vs. restoration-oriented coping

loss

morbidity of grief

inner representations

linking objects

mortality of bereavement

mourning

multiple losses

narrative model of grief

pathological grief

perceived similarity

secondary morbidity

somatic symptomatology

survivor guilt

survivor support groups

tasks of mourning

trigger events

unfinished business

Questions for Guided Study and Review

1. How can we distinguish between the terms *grief, bereavement*, and *mourning*?
2. How do social and cultural norms influence mourning practices?
3. What is the "grief work" model?
4. How does *attachment theory* relate to understanding the dynamics of grief?
5. In what way is bereavement a type of *psychosocial transition*?
6. What are the four tasks of mourning described by William Worden?
7. What are the six Rs described by Therese Rando?
8. Is it necessary to "break the bonds" to adjust to grief?
9. In what way is the notion of "maintaining bonds with the deceased" a useful addition to our understanding of grief?
10. How do bereaved people in different cultures maintain connections with deceased loved ones?
11. How is "telling the story" related to coping with grief?
12. What is the dual-process model of grief, and what are the two processes?
13. How does the dual-process model posit grief as a dynamic process?
14. How does grief manifest in various ways?
15. How does grief tend to progress in phases?
16. What special issues are typically associated with the acute, middle, and final phases of grief?

17. What kinds of events may reactivate grief for a loss previously mourned?
18. What factors potentially result in complicated grief?
19. What factors potentially influence the "mortality of bereavement," and why is it a concern?
20. How might conflict occur between emotional versus intellectual responses to grief?
21. What are some of the main variables influencing the experience of grief, and how might they affect the bereaved?
22. How do personality and social roles influence grief?
23. How is grief likely to be affected by factors such as the nature of the relationship (i.e., central versus peripheral) and beliefs about the circumstances of the death (i.e., preventable versus unavoidable)?
24. What effect might *perceived similarity* have on grief?
25. How does the *mode of death* influence grief?
26. What is *anticipatory grief*?
27. In what ways might suicide and homicide effect the course of grief?
28. What is *disenfranchised grief*?
29. What is the role of social support in coping with grief?
30. What is *unfinished business*, and under what circumstances might it be a factor in grief?
31. How do funerals and other leave-taking rituals and activities provide a framework for social support?
32. What are *linking objects*?
33. In what ways might bereavement lead to personal growth?

Practice Test Questions

MULTIPLE CHOICE

1. Which of the following contains the three primary tasks identified by Erich Lindemann necessary for successfully managing grief?
   a. a feeling of loss, a feeling of loneliness, a feeling of acceptance
   b. accepting the fact of loss, adjusting to life without the deceased, forming new relationships
   c. sense of anger, sense of guilt, sense of sadness
   d. allowing oneself to feel the emotions of grief, expressing grief emotions, understanding one's emotions of grief

2. Anniversaries, birthdays, and holidays
   a. are usually happy times even in the midst of mourning.
   b. do well to mark the time of a loved one's absence.
   c. can reawaken unexpected feelings of grief.
   d. have to be celebrated just as before the death.

3. Feelings of anger toward a deceased loved one should be
    a. denied until they go away.
    b. neutralized by thought and understanding.
    c. given no attention.
    d. experienced and expressed.

4. *Unfinished business* is a term that refers to the
    a. process that leads to probate.
    b. financial aspects of funeral plans.
    c. clearing of emotional conflicts and questions.
    d. need to act on the wishes of a will.

5. Why have bereavement support groups developed in modern society?
    a. With death becoming less acceptable, friends and family are reluctant to talk about emotions of grief.
    b. With urbanization and specialization, society is impersonal, with professionals providing services previously provided by family and friends.
    c. With a greater understanding of human psychology, professionals are better able to provide guidance through support groups.
    d. With traditional means of community support lacking, survivors seek other avenues for gaining social support.

True/False

_____ 1. The basic stages of the grieving process are well defined and most individuals proceed through them in a specified order.

_____ 2. Evidence suggests that the reaction to loss of a loved one may enhance the body's ability to fight disease.

_____ 3. An individual's ability to cope with the loss of a loved one is NOT related to his or her ability to cope with day-to-day problems.

_____ 4. People who care for dying patients may experience *secondary morbidity*, which refers to difficulties in physical, cognitive, emotional, or social spheres of functioning.

_____ 5. Different cultures tend to express grief in a similar emotional fashion throughout the world.

MATCHING

Match each of the following terms on the left with the most appropriate description on the right. Each description may be used only once.

_____ 1. Disenfranchised grief

_____ 2. High-grief death

_____ 3. Anticipatory grief

_____ 4. Funeral

_____ 5. Mourning

a. allows an orderly and acceptable framework for dealing with loss

b. consequence of lacking social support or acknowledgment of loss

c. a response to prior knowledge of an impending death

d. incorporates the loss of a loved one into one's ongoing life

e. produces an intense emotional and physical reaction

❧ Answers to practice questions can be found in Part IV ☙

Related Readings

📖 Indicates selection from *The Path Ahead: Readings in Death and Dying*, eds. Lynne Ann DeSpelder and Albert Lee Strickland (Mountain View, Calif.: Mayfield, 1995).

THE EXPERIENCE OF GRIEF

Thomas W. Attig. *How We Grieve: Relearning the World*. New York: Oxford University Press, 1996.

📖 Sandra L. Bertman, "Bearing the Unbearable: From Loss, the Gain," pp. 348–354.

📖 Kenneth J. Doka, "Disenfranchised Grief," pp. 271–275.

Kenneth J. Doka and Joyce D. Davidson, eds. *Living with Grief: Who We Are, How We Grieve*. Washington, D.C.: Hospice Foundation of America, 1998.

Charles R. Figley, Brian E. Bride, and Nicholas Mazza, eds. *Death and Trauma: The Traumatology of Grieving*. Washington, D.C.: Taylor & Francis, 1997.

📖 John D. Kelly, "Grief: Re-forming Life's Story," pp. 242–245.

Dennis Klass, Phyllis R. Silverman, and Steven Nickman, eds. *Continuing Bonds: New Understandings of Grief*. Washington, D.C.: Taylor & Francis, 1996.

Colin Murray Parkes. *Bereavement: Studies of Grief in Adult Life*, 3rd ed. New York: Routledge, 1996.

Therese Rando. *Grieving: How to Go On Living When Someone You Love Dies*. Lexington, Mass.: Lexington Books, 1988.

📖 Margaret Stroebe, Mary M. Gergen, Kenneth J. Gergen, and Wolfgang Stroebe, "Broken Hearts or Broken Bonds: Love and Death in Historical Perspective," pp. 231–241.

Margaret S. Stroebe, Robert O. Hansson, Wolfgang Stroebe, and Henk Schut, eds. *Handbook of Bereavement Research: Consequences, Coping, and Care.* Washington, D.C.: American Psychological Association, 2001.

Vamik D. Volkan and Elizabeth Zintl. *Life After Loss: The Lessons of Grief.* New York: Collier, 1994.

SPECIFIC TYPES OF BEREAVEMENT

📖 Dennis Klass, "Solace and Immortality: Bereaved Parents' Continuing Bond with Their Children," pp. 246–259.

📖 Sandra Jacoby Klein. *Heavenly Hurts: Surviving AIDS-Related Deaths and Losses.* Amityville, N.Y.: Baywood, 1998.

Catherine M. Sanders. *Grief, The Mourning After: Dealing with Adult Bereavement.* New York: John Wiley and Sons, 1989.

📖 Nancy Scheper-Hughes, "Death Without Weeping: The Violence of Everyday Life in Brazil," pp. 41–58.

📖 Phyllis R. Silverman, Steven Nickman, and J. William Worden, "Detachment Revisited: The Child's Reconstruction of a Dead Parent," pp. 260–270.

📖 Avery D. Weisman, "Bereavement and Companion Animals," pp. 276–280.

SOCIAL SUPPORT AND FAMILIES

📖 Stephen J. Fleming and Leslie Balmer, "Bereaved Families of Ontario: A Mutual-Help Model for Families Experiencing Death," pp. 281–288.

Janice Winchester Nadeau. *Families Making Sense of Death.* Thousand Oaks, Calif.: Sage, 1997.

Major Points in This Chapter

- Surviving a loss, whether a "little death" or a major bereavement experience, brings with it the possibility of grief and mourning.
- Awareness of cultural context and the multiplicity of mourning behaviors is essential to understanding the range of human responses to bereavement.
- The human response to loss is complex; it encompasses a multitude of personal, familial, and social factors.
- Manifestations of grief include both physical and psychological distress.
- Complicated mourning may occur when certain high-risk factors are present in the bereaved's experience of loss.
- Various models of grief—including Kübler-Ross's five stages, Lindemann's "working through" grief, Worden's tasks of mourning, and Rando's 6R processes of mourning—have guided the search for patterns in bereavement.
- The notion that resolving grief means "letting go" is being revised in light of the recognition that people generally "relocate" the deceased in some fashion into their ongoing lives.
- Narrative approaches to grief use talking about the death and the deceased as an important component.

- Variables influencing grief include the survivor's model of the world (such as his or her values, personality, social roles, and perception of the deceased's importance), the mode of death (sudden, anticipated, suicide, or homicide), the nature of the survivor's relationship to the deceased, the presence of social support, and whether the survivor has a sense of "unfinished business" with the deceased.
- Disenfranchised grief typically occurs when the significance of a loss is not socially recognized or when the relationship between the deceased and the survivor is not socially sanctioned.
- Funerals and other leave-taking rituals, along with survivor support groups, can be important aids to coping with bereavement.
- Bereavement can be an opportunity for personal growth.

Observations and Reflections

The possibility of evoking strong emotions exists during activities and discussions and bereavement and grief. Voices may become choked. Tears may be shed. Keep in mind that there is no need to become alarmed simply because someone is expressing difficult painful memories or emotions. Pause and take a couple of slow, deep breaths. The rest of the story will come out.

Use the space below to make notes about the material covered in this chapter.

➠ *The 5L Model for Companioning the Bereaved*

Directions   *Read Patrick Dean's 5L Model. Answer the questions in the space provided.*

Love. Ultimately, when all is said and done, love is the only happiness. While we can and do come to terms with the death of someone we love, in our own ways and our own time spaces, we need to remember that, while people die, love does not. Vincent van Gogh said it wonderfully when he taught that the best way to know life was to love many things.

Laugh. Numerous studies have shown the powerful healing and palliative effect of a good laugh or, even better, a shared laugh. A hallmark of the grief and healing process is the ability, in the midst of intense feelings of loss, to be able to find humor or allow the presence of laughter to balance sadness. Bereaved people will often deny themselves the pleasure that accompanies laughing in an unhealthy attempt to show the outside world the fact of their mourning. They may even deny themselves the gift of feeling pleasure as a way to stay connected to their sadness and to the deceased.

Live. As companions to the bereaved, it is critical that we model an "attitude of gratitude" towards the gift that is life. In so doing, we honor not only the death that has happened, but also the life that was lived. When we couple this attitude with the religious or secular beliefs of our bereaved companion, we are modeling a truly high level of spirituality.

Learn. We need to learn to cultivate curiosity. This "client as teacher" attitude allows the narrative that is every bereaved person's story of loss to unfold from and by the expert—that is, the person surviving any particular loss. This frees us as companions to the bereaved from having to say the right thing or to be some particular way that we may or may not be comfortable with when we assume total responsibility for "fixing" the necessary sadness that is grief.

Listen. We have been given two ears and one mouth and we ought to use them in that proportion, listening more than talking. We need to listen with our head and our heart. Listening with our head is an important "academic part" of helping. Equally important, and its perfect compliment, is listening with the heart. Finding the balance between the science of head knowledge and the art of listening with the heart is a skill developed with practice, patience, and prayer.

1. Is "companioning the bereaved" the same thing as being with a person who is grieving? Why or why not?

   _____

   _____

   _____

   _____

   _____

   _____

   _____

2. When Dean talks about a "client", do you think this would also apply to a friend or family member? Explain.

_____

_____

_____

3. Which is your favorite "L"?_____. Describe your interest.

_____

_____

_____

4. Rank order the "5 Ls" from 1–5 (1 being the most important and 5 the least important). Notice how your ranking is related to your own coping skills.

_____

_____

_____

_____

_____

5. Can you think of any other "L" that belongs on this list? What would it be? Explain why it should be included.

_____

_____

_____

_____

_____

⇒ *Survivor Interview*

Directions   Find a person who has experienced a death and who is willing to share his or her experience. The interviewee need not share anything that makes him or her uncomfortable. The person may become emotional at times. Begin the interview by asking the following questions.

Who was the person who died? _____

_____

When did the death occur? _____

_____

Where did the death occur? _____

_____

How did you react at first? _____

_____

_____

_____

_____

_____

How did this initial reaction change over time? _____

_____

_____

_____

_____

_____

What helped you cope with your grief? _____

_____

_____

_____

_____

_____

What didn't help? _____

_____

_____

_____

_____

What did you learn from the experience? _____

_____

_____

_____

_____

_____

_____

_____

_____

💻 *Internet Survivor Support*

Directions   *The Internet functions, on some level, as a survivor support group. There are numerous web pages designed to memorialize a loved one, and many of them have resources about a particular type of loss. Other sites contain opportunities for survivors to tell the stories of their loss. Here, you will search the Web to identify five "survivor sites." Please rate each listing from 1 (very good) to 5 (useless) and give a summary of the information to be found on the site.*

You may begin your Internet web search at: <http://www.webhealing.com/honor.html> *or* <http://www.kiva.net/~markh/memorial.html> *or the homepage of The Ring of Death, which is a network of death, dying, and bereavement pages on the web at* <http://www.alsirat.com/silence/ring/>

1. URL_____ Rating_____

   _____

   _____

   _____

   _____

   _____

   _____

   _____

2. URL_____ Rating_____

   _____

   _____

   _____

   _____

   _____

   _____

   _____

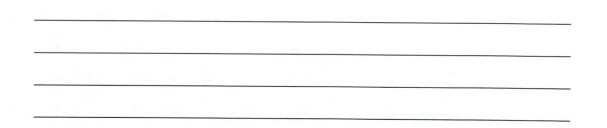

3. URL_____ Rating_____

_____

_____

_____

_____

_____

_____

_____

4. URL_____ Rating_____

_____

_____

_____

_____

_____

_____

_____

_____

5. URL_____ Rating_____

_____

_____

_____

_____

_____

_____

_____

Last Rites:
Funerals and Body Disposition

Chapter Summary

Chapter 8 examines the structure, symbolic content, and function of funeral rituals. In a broad sense, funerals are rites that denote a change in status of both the deceased and his or her survivors. In modern societies, funerals have come to be seen largely as a means whereby social support is made available to survivors. The social aspects of last rites begin with notification of the death, a process that extends from relatives and close friends to those who were less intimately related to the deceased. Gathering together to comfort the bereaved during the various events associated with the funeral provides reassurance that the death of an individual—and the survivors' grief— are part of a larger whole. In this sense, funerals and other such rites of passage are seen as occurring within a caring community.

Although funerals typically fulfill an important function as a means for coping with loss, the modern funeral has been criticized for its cost as well as its tendency to "prettify" or deny death by cosmetically restoring the corpse, engaging in euphemistic language to describe the facts of death, and creating a "staged" ceremony. Studies have shown that most people are satisfied with current funeral practices and feel they have been treated fairly by funeral-service personnel. Still, because most people are unfamiliar with the various choices and costs surrounding funeral and mortuary services, there is lingering concern that customers could be taken advantage of by the funeral industry.

Becoming familiar with the historical evolution of funeral practices aids our understanding of the shape of present-day practices. Undertakers were initially tradespeople who supplied funeral paraphernalia to families, usually as a sideline to some other business. Undertakers essentially provided a service to families who were, in effect, their own funeral directors. Over time, the growth of urbanization and other social changes altered this traditional relationship, with professional morticians taking on an ever-larger role in caring for the dead as family involvement diminished. Indeed, in some cases, the primary involvement of families in modern funeral rituals is to pay for services arranged by professional funeral directors.

Even when individuals do not wish to assume a larger role in designing their own funerals or creating appropriate farewells for their deceased loved ones, it is still prudent to become acquainted with the options available in funeral services. The purpose of the funeral—as an occasion for acknowledging publicly that a member of the community has died and to effect closure on that person's life for the bereaved—can be realized whether it is garnished with diamonds and rubies, or with poetry and a song. As a transaction unique in commerce, the contract for funeral services is usually entered into during a time of crisis, and the decision, once made, is final. Preparing oneself in advance by acquiring knowledge about the various funeral service charges and their approximate costs can help in making meaningful decisions when the need arises.

Funeral service charges typically include categories for professional services (covering mortuary staff services and general overhead), intake charges (for transporting remains), embalming or refrigeration of the body, other body preparation (cosmetology, hairstyling, dressing the corpse, and the like), the casket (of which there is a wide range of choices), facilities (use of a visitation or viewing room, or the mortuary chapel), vehicles (hearse, family cars), and a miscellaneous category that might include the costs of newspaper death notices, acknowledgment cards, floral arrangements, honoraria for pallbearers or clergy, and burial garments purchased from the mortuary.

Purchasers of mortuary services are also advised to learn something about the various options for body disposition. Burial, entombment, and cremation are the most common in North America. Finally, costs associated with placing grave markers or erecting more elaborate memorials at the gravesite need to be considered, along with any fees for "perpetual care" that may be assessed by cemeteries or mausoleums.

As a response to death, funerals range from the simple to the elaborate, from the few essentials needed for proper disposal of the body to ornate ceremonies that span several days, or even longer. Some people prefer minimal involvement in caring for their deceased loved ones; others seek more active participation. In a pluralistic society, there are many ways of dealing meaningfully with death. Becoming aware of the choices available enables us to make more informed, and more gratifying, choices about last rites.

Objectives

- To describe the function of funeral rituals, including their psychosocial aspects.
- To describe the historical changes in American funeral rituals and to assess the relevance of criticism with respect to current practices.
- To examine practices and costs of various mortuary and cemetery options.
- To design a personally meaningful funeral ritual for oneself.

Key Terms and Concepts

aftercare
body disposition
burial
casket
cemetery
coffin
columbarium
cosmetic restoration
cremains
cremation
crematory
cryogenic suspension
crypt
cybermourners
death notification
embalming
entombment
FTC Funeral Rule
funeral parlor

funerary artifacts
funeral and memorial societies
grave goods
grave liner
grave marker
indigent burial funds
itemized pricing
last rites
mausoleum
memorialization
mortician
mortuary
niche
pallbearers
single-unit pricing
undertaker
vigil
wake

Questions for Guided Study and Review

1. According to Vanderlyn Pine, what are the four major social functions historically addressed by funerals?
2. What purpose did embalming and preservation of the body have for the ancient Egyptians?
3. What are the main purposes—socially and psychologically—of last rites?
4. How does the gathering of the community serve the psychosocial aspects of last rites?
5. What seven elements of funeral rituals are described in the text?
6. How does notification of a death take place?
7. Why is death notification, and the manner in which it takes place, important?
8. How are themes of separation and integration evident in funeral rites?
9. How does the notion of a "change of status" apply to funeral rites?
10. How are funeral rites an impetus to cope with a loss?
11. What are the main criticisms voiced about funerals?
12. What major changes occurred in funerals during the twentieth century?
13. How has the role of the undertaker changed since the end of the nineteenth century?
14. How did the term "funeral parlor" come into being?
15. In what way is the purchase of funeral goods and services a unique commercial transaction?
16. What are the four categories of costs related to a standard American funeral, as outlined by the National Funeral Directors Association?
17. What is the Funeral Rule, and what does it require?
18. How did the practice of embalming develop in the United States?

19. In modern usage, how is embalming done?
20. What is the purpose of embalming, and when is it required?
21. What types of caskets are generally available?
22. What are the requirements for using a casket when a body is to be cremated?
23. How do direct cremations and immediate burials differ from the standard funeral?
24. What are the main choices for body disposition?
25. How do religious beliefs potentially affect the method of body disposition?
26. What is *cryogenic suspension*?
27. How is the process of cremation accomplished?
28. What are the choices for disposition of cremated remains?
29. What is *memorialization*?
30. What are some of the recent innovations in funeral and memorialization practices?
31. Does the definition of funerals as "an organized, purposeful, time-limited, flexible, group-centered response to death" apply to current approaches to caring for the dead?

Practice Test Questions

MULTIPLE CHOICE

1. The death customs of the ancient Egyptians reveal
   a. that they welcomed death because they thought it would be a rewarding experience for those who had served the gods well.
   b. a culture preoccupied with acquiring mortuary goods and preparing for the afterlife.
   c. that most Egyptians did not include religion as a dominant theme in their transition of death.
   d. a preoccupation with the fear of death, which influenced its population to serve the pharaohs in hope of pleasing the gods.

2. Itemizing funeral costs is designed to change the pattern of
   a. equating the most expensive casket with the most elaborate funeral.
   b. selecting funeral services "a la carte."
   c. paying for unnecessary and unwanted services.
   d. using the layaway payment schedule.

3. Funeral parlors acquired that name because
   a. parlor is a pun as it comes from the same root word as pale or dead.
   b. undertakers wanted to disguise the reality of death.
   c. church officials wanted a separate place for funeral services.
   d. viewing of the body used to take place in the parlor of the family home.

4. Funeral and memorial societies are organized to
   a. offer a wider range of options in funeral care.
   b. host annual conventions for funeral directors.
   c. hold gatherings to honor dead friends and relatives.
   d. provide body disposition services at lower cost based on volume purchases.

5. The "ashes" left from the cremation process are
   a. 20 to 30 pounds in weight.
   b. as fine as dust.
   c. like coarse coral sand.
   d. different shades according to the person's ethnicity.

TRUE/FALSE

_____ 1. Our choices regarding last rites reflect our attitudes and beliefs about death.

_____ 2. According to the FTC Funeral Rule, if direct cremation or immediate burial is chosen, there is no need to include any fee charged for professional services in the price quoted for those methods of disposition.

_____ 3. Embalming is always required in the United States today.

_____ 4. Burial vaults or grave liners are NOT required in all American cemeteries.

_____ 5. The Parsi community in India disposes of the dead by allowing corpses to be consumed by vultures.

MATCHING

Match each of the following societies with its associated characteristics.

_____ 1. United States   a. views cremation as a symbol of the transitory nature of human life

_____ 2. Egyptian   b. immediacy of death notification is equated with importance and respect

_____ 3. Hindu   c. Ka and Ba are immortal elements within the body

_____ 4. African American   d. criticized for excessive materialism in funeral rites

❧ Answers to practice questions can be found in Part IV ❧

Related Readings

📖 Indicates selection from *The Path Ahead: Readings in Death and Dying*, eds. Lynne Ann DeSpelder and Albert Lee Strickland (Mountain View, Calif.: Mayfield, 1995).

FUNERAL PRACTICES: GENERAL

Xavier A. Cronin. *Grave Exodus: Tending to Our Dead in the 21st Century*. New York: Barricade Books, 1996.

📖 Stephen J. Fleming and Leslie Balmer, "Bereaved Families of Ontario: A Mutual-Help Model for Families Experiencing Death," pp. 281–288.

Glennys Howarth. *Last Rites: The Work of the Modern Funeral Director*. Amityville, N.Y.: Baywood, 1996.

Kenneth V. Iserson. *Death to Dust: What Happens to Dead Bodies?* Tucson: Galen Press, 1994.

Thomas Lynch. *The Undertaking: Life Studies from the Dismal Trade*. New York: Norton, 1997.

Ernest Morgan. *Dealing Creatively with Death: A Manual of Death Education and Simple Burial*. 11th ed. Burnsville, N.C.: Celo Press, 1988.

Phyllis Theroux. *The Book of Eulogies*. New York: Simon & Schuster, 1997.

FUNERAL PRACTICES: CULTURAL STUDIES

Ronald K. Barrett, "Contemporary African-American Funeral Rites and Traditions," pp. 80–92.

Robert W. Habenstein and William M. Lamers. *The History of American Funeral Directing*. Milwaukee: Bulfin Printers, 1962.

Robert W. Habenstein and William M. Lamers. *Funeral Customs the World Over*. Rev. ed. Milwaukee: Bulfin Printers, 1974.

Christopher L. Hayes and Richard A. Kalish, "Death-Related Experiences and Funerary Practices of the Hmong Refugee in the United States," pp. 75–79.

Douglas Keister. *Going Out in Style: The Architecture of Eternity*. New York: Facts on File, 1997.

Elaine Nichols, ed. *The Last Miles of the Way: African-American Homegoing Traditions, 1890-Present*. Columbia, S.C.: South Carolina State Museum, 1989.

Major Points in This Chapter

- The choices people make involving funeral rituals and body disposition reflect their attitudes and beliefs about death.

- The psychosocial aspects of funeral rites include death notification (including obituaries and death notices), as well as mutual support as an impetus for coping with loss.

- The American funeral has evolved from handmade coffins and wakes held in the parlor of the family home to ornate caskets and ceremonies managed by funeral directors. Critics maintain that modern funerals are prone to unnecessarily high costs.

- Well-informed consumers of funeral services are knowledgeable about costs and are able to compare prices and evaluate the variety of services offered in the marketplace.

- Funeral and memorial societies are organized to serve their members or customers by negotiating reduced prices for basic services.

- The laws regulating the disposition of human remains generally specify where and how burials and disposal of cremated remains can be accomplished.

Observations and Reflections

Many local funeral directors will be pleased to meet with you individually to answer your questions and give you a tour of the facilities. Some students express in "ughs" and sighs their discomfort in visiting a mortuary. If you are uncomfortable, it is good to realize that the experience probably will not match your worst expectations. You may be afraid of seeing a dead body, embalming equipment, or the like. The visit should be arranged with the mortician beforehand so that you can have choices about what you will see. In fact, though, it is unlikely that you will see any dead bodies since mortuary personnel are careful to protect the rights of the families using their facilities. Be aware that mourners may be present during your visit.

Use the space below and on the following page to make notes about what you have learned about funerals and body disposition.

⮞ *Creating a Funeral Home*

Directions   *To your surprise you have just found out that you have inherited the funeral home of a long-lost relative. The will states that, if you can keep the funeral home business for five years and make a profit, you will receive an inheritance of $1,000,000! You now have some decisions to make about your new business.*

1. You must hire five new funeral directors. What characteristics do you want them to have?

   _____

   _____

   _____

   _____

2. What would your casket selection room look like?

   _____

   _____

   _____

   _____

3. What would the entryway of your mortuary look like?

   _____

   _____

   _____

   _____

4. Would your funeral home provide "aftercare"? Why or why not?

   _____

   _____

   _____

   _____

5. Would you be personally active in the business (for example, being present at funerals)?

_____

_____

_____

_____

6. How would you try to reduce criticisms of the funeral industry?

_____

_____

_____

_____

_____

_____

_____

7. What innovations would you bring to your new enterprise to make it the "best funeral home in the nation"?

_____

_____

_____

_____

_____

_____

_____

⇒ *Questionnaire: Funeral Planning*

Directions   *Indicate your funeral wishes by completing the following sentences:*

- I would like my body to be (embalmed, viewed at home, not viewed, cremated, buried, entombed) _____

- I'd like to be wearing _____

- Please transport my body in a _____

- The mortuary, crematory, or memorial society I prefer is _____

- The price range I would want spent on my funeral is _____
  _____

- I would like the final disposition of my body to be _____
  _____

- If I were cremated, I would want my ashes _____
  _____

- I'd like a tombstone or marker that reads _____
  _____

- I (would/would not) like flowers sent _____
  and/or donations made to
  _____

- I would like a funeral or memorial service led by _____
  _____

  at _____

- I'd like a (religious/secular) service that would include (open casket, flowers, music, quotes, speakers) _____
  _____

- I'd prefer to leave the arrangements for my funeral to _____
  _____

ETHICAL WILL

What I'd most like my family and friends to understand about my life, what was important to me, and what I learned are described below. The last thing I'd like to say is

_____

_____

_____

_____

_____

_____

_____

_____

💻 *Underground Humor*

Directions   *Funerals, graves, tombstones, epitaphs, and body disposition are the focus for many kinds of humor. Complete a search of the Internet and find at least five web sites devoted to these subjects. Please rate each one, from 1 (very good) to 5 (useless), and give a summary of the information to be found on the site. You can start with:*

<http//members.aol.com/OFFbeatPub/Underground_Humor.html>.

1. URL_____ Rating_____

_____

_____

_____

_____

_____

_____

_____

2. URL_____ Rating_____

_____

_____

_____

_____

_____

_____

3. URL_____ Rating_____

_____

_____

_____

_____

_____

_____

_____

_____

4. URL_____ Rating_____

_____

_____

_____

_____

_____

_____

_____

5. URL_____ Rating_____

_____

_____

_____

_____

_____

_____

_____

➠ *Interview with a Funeral Director*

Directions   Make arrangements to visit a funeral home and talk to one of the funeral directors. This interview is designed to give you first-hand knowledge about the business of funeral directing, including the services offered by a mortuary. The following interview pertains to the three areas of personal history, services offered, and business realities. Add any additional questions you may have. Report on what you learned from your interview.

- Many children say what they want to be when they grow up. I would imagine they don't often say "a mortician." When did you know that you wanted to be a mortician? What prompted you to choose this career over, say, being a firefighter or a doctor?

- Will you tell me about the first time you saw a dead body? What were the circumstances and how did you feel?

- What allows you to handle so much exposure to death? How do you cope?

- How does the public perceive you? For example, how do children react to your occupation? What about acquaintances, close friends, and relatives?

- What training did you receive for your job?

- Did you receive training in grief counseling?

- Would you describe the embalming process? Is it required by law and, if so, under what circumstances?

- Can refrigeration substitute for embalming? How do the costs compare?

- What is the longest period of time you've kept a body before final disposition?

- Would you say something about body viewing? For example, under what circumstances would you recommend not viewing a body? When do you think body viewing is most beneficial for survivors? What are your feelings about the importance of viewing the body?

- Should children view a dead body? Have there been situations when you thought they should not have viewed the body? What were the circumstances?

- What about cosmetics? Are they required? What do you think are the advantages? Any disadvantages?

- Making funeral rituals personally meaningful can be valuable for survivors. What requests do people make? What would be an unconventional request?

- Could survivors handle all the details of a funeral themselves? How would it be done? What would be the costs?

- What do you find to be the most difficult deaths? How do you personally cope?

- What are some of the costs in operating this business?

- Do you think the stereotype of the rich mortician making money from others' pain is ever accurate?

- What kinds of malpractice suits is a mortuary subject to?

- How do funeral directors build their businesses?

ADDITIONAL QUESTIONS

_____

_____

_____

_____

REPORT ON INTERVIEW

Use this space (and additional sheets if needed) to make notes from your interview.

_____

_____

_____

_____

_____

_____

_____

_____

_____

_____

_____

_____

_____

CHAPTER 9

The Law and Death

Chapter Summary

Chapter 9 surveys a variety of legal and administrative matters pertaining to death and dying. The topics discussed in this chapter include legislation defining death, advance directives, and physician-assisted suicide, as well as rules governing death certification, the roles of the coroner and medical examiner, autopsies, wills and probate, and "death benefits" such as life insurance.

Recent decades have seen the enactment of legislation recognizing the fact that, with the advent of modern medical technologies, the conventional definition of death—that is, irreversible cessation of heartbeat and breathing—sometimes proves inadequate. The convention definition of death remains a sufficient basis for determining death in most cases. However, for respirator-maintained bodies, death is now defined as the irreversible cessation of all functions of the entire brain, including the brain stem. Some experts suggest that this "whole-brain" formulation be replaced with a "higher-brain" criterion—that is, one that focuses on an individual's capacity for consciousness, social interaction, or personhood. At present, there seems to be insufficient enthusiasm for making such a change in defining death.

Advances in medical technology have also resulted in widespread attention to *advance directives*, a category that encompasses living wills, natural death directives, and durable powers of attorney for health care. Advance directives express a person's desire that medical heroics be avoided when death is imminent, or that life-sustaining or extraordinary procedures not be used when there is no chance of recovery. Such directives are completed while the person is able to make informed decisions and can be important in shaping the circumstances of a person's dying. In the wake of the Nancy Beth Cruzan case, and after enactment of the Patient Self-Determination Act, advance directives have not only received considerable public attention, but have also increasingly become part of mainstream health care.

Less accepted, but widely discussed and debated, is the topic of physician-assisted suicide. Due to the sustained efforts of various right-to-die organizations, as well as the highly publicized activities of Michigan pathologist Jack Kevorkian, considerable attention has been drawn to an ongoing debate about the ethical and legal issues involved in physicians providing aid in dying. At present, such aid can be legally provided in only one state, Oregon, where physicians are allowed to prescribe lethal medications to terminally ill patients who satisfy the law's requirements. Although the U.S. Supreme Court has ruled that there is no constitutional right to physician-assisted suicide, the debate about legalization of aid-in-dying and its acceptance within medical practice continues.

The official registration of death by means of the death certificate is considered to be the most important legal procedure following a death. Though often taken for granted, the death certificate can have far-reaching effects with respect to such diverse matters as distributing property and benefits to heirs, aiding in the detection of crime, tracing family genealogy, and promoting efforts to understand and prevent disease. The modes of death usually recognized by law include natural, accidental, suicidal, and homicidal. Yet the cause of death is not always the same as the mode of death. A death caused by asphyxiation due to drowning, for example, might be classified as an accident, a suicide, or a homicide, depending on the circumstances.

The coroner or medical examiner plays an important role in determining the cause and mode of death in doubtful circumstances. The cause of death is determined by the use of various scientific procedures, and may include an autopsy as well as other tests, analyses, and studies. Autopsy, or the medical examination of a body after death to determine the cause of death or to investigate the extent and nature of changes caused by disease, is also an important tool for both medical research and training.

Wills provide a legal means for expressing a person's intentions regarding the disposition of his or her property after death. As such, the will is a valuable tool for planning one's estate and for conveying property to one's beneficiaries. The conventional document for specifying such intentions is the formally executed will, which is usually completed in consultation with an attorney who is conversant with any requirements established by the laws of the state in which the will is executed. The making and probating of a will can be symbolically significant for both the testator and his or her survivors.

During the course of probate, the validity of the will is proved, the matters necessary to settling the estate are carried out by the executor or administrator, and, with the probate court's approval, the deceased's property is distributed to his or her beneficiaries. In the absence of a will, the distribution will be made according to the applicable laws of intestate succession.

Life insurance can provide a basic estate for one's beneficiaries, or it may be part of a more comprehensive estate. Insurance plans can be designed in a variety of ways to suit many different purposes. Unlike some other assets, life insurance benefits usually become available to beneficiaries immediately following the insured's death, thus providing funds and perhaps a sense of security to survivors. Other death benefits may be payable through governmental programs, such as Social Security and the Veterans Administration, or through pension plans resulting from employment.

As the variety of topics covered in this chapter makes clear, the law and legalities impinge in many ways on our experiences of death and dying. In some cases, laws increase our options; in other cases, they restrict them. Either way, a basic knowledge of the legalities concerning death and dying can provide for more informed choices and potentially more satisfying outcomes.

Objectives

- To describe the history of legislation defining death and the major points of view involved in its evolution.
- To appraise one's own death in terms of advance directives.
- To evaluate the arguments for and against physician-assisted suicide.
- To describe the functions of the coroner and the medical examiner.
- To identify the functions of the death certificate and the purposes of the autopsy.
- To identify the types, content, and purposes of wills.
- To explain the processes of probate and to evaluate the consequences of dying intestate.
- To assess the value to survivors of a comprehensive plan that includes trusts, life insurance, and other death benefits.

Key Terms and Concepts

advance directives
autopsy
beneficiary
bequest
codicil
conditional will
coroner
death benefits
death certificate
double effect
durable power of attorney for health care
estate
executor/administrator
forensic pathology
formally executed will
health care proxy
holographic will

intestate
life insurance
living will
medical examiner
mutual will
next of kin
nuncupative will
Oregon Death with Dignity Act
Patient Self-Determination Act
persistent vegetative state
physician-assisted suicide
postmortem
probate
testator
Uniform Determination of Death Act
viatical settlement

Questions for Guided Study and Review

1. In what ways does the law significantly affect our experiences of death and dying?
2. What is the recent history of legislation defining death?
3. What is the purpose of the Uniform Determination of Death Act?
4. Distinguish between the "whole-brain" and "higher-brain" definitions of death?
5. What three causes generally result in irreversible loss of functions of the whole brain?
6. What is the purpose of an advance directive?
7. What are the different types of advance directives?
8. What is a living will, and what is it meant to accomplish?
9. What is an advance proxy directive, or durable power of attorney for health care?
10. How do advance proxy directives differ from living wills?
11. What is the purpose of the Patient Self-Determination Act, and what does it require of health care providers?

12. What is the current legal standing of physician-assisted suicide?
13. What are the requirements of the Oregon Death with Dignity Act?
14. Summarize the U.S. Supreme Court's 1997 ruling on physician-assisted suicide.
15. What are the main functions of a death certificate?
16. What are the four modes of death listed on the typical death certificate?
17. How does the *cause* of death differ from the *mode* of death?
18. What role do coroners and medical examiners have when a death occurs?
19. How do coroners and medical examiners differ?
20. What is *forensic pathology*?
21. What is an autopsy?
22. Why are autopsies performed?
23. What is the responsibility of the Army Central Identification Laboratory (CILHI), and how does it carry out its mission?
24. What is the purpose of making a will?
25. What are the requirements for making a will?
26. What is the meaning of the terms *codicil, intestate, executor,* and *administrator*?
27. Can a legally executed will be amended or revoked?
28. How does an executor differ from an administrator?
29. What is probate?
30. How do laws of intestate succession function?
31. In what way is life insurance a death benefit?
32. What is a *viatical settlement*?
33. What are some of the main categories or types of death benefits that may be available to survivors?
34. Why is attention to the legal aspects of death and dying important for the bereaved?

Practice Test Questions

Multiple Choice

1. The Durable Power of Attorney for Health Care involves an agent who is
   a. recommended by health professionals.
   b. assigned by the court.
   c. chosen by the patient's family.
   d. designated by the person executing the document.

2. The most important legal procedure following a death is considered to be the
   a. reading of the will of the deceased.
   b. official registration of the death.
   c. administration of the funeral.
   d. distribution of the property of the deceased.

3. The modes of death recognized by law include all of the following categories EXCEPT
   a. accident.
   b. homicide.
   c. suicide.
   d. mature death.

4. The text cites the example of forensic scientists helping to identify remains of the "disappeared" in Argentina to show
   a. the disaster of military rule and terrorism.
   b. that governments are held accountable for their actions.
   c. the application of forensic science to human rights violations.
   d. that forensic scientists in Argentina are among the world's best.

5. If a person dies without leaving a will, his or her property will be distributed according to
   a. local custom.
   b. familial wishes.
   c. state law.
   d. federal law.

TRUE/FALSE

_____ 1. Because it is legally binding, a person's living will must always be obeyed.

_____ 2. Completing an advance proxy directive, or durable power of attorney for health care, does NOT require the assistance of an attorney.

_____ 3. If the contents of a will conflict with ordinary standards of social policy, its provisions may not be followed.

_____ 4. The right of an individual to determine the distribution of his or her property is NOT available in all societies.

_____ 5. An administrator is an agent appointed by the court while an executor is specifically named in the will.

MATCHING

Match each of the following definitions with its appropriate legal term. Only four of the five terms will be used.

_____ 1. amendment to a will   a. intestate

_____ 2. expression of the desire to avoid medical heroics when   b. probate
death is imminent

_____ 3. situation of dying without having made a valid will   c. testator

_____ 4. process by which an estate is settled and property   e. codicil
distributed d. advance directive

꘡ Answers to practice questions can be found in Part IV ꘡

Related Readings

📖 Indicates selection from *The Path Ahead: Readings in Death and Dying,* ed. Lynne Ann DeSpelder and Albert Lee Strickland (Mountain View, Calif.: Mayfield, 1995).

PHYSICIAN-ASSISTED SUICIDE

Howard Brody. "Assisted Death: A Compassionate Response to Medical Failure." *New England Journal of Medicine* 327, no. 19 (5 November 1992): 1384–1388.

📖 Charles J. Dougherty. "The Common Good, Terminal Illness, and Euthanasia," pp. 154–164.

Thane Josef Messinger. "A Gentle and Easy Death: From Ancient Greece to Beyond Cruzan Toward a Reasoned Legal Response to the Societal Dilemma of Euthanasia." *Denver University Law Review* 71, no. 1 (1993): 175–251.

DEATH CERTIFICATION

📖 Jack Lule. "News Strategies and the Death of Huey Newton," pp. 33–40.

Frank Smith. *Cause of Death: The Story of Forensic Science.* New York: Van Nostrand Reinhold, 1980.

Cyril Wecht. *Cause of Death.* New York: Dutton, 1993.

WILLS AND ESTATE PLANNING

Paul P. Ashley. *You and Your Will: The Planning and Management of Your Estate,* Rev. ed. New York: New American Library, 1985.

Joseph M. Belth. *Life Insurance: A Consumer's Handbook,* 2nd ed. Bloomington: Indiana University Press, 1985.

Edward F. Sutkowski. *Estate Planning: A Basic Guide.* Chicago: American Bar Association, 1986.

Major Points in This Chapter

- Legislation defining death has evolved with the expansion of sophisticated medical technologies.
- Advance directives such as living wills and durable powers of attorney for health care provide a means for individuals to express their wishes about the use of life-sustaining treatment.
- The Patient Self-Determination Act, enacted into law by Congress in 1990, requires health care providers who receive federal funds to give information to patients concerning advance directives.
- Physician-assisted suicide, as exemplified in the highly publicized actions of Dr. Jack Kevorkian, is increasingly an issue for national debate and legislative initiatives. In 1994, Oregon voters passed the Oregon Death with Dignity Act, making that state the first to legalize aid-in-dying. In March 1998, an elderly woman with breast cancer became the first known person to die under the law, having taken a lethal dose of barbituates prescribed by her doctor.

- Death certification, along with autopsies conducted at the direction of coroners and medical examiners, involves a legal process for reporting the cause and mode of death.
- A will is a legal document expressing an individual's wishes and intentions with respect to the disposition of his or her property after death.
- Probate is the legal process whereby a will is proved valid and an estate is distributed to its beneficiaries; it is conducted by an administrator or executor under supervision of a court.
- Life insurance and other death benefits provide funds to survivors who have been named by the deceased as beneficiaries or who are otherwise entitled to the proceeds from such benefits.

Observations and Reflections

After reading the section about wills, you now have more information about their importance. You are now aware of the form and content of a will. You also understand the potential ramifications of dying intestate, even at a young age. Think about the importance of the nonmaterial aspects of will-making, as well as those involving the distribution of material goods. In this way, you can understand that it is not merely the amount of wealth you have to distribute that might motivate you to make a will.

If you already have a will, consider reviewing it in light of the information you now have. Is it time for a change?

You might have noticed some aversion to exploring topics like homicide, suicide, and autopsies as they relate to the legal issues surrounding death. In reading about these topics, keep in mind that emotional responses are sometimes triggered by a past experience. Often, however, the aversion results from a lack of information, rather than too much information. It is important to be sensitive to your emotional response, but keep in mind that information in itself is not harmful. Indeed, it may provide relief from the pain that you feel in connection with a personal experience of death.

Use the space below and on the following page to make notes about this chapter.

⇒ *Attorney Interview*

Directions   *Locate an attorney who specializes in estate planning and probate. Tell him or her about the course that you are taking and ask if you may conduct an interview, either in person or over the phone. During the interview, you will be concentrating on dying intestate, probate, durable power of attorney, education, and personal experience. Sample questions follow.*

- ■ I've read about a number of different kinds of wills in our text. Some students in the class have made wills, but, statistically, seven out of ten people die intestate. Perhaps some of us have not made a will because we have little property to leave our friends and loved ones and so believe that wills are for others and not for us. Would you describe the average person for whom you draw up a formally executed will? For instance, what is his or her socio-economic status?

_____

_____

_____

_____

_____

_____

- ■ What is contained in a typical will, with respect to both material and nonmaterial considerations? Besides the distribution of the testator's property, what are the benefits of drawing up a will? Is there an emotional value for the testator and for his or her survivors?

_____

_____

_____

_____

_____

_____

■ Under what circumstances would a mutual will or a conditional will be executed? What about a holographic or a nuncupative will? When would it be appropriate to make one of these types of wills?

_____

_____

_____

_____

_____

_____

■ What occurs in this state when a person dies without leaving a will? In other words, what are the laws of succession? Let's take a hypothetical case: Suppose a middle-aged corporation officer with two grown children divorces his wife to marry another woman. Then he adopts the new wife's two children from her previous marriage. The next year he dies of a heart attack, intestate. How would his estate be divided? For instance, would the line of succession go from his present spouse to the four children? What about the former wife to whom he may have been married for more than twenty years? If a former spouse is not included in the laws of succession, does she or he have any recourse? How would a court determine the distribution of property in such cases?

_____

_____

_____

_____

_____

_____

■ In turning to the subject of probate, would you describe the legal procedures that occur when a client dies? What actions do you take? Under what circumstances might you be named as executor? What does an executor do? What is the cost of probate and is there any way to reasonably avoid it? Are there any pitfalls in trying to avoid probate?

_____

_____

_____

_____

_____

_____

■ Are you familiar with living wills or advance death directives? Have you been asked to draw one up? Under what circumstances do you find them to be valuable? Do you believe that having an advance directive will result in an individual experiencing a "better" death? Is the living will legally enforceable? Are individuals truly able to exercise choice about life support? What do you think are some problems with advance directives and similar documents?

_____

_____

_____

_____

_____

_____

■ What was the most complicated or difficult will for you to draw up? Why?

_____

_____

_____

_____

_____

_____

_____

■ As a professional, how do you cope with the loss when a client dies? Can you describe any particularly difficult experiences related to the issue of loss?

_____

_____

_____

_____

_____

_____

■ In your experience, does law school prepare attorneys for dealing with survivors? One might imagine a course called "Survivors 102." If there is some preparation, how is the topic of death dealt with? Has this aspect of your work ever been a problem to you?

_____

_____

_____

_____

_____

_____

You can use the space between questions to make notes about your interview. If this assignment is to be handed in, type up what you have learned.

🖥 *Internet: Advanced Directives*

Directions *Use the Internet to find state-specific advance directive forms. Locate five web sites that have information on advance directives or living wills. List each site along with a summary of the information found. Rate each site's usefulness on a scale from 1 (very helpful) to 5 (useless).*

Here are some suggestions for beginning your search:

Partnership for Caring:	\<http://www.choices.org/>
Final Thoughts:	\<http://www.finalthoughts.com/>
Five Wishes:	\<http://www.agingwithdignity.org/5wishe.html>

1. URL_____ Rating_____

   _____

   _____

   _____

   _____

   _____

   _____

   _____

   _____

2. URL_____ Rating_____

   _____

   _____

   _____

   _____

   _____

   _____

   _____

   _____

3. URL_____ Rating_____

_____

_____

_____

_____

_____

_____

_____

4. URL_____ Rating_____

_____

_____

_____

_____

_____

_____

_____

5. URL_____ Rating_____

_____

_____

_____

_____

_____

_____

_____

🖥 *Physician-Assisted Suicide (PAS)*

Directions: *Information about the status of physician-assisted suicide laws along with information for and against such laws can be found on the Internet. Select five sites, summarize the information found, and rate each site on a scale from 1 (very helpful) to 5 (useless). Starting with the Hemlock Society's site [http://www.hemlock.org/], review the latest on the laws and arguments for legalization of physician-assisted suicide.*

1. URL_____ Rating_____

_____

_____

_____

_____

_____

_____

_____

2. URL_____ Rating_____

_____

_____

_____

_____

_____

_____

_____

3. URL_____ Rating_____

_____

_____

_____

_____

_____

_____

_____

_____

4. URL_____ Rating_____

_____

_____

_____

_____

_____

_____

_____

5. URL_____ Rating_____

_____

_____

_____

_____

_____

_____

_____

ⅲ▶ *Death Certificate*

Directions   *Obtain a copy of a death certificate for your state. Below is an example from the state of California. Review the categories of required information. Give close attention to the information provided by the coroner or medical examiner in items #101–#128. You might find it interesting to fill out this certificate as if it were being used to record your death.*

CERTIFICATE OF DEATH
STATE OF CALIFORNIA
USE BLACK INK ONLY/NO ERASURES, WHITEOUTS OR ALTERATIONS
VS-11 (REV. 1/00)

STATE FILE NUMBER   LOCAL REGISTRATION NUMBER

DECEDENT PERSONAL DATA

1. NAME OF DECEDENT—FIRST (GIVEN) | 2. MIDDLE | 3. LAST (FAMILY)

4. DATE OF BIRTH M M / D D / C C Y Y | 5. AGE YRS. | IF UNDER 1 YEAR (MONTHS / DAYS) | IF UNDER 24 HOURS (HOURS / MINUTES) | 6. SEX | 7. DATE OF DEATH M M / D D / C C Y Y | 8. HOUR

9. STATE OF BIRTH | 10. SOCIAL SECURITY NO. | 11. MILITARY SERVICE YES ☐ NO ☐ UNK ☐ | 12. MARITAL STATUS | 13. EDUCATION—YEARS COMPLETED

14. RACE | 15. HISPANIC—SPECIFY YES ☐ _____ NO ☐ | 16. USUAL EMPLOYER

17. OCCUPATION | 18. KIND OF BUSINESS | 19. YEARS IN OCCUPATION

USUAL RESIDENCE

20. RESIDENCE—(STREET AND NUMBER OR LOCATION)

21. CITY | 22. COUNTY | 23. ZIP CODE | 24. YRS IN COUNTY | 25. STATE OR FOREIGN COUNTRY

INFORMANT

26. NAME, RELATIONSHIP | 27. MAILING ADDRESS (STREET AND NUMBER OR RURAL ROUTE NUMBER, CITY OR TOWN, STATE, ZIP)

SPOUSE AND PARENT INFORMATION

28. NAME OF SURVIVING SPOUSE—FIRST | 29. MIDDLE | 30. LAST (MAIDEN NAME)

31. NAME OF FATHER—FIRST | 32. MIDDLE | 33. LAST | 34. BIRTH STATE

35. NAME OF MOTHER—FIRST | 36. MIDDLE | 37. LAST (MAIDEN) | 38. BIRTH STATE

DISPOSITION(S)

39. DATE M M / D D / C C Y Y | 40. PLACE OF FINAL DISPOSITION

FUNERAL DIRECTOR AND LOCAL REGISTRAR

41. TYPE OF DISPOSITION(S) | 42. SIGNATURE OF EMBALMER ▶ | 43. LICENSE NO.

44. NAME OF FUNERAL DIRECTOR | 45. LICENSE NO. | 46. SIGNATURE OF LOCAL REGISTRAR ▶ | 47. DATE M M / D D / C C Y Y

PLACE OF DEATH

101. PLACE OF DEATH | 102. IF HOSPITAL, SPECIFY ONE: ☐ IP ☐ ER/OP ☐ DOA | 103. FACILITY OTHER THAN HOSPITAL: ☐ CONV. HOSP. ☐ RES. CARE ☐ OTHER | 104. COUNTY

105. STREET ADDRESS—(STREET AND NUMBER OR LOCATION) | 106. CITY

CAUSE OF DEATH

107. DEATH WAS CAUSED BY: (ENTER ONLY ONE CAUSE PER LINE FOR A, B, C, AND D) | TIME INTERVAL BETWEEN ONSET AND DEATH | 108. DEATH REPORTED TO CORONER YES ☐ NO ☐ REFERRAL NUMBER

IMMEDIATE CAUSE (A)

DUE TO (B) | 109. BIOPSY PERFORMED YES ☐ NO ☐

DUE TO (C) | 110. AUTOPSY PERFORMED YES ☐ NO ☐

DUE TO (D) | 111. USED IN DETERMINING CAUSE YES ☐ NO ☐

112. OTHER SIGNIFICANT CONDITIONS CONTRIBUTING TO DEATH BUT NOT RELATED TO CAUSE GIVEN IN 107

113. WAS OPERATION PERFORMED FOR ANY CONDITION IN ITEM 107 OR 112? IF YES, LIST TYPE OF OPERATION AND DATE.

PHYSICIAN'S CERTIFICATION

114. I CERTIFY THAT TO THE BEST OF MY KNOWLEDGE DEATH OCCURRED AT THE HOUR, DATE AND PLACE STATED FROM THE CAUSES STATED. DECEDENT ATTENDED SINCE M M / D D / C C Y Y DECEDENT LAST SEEN ALIVE M M / D D / C C Y Y | 115. SIGNATURE AND TITLE OF CERTIFIER ▶ | 116. LICENSE NO. | 117. DATE M M / D D / C C Y Y

118. TYPE ATTENDING PHYSICIAN'S NAME, MAILING ADDRESS, ZIP

CORONER'S USE ONLY

I CERTIFY THAT IN MY OPINION DEATH OCCURRED AT THE HOUR, DATE AND PLACE STATED FROM THE CAUSES STATED. | 120. INJURY AT WORK YES ☐ NO ☐ | 121. INJURY DATE M M / D D / C C Y Y | 122. HOUR | 123. PLACE OF INJURY

119. MANNER OF DEATH ☐ NATURAL ☐ SUICIDE ☐ HOMICIDE ☐ ACCIDENT ☐ PENDING INVESTIGATION ☐ COULD NOT BE DETERMINED | 124. DESCRIBE HOW INJURY OCCURRED (EVENTS WHICH RESULTED IN INJURY)

125. LOCATION (STREET AND NUMBER OR LOCATION AND CITY, ZIP)

126. SIGNATURE OF CORONER OR DEPUTY CORONER ▶ | 127. DATE M M / D D / C C Y Y | 128. TYPED NAME, TITLE OF CORONER OR DEPUTY CORONER

STATE REGISTRAR

A | B | C | D | E | F | G | H | FAX AUTH. # | CENSUS TRACT

Use this page to record your notes and responses to the Death Certificate activity.

Death in the Lives of Children and Adolescents

Chapter Summary

Chapter 10 looks at experiences of loss in the lives of children and adolescents. In providing a life-span approach to the issues, this chapter builds on material presented in earlier chapters—particularly those dealing with how children are socialized about death, how individuals cope with serious illness, and how survivors cope with loss and bereavement. Change is a common component of children's lives. They may experience separations from friends and neighborhoods to which they have become attached. Changes in the composition of the family unit, through death, divorce, or the departure of a sibling, require children to adapt to unfamiliar and sometimes painful circumstances.

A child's understanding of death is influenced by his or her level of psychosocial and cognitive development, as well as by attitudes and experiences encountered in the environment. The role of developmental factors is explored by focusing on the models of child development devised by Erik Erikson and Jean Piaget. These models are applied to the ways that children understand death at different stages of development, beginning with infancy and toddlerhood, through the early and middle years of childhood, to adolescence—by which time children have generally acquired a mature concept of death. Even young children may recognize the essential elements of a mature concept of death, although the more abstract or symbolic thoughts about death usually take longer to develop. A child's experiences can have great impact on his or her understanding of death. The death of a close family member, for example, may cause a child to come to an understanding of death that would usually be associated with a later period of development.

When a child is diagnosed with a serious and possibly life-threatening illness, confusion and emotional upheaval usually result—for the child as well as his or her family. A child's natural curiosity about the seriousness of his or her condition is sometimes met with silence or attempts to avert disclosure on the part of adults. The need to comply with a discomforting medical regimen typically adds to the child's fears and anxieties. As with adults, children use a range of coping strategies as they adjust to difficult and painful circumstances. How a child perceives an illness and the manner in which he or she responds to it depends on such factors as age (or developmental level), patterns of social interaction, family relationships, and past experiences, as well as the nature of the illness and its treatment.

When a child's life is threatened by serious illness, it affects the whole of family life. Caring for a seriously ill child involves attending not only to his or her physical needs but also to his or her emotional and psychological needs. While trained personnel best provide the technical aspects of medical care, family members can participate in the crucial nontechnical aspects of care, such as those involving emotional support and encouragement.

Although not all children experience serious injury or illness, most do become survivors of a death, whether it is the death of a pet, a parent or grandparent, a sibling, or other close relation. A child's response to such losses will reflect such factors as his or her stage of mental and emotional development as well as previous experiences with death. Children of the same age may exhibit significant differences in their abilities to comprehend death and cope with its effects on them as survivors. Experiencing a close death may stimulate the development of more mature concepts about death as a child copes with the fact of loss in his or her life.

Children typically look to parents and other adults as examples of how to deal with loss. Children should be given opportunities to express their grief. Feelings need to be openly explored in a supportive atmosphere. Children seem to cope more easily with their feelings about a close death or other traumatic event when they are allowed to participate in the unfolding experience. When children are excluded, or when their questions go unanswered, they may experience greater confusion and pain.

Foremost among the guidelines for helping a child cope with crisis is a willingness to listen. Acknowledge the child's feelings. Discover what he or she thinks and feels. Questions should be answered honestly and directly, without overwhelming the child with information beyond his or her ability to comprehend. Age-appropriate books dealing with various situations involving dying and death can provide opportunities to explore issues and experiences with children. A variety of organizations provide social support to children who are coping with life-threatening illness or with a significant death. As much as we might wish it were otherwise, children cannot ultimately be shielded from painful experiences involving loss. The material covered in this chapter can provide a basis for helping children cope with their experiences of change and loss.

Even absent significant death-related experiences, children are naturally curious and inquisitive about death. Adults who are prepared to discuss the subject openly and honestly, and in a way appropriate to the child's level of understanding, can play a crucial supportive role in the child's efforts to come to terms with the reality of death and the emotions engendered by loss.

Objectives

- To describe the psychosocial and cognitive models of development and to demonstrate their value in comprehending a child's understanding of death.
- To identify the factors that influence a child's understanding of and attitude toward death.
- To describe the child's perception of illness.
- To explain how a terminally ill child's fears and anxieties are developmentally related.
- To identify the various coping mechanisms used by terminally ill children and to assess the value of each.
- To identify factors influencing a child's experience of grief.
- To illustrate ways of helping children cope with death.

Key Terms and Concepts

bibliotherapy
cognitive transformations
concrete operational
coping mechanisms
distancing strategies
formal operational
goal substitution
magical thinking
mature concept of death
metaphorical explanation
parent death

pet death
preoperational
protothanatic
psychosocial development
reversibility
selective memory
sensorimotor
separation anxiety
sibling death
sublimation
support groups

Questions for Guided Study and Review

1. What are some of the ways that young children encounter loss and death?
2. When do children generally become aware of death?
3. How does the "peekaboo" game or a child's statement "no more" reflect death-related understandings?
4. What is the contribution of psychoanalytic theory to our understanding of death-related anxieties?
5. What is the premise of *magical thinking*?
6. How do play activities help children reach some understanding of death?
7. At what age do children begin to make efforts to come to terms with death-related experiences?
8. How does Erik Erikson's model of psychosocial development help us understand children's concerns about death?
9. How does Jean Piaget's model of cognitive development help us understand children's concerns about death?
10. Briefly describe the sequence of psychosocial and cognitive stages during childhood and how they relate to a child's understanding of death.

11. How does the adolescent sense of invulnerability relate to the concept of personal death?
12. How might "mental first aid" be offered to help a seriously ill child?
13. How does development of a "death concept" relate to the concerns expressed by seriously ill children?
14. What methods of coping are typically used by seriously ill children?
15. How are distancing and sublimation used as coping mechanism?
16. What are some issues that deserve consideration in caring for a seriously ill or dying child?
17. What factors influence a bereaved child's experience of grief?
18. How might guilt complicate childhood grief?
19. Why is the death of a pet often experienced as a significant loss?
20. What are some ways that children can be helped in coping with the death of a parent?
21. What is an "inner representation of the deceased" and how is it related to a child's grief for a parent's death?
22. What are some issues that should be considered in a child's experience of a parent's death?
23. How does the death of a sibling potentially affect the surviving child's sense of vulnerability?
24. What are some issues that should be considered in a child's experience of a sibling's death?
25. How might parental responses influence a child's ability to cope with a sibling's death?
26. Why is it important to share information about change and loss with children?
27. What are the main guidelines for sharing information about death with children?
28. What are some of the important considerations in talking with children about death before a crisis occurs, when a family member is seriously ill, and in the aftermath of a loss?
29. When discussing death with children, why is listening often more important than speaking?
30. Why is it important to verify that a child understands what you've said about death?
31. What are some factors to consider when discussing *beliefs* with children?
32. How might books be used with children as an aid to their understanding of and coping with death?
33. What are some of the support groups for ill and bereaved children?
34. How do you interpret Erik Erikson's statement, "Healthy children will not fear life if their parents have the integrity not to fear death"?

Practice Test Questions

MULTIPLE CHOICE

1. Early experiences with death during childhood influence concepts about death in later life
   a. inconsistently.
   b. greatly.
   c. only when they are traumatic.
   d. insignificantly.

2. According to Piaget's theory, when a child first becomes able to name realistic ways that people die, he or she is probably between the ages of
   a. 3 and 5.
   b. 7 and 12.
   c. 10 and 13.
   d. 14 and 17.

3. It is important for individuals who have lost a pet to
   a. gain insight into the animal-human bond.
   b. acknowledge the role of pet death in the overall scheme of things.
   c. acquire a new pet as soon as possible.
   d. express feelings about the loss.

4. The text uses the example of the young woman who avoided fruit seeds into adulthood to illustrate how
   a. common items can scare children.
   b. childhood fears sometimes never disappear.
   c. children can become confused by metaphors.
   d. illogical children's perceptions of death can be.

5. When talking to children about a potentially painful situation, it is best to
   a. rely as much as possible on the child's intuition.
   b. speak freely, knowing that they will hear only what they are ready for.
   c. let the child's questions be a guide to what you say.
   d. relate to how you felt at their age.

TRUE/FALSE

_____ 1. Changes in family relationships, such as divorce or separation, may be experienced as a kind of death.

_____ 2. According to Piaget's theory, all children do NOT move through the stages of cognitive development in the same sequence.

_____ 3. Some children cope with life-threatening illnesses and painful treatment by regressing to a pattern of behaviors that reflects a less-demanding, more comfortable time in their lives.

_____ 4. A sibling's death usually represents a loss of security for the surviving child.

_____ 5. When talking with children about death, the liberal use of euphemism and metaphor is the best way to help them understand death.

MATCHING

Match each of Jean Piaget's stages with its corresponding characteristic.

_____ 1. Concrete operational .   a. The child is able to think abstractly or symbolically

_____ 2. Formal operational   b. The child acquires a stable concept of death.

_____ 3. Preoperational   c. The child begins to use logic to solve problems.

_____ 4. Sensorimotor   d. The child appraises his or her situation in the world and begins to seek explanations.

                                         e. The child becomes acquainted with his or her body and the environment.

❧ Answers to practice questions can be found in Part IV ❧

Related Readings

Indicates selection from *The Path Ahead: Readings in Death and Dying*, eds. Lynne Ann DeSpelder and Albert Lee Strickland (Mountain View, Calif.: Mayfield, 1995).

CHILDREN: GENERAL WORKS

David W. Adams and Eleanor J. Deveau, eds. *Beyond the Innocence of Childhood*. 3 vols. Amityville, N.Y.: Baywood, 1995.

Charles A. Corr and David E. Balk, eds. *Handbook of Adolescent Death and Bereavement*. New York: Springer, 1996.

Charles A. Corr and Donna M. Corr, eds. *Handbook of Childhood Death and Bereavement*. New York: Springer, 1996.

CHILDREN AND GRIEF

Myra Bluebond-Langner. *In the Shadow of Illness: Parents and Siblings of the Chronically Ill Child*. Princeton, N.J.: Princeton University Press, 1996.

Betty Davies. *Shadows in the Sun: The Experience of Sibling Bereavement in Childhood*. Washington, D.C.: Taylor & Francis, 1998.

Kenneth J. Doka, ed. *Children Mourning, Mourning Children*. Washington, D.C.: Hospice Foundation of America, 1995.

Dianne McKissock. *The Grief of Our Children*. Sidney: Australian Broadcasting Commission, 1998.

Phyllis R. Silverman, Steven Nickman, and J. William Worden. "Detachment Revisited: The Child's Reconstruction of a Dead Parent," pp. 260–270.

Avery D. Weisman, "Bereavement and Companion Animals," pp. 276–280.

J. William Worden. *Children and Grief: When a Parent Dies*. New York: Guilford Press, 1996.

CHILDREN AND LIFE-THREATENING ILLNESS

William G. Bartholome. "Care of the Dying Child: The Demands of Ethics," pp. 133–143.

Robert W. Buckingham. *Care of the Dying Child: A Practical Guide for Those Who Help Others*. New York: Continuum, 1989.

Shelley Geballe, Janice Gruendel, and Warren Andiman, eds. *Forgotten Children of the AIDS Epidemic*. New Haven, Conn.: Yale University Press, 1995.

Barbara M. Sourkes. *Armfuls of Time: The Psychological Experience of the Child with a Life-Threatening Illness*. Pittsburgh: University of Pittsburgh Press, 1996.

CHILDREN AND OTHER ENCOUNTERS WITH DEATH

📖 Zlata Filipovic. "Zlata's Diary: A Child's Life in Sarajevo," pp. 175–178.

📖 James Garbarino. "Challenges We Face in Understanding Children and War: A Personal Essay," pp. 169–174.

📖 Ice T. "The Killing Fields," pp. 178–181.

Major Points in This Chapter

- Theoretical frameworks such as Erikson's "psychosocial development" and Piaget's "cognitive transformations" are useful for comprehending the developmental sequence relative to the acquisition of a mature concept of death.

- Children with life-threatening illness are usually able to guess their condition by observing and interpreting the behavior of adults in their environment.

- Sick children use a variety of coping mechanisms to deal with anxiety, confusion, and the sometimes painful treatments that accompany life-threatening illness.

- Bereaved children's responses to loss are similar to those of adults. A particular child's experience of grief is influenced by such factors as age, stage of mental development, patterns of family interaction and communication, the nature of the relationship with the person (or pet) who has died, and previous experiences with death.

- Grief in response to the death of a pet is a normal and authentic experience for adults as well as children.

- Longitudinal studies of children who have experienced a parent's death reveal that children typically construct an "inner representation" (manifested in memories, feelings, and actions) that is used to maintain a relationship with the dead parent. The nature of this relationship changes as the child grows older and acute grief diminishes.

- Books for children and adolescents are a source of information and insight about dying, death, and bereavement; they offer opportunities for sharing between adults and young people.

- Honest communication tailored to a child's level of comprehension can promote healthy coping with life-threatening illness and grief.

- In discussing death with children, it is important to listen carefully and verify what you believe they are saying. Accept the reality of the child's grief and answer questions honestly and directly, taking care not to use metaphorical explanations that may confuse or mislead the child.

- Social support for children includes many of the same kinds of options avail-able to adults who are coping with life-threatening illness or bereavement. In addition to a variety of peer-oriented support groups, there are programs that focus on the needs of specific populations (such as inner-city children bereaved as a result of drive-by shootings and other types of "street" violence) and programs that seek to "grant the wishes" of children with serious illness.

Observations and Reflections

As you read about the developmental models, notice the differences between each of them relative to a child's understanding of death and dying. In reading the material in this chapter, you may recall experiences with loss in your own childhood. Consider whether you have experienced "magical thinking" even as an adult.

After reading this chapter, many students are eager to explore children's thoughts and experiences. For young children, books about death can be used to begin a dialogue. However, remember to first talk with the child's parent(s) before you embark upon a conversation about death.

Use the space below to record your notes and responses to the topics covered in this chapter.

⇒ *Explaining Death to Children:*
An Example from the Popular Press

Directions As you read the following excerpt from a contemporary paperback horror novel, think about your readings from **The Last Dance**. After you read the excerpt, respond to the review questions in the spaces provided on the following page.

Tuck wiped the tears from his eyes as he pondered this. "Daddy?"

"Yes, Tuck?"

"Are we still going to move?"

"Not for the time being. Maybe in a little while."

Tuck fiddled with a button on his shirt. "I'm glad we didn't leave," he returned. "You know why."

"Why?"

"Because that would have meant that we were leaving Ben behind." After this remark Tuck continued to fumble distractedly with his shirt button, gazing meditatively off into space. David drew in his breath, grateful at least that Tuck had not phrased the remark in the form of a question, and hugged his son tighter. Nonetheless, a moment later David noticed that Tuck's expression had taken on a darker cast, and as he continued to stare off into the distance some inner voice seemed to be speaking to him, prodding him with things he found painful.

"Daddy?"

"Yes, Tuck?"

"Is Ben ever coming back?"

David closed his eyes as he embraced his son tighter still. It was the question he had been dreading. As long as he himself had been ignorant of Ben's fate it had been easy to be evasive, to postpone confronting the matter. But now that he knew the truth he was left in a quandary. The last thing in the world he wanted to do was tell Tuck the truth, for he feared it would send Tuck even further into his ever-increasing depressions. But after what he had said about Mrs. Comfrey he felt he had no right to lie. He took a deep breath.

"No, Tuck. Ben isn't coming back."

Tuck remained absolutely motionless, absorbing the information with no visible sign of distress.

"Why not?" he asked.

David took another deep breath. "Do you know how every fall the flowers die and the leaves fall off the trees? Do you know why they do that?"

Tuck shook his head in the negative. "'Cause winter's coming?" he offered tentatively.

"Partly because the winter's coming," David returned. "But partly because they have to make room for the new flowers and leaves. You see, that's the way nature works. Everything has a beginning and an end. If it didn't the world would become stagnant, like a bucket of water that you just let sit and sit. Can you imagine what the world would be like if everything lasted forever? Just think about it. Every bee that ever lived, every tree and every person would still be here, and what a crowded place it would be. The only problem is that it's painful when things we love go away. We miss them and that's okay. But what's not okay is to think that it's bad that things have to go away, because it's not bad. It's a very important thing. It's what allows new flowers to grow, and new leaves to replace the old, and the world to renew itself."

"And Ben went away?"

"Yes, Ben went away."

"Where did he go?"

"To heaven," David replied.

Tuck's lower lip started to quiver. "But why did he have to go to heaven?"

"Because it was his time to go."

A large tear rolled down Tuck's cheek and hit David's arm, and he gave his son another reassuring hug. "Hey, now, I don't want you to be upset about this. I told you the truth about Ben because I don't want you to be afraid when things have to go to heaven. Too many people in this world spend too much time being afraid of that, and it's just silly. When something goes to heaven it's a scary thing, and it's a painful thing. But you've got to be brave about it. Things don't go to heaven very often, but when they do, you've got to face it like a man."

Tuck wiped the tear from his eye. "I've got to have moxie, huh, Dad?"

David smiled. He had forgotten about that. "Yes, Tuck. You've got to have moxie."

⇒ *Review Questions for* The Bog

1. Which euphemism does the father use when describing what happened to Ben? _____
   _____ (Underline each appearance in the excerpt.)

2. Review Table 1.2 in Chapter 1 of The Last Dance. Pick another euphemism and substitute it for the one in the story excerpt. How does the discussion read now? _____
   _____

3. Using Piaget's model of cognitive development, what developmental phase is presumed in the father's explanation? _____

   What age range is associated with this developmental phase? _____

   What are the characteristics of this phase? _____
   _____

4. What is the parental message about death that is being communicated in this story? _____
   _____

5. Based on the information given in the text and in class, evaluate the parental communication. Using specific examples, which elements of the communication do you believe are appropriate? _____
   _____
   _____

   Which are inadequate? _____

6. Given that the child in this story is a survivor of a high-grief death, what are at least five possible benefits to him that might result from this conversation? _____
   _____
   _____
   _____
   _____
   _____
   _____
   _____
   _____
   _____
   _____

7. Does it seem that descriptions of talking with children about death are rare in contemporary paperback novels? _____

8. What editorial advice would you give to the author if you knew that the child in this story was five years old? _____

_____

_____

_____

_____

_____

_____

_____

_____

_____

_____

_____

_____

⇒ *Factors and Variables that Influence Grief Reactions in Bereaved Children*

Directions: Read Carol Berns's list of factors that can influence a child's grief. Circle the numbers of those you identify as particularly important. In the space provided following this text, add your own factors to the list.

1. **Age, cognitive development, and life experiences:** Can the child verbalize his or her sense of what has occurred? Does the child have a mature understanding of death?

2. **Early attachment patterns:** Researchers identify early patterns of attachment as determinants of whether a child may be resilient or vulnerable to later stressful life events.

3. **Genetic factors and medical history:** The role of genetic factors is difficult to determine; however, children with genetic susceptibility, such as depression, may have their vulnerability triggered by bereavement.

4. **Previous losses:** Has the child experienced prior losses? If those losses have been unaddressed or poorly managed, the risk of poor resolution in this loss may be increased.

5. **The role of the child's personality prior to bereavement:** How does this child see himself or herself? Children who perceive themselves as capable and take responsibility for themselves after a death often gain mastery over their environment. Having *acted* rather than *reacted* to the loss, they can develop self-esteem, strength, and confidence that helps with later stresses.

6. **The preexisting relationship between the bereaved and the deceased:** The more ambivalent or dependent the relationship, the more complex the mourning and greater probability of a poor outcome. The level of intimacy and the complexity of the relationship will affect grief.

7. **The amount of "unfinished business" between the bereaved and the deceased:** Unfinished business refers to those issues left unsettled or never addressed.

8. **The type of death:** Sudden, unexpected, and untimely deaths are more likely to be associated with difficult outcomes than are anticipated deaths. However, death from a lingering, terminal illness may also lead to difficult outcomes. Is this death viewed as preventable, as with an accidental poisoning or suicide?

9. **The circumstances and nature of the death:** How, when, and where did the person die? Is the death in the natural order of expected deaths in the family? Have older members already died? Was the child present at the time of death? Did the deceased suffer in dying, or was he or she disfigured in death? Was this loss violent, the result of suicide or murder? Did it occur in wartime, or in a faraway location? Was the body found? If the death was caused by homicide, the child can have vengeful thoughts, intense anger, and revenge fantasies towards the killer. When the killer cannot be identified, the fantasies may be greater and the grief more difficult.

10. **Intensity of guilt or responsibility:** What intensity of guilt or responsibility is the child experiencing? Children often ask, "Could I have saved him or her?" Magical thinking and confused notions of what happened will need clarification.

11. **Change in child's role:** To what extent has the child's role changed since the death? The child whose only sibling dies becomes an only child, perhaps having to take on more

responsibility in his or her parents' eyes. The child may place added pressure on himself or herself. Can the child be helped to move through the grief naturally, rather than be subject to unnecessary pressure?

12. **Current stress or crises:** Stress, crises, or other losses occurring during bereavement may demand the child's resources, thereby creating extra pressure and impeding healing.

13. **Sanctioned by society:** Is this a disenfranchised grief, or does society or the social/cultural group sanction this loss? When a loss is not socially validated—that is, not acknowledged by society as an important loss to be mourned—the child is put in a difficult situation. This may be the case when the relationship is unrecognized, not understood, or largely unaccepted by society. Examples may include a child losing a pet, a grandparent, a newborn sibling to SIDS (sudden infant death syndrome), a best friend or classmate, a parent's former live-in mate, a nanny, or a non-relative caregiver.

14. **Availability of community support:** Is there an aftercare program or school awareness program? Is there a church, community, or school bereavement group?

15. **Coincidental deaths or losses:** Were there simultaneous deaths in a family or community? For example, a multiple car accident or major disaster? In such cases, the grief is more complex and there may be less comfort and support available. Coincidental losses render the child especially vulnerable because the different losses each need to be individually grieved and support may not be available.

16. **The responses of the family and social network:** A poor outcome is more likely when the child perceives his or her family and social network as nonsupportive in terms of sharing in or allowing for expression of grief, or when there is chaos in the family and members fail to support each other. Enmeshed or disengaged family patterns, in which individuals lack tolerance for different responses or cohesion for mutual support, is problematic. Is there healthy family modeling? Is there support for emotional expression?

17. **Religious-cultural-ethnic influence and accessibility:** Does the religious, cultural, or ethnic identification affect how grief is acknowledged? The child's responses to loss and death generally reflect the norms, mores, and sanctions of the immediate sociocultural environment. Religious faith or belief may increase the comfort, support, and hope, or may instead increase guilt, regret, and despair. Is a spiritual leader available?

18. **Successive deaths or losses:** When losses, death, or disaster follow in quick succession, the grief over one may be distracted or disturbed by the shock and grief over the next. "Bereavement overload" can occur when an individual has experienced too many deaths, either as serial losses or simultaneous losses.

19. **The behavior, attitudes, and responsiveness of parents and other significant adults in the child's environment:** Is an open display of emotions allowed? Is communication encouraged? Are there secrets, myths, or taboos surrounding death? Does the family belief system invoke blame, shame, or guilt surrounding death? Is healing, growth, laughter encouraged?

20. **Sociodemographic factors:** Chronological and developmental age, gender, religion, culture, and parental occupation and economic position are factors that influence outcome.

21. **Environmental factors:** Is the child in a dangerous home environment or neighborhood? Does he or she see movies or television programs that show destruction and violence? Is the household unstable?

22. **New losses or changes:** What other losses or changes might occur because of this death? "Secondary losses" are those losses that develop as a consequence of a loved one's death. Will a surviving parent have to work away from home or be away longer hours? Will the child's extracurricular activities be changed or terminated? Will family activities be altered? Will there be a change in economic status?

23. **Subsequent life circumstances for the child:** Have siblings or friends reacted by withdrawing from the child? Will there be a change in schools? Is the surviving parent dating or thinking of remarriage?

24. **Involvement by the media:** Children may experience discomfort when what is private for them is made public.

Use the space below and on the following page to list and describe additional factors that you think are important in dealing with a child's grief:

_____

_____

_____

_____

_____

_____

_____

_____

_____

_____

_____

_____

_____

_____

_____

⇒ *Tools for Helping Bereaved Children*

Directions: Read each of the items below. (Notice how most also apply to children who have a life-threatening illness or who have a seriously ill loved one). In the blank next to the each statement, use the following codes to indicate your opinion.

SA = Strongly Agree

A = Agree

NA = No Opinion

D = Disagree

SD = Strongly Disagree

_____ 1. Know your own feelings.

_____ 2. Know your expectations. What do you expect to give? What do you expect in return? Why are you offering it?

_____ 3. Be guided by the child's needs, not your own.

_____ 4. Be a good observer. Watch body language and emotional expression.

_____ 5. Listen to unspoken as well as verbal language. Listen for abstracts, themes, cues, fantasies, and feelings.

_____ 6. Realize that responses may not be obvious and immediate.

_____ 7. Give permission for the child to feel anything. Allow him or her to hurt, grieve, and express grief.

_____ 8. Don't rush through the "stages." Keep in check your impulse to guide the grief process. Each child grieves at his or her own pace and in his/her own way.

_____ 9. Remember that there are no right or wrong ways to grieve.

_____ 10. Help find constructive outlets for energy, anger, fears, and tears.

_____ 11. Maintain discipline. Consistency and strong guides are comforting in a world where everything else seems shattered, confused, and chaotic.

_____ 12. Regressive or aggressive behaviors are common. Be supportive rather than punitive.

_____ 13. Do not condone misbehavior. Change or grief should never be excuses for antisocial conduct.

_____ 14. Continue to expect appropriate behaviors. Temper your expectations with kindness and understanding, but continue to expect functioning and participation.

_____ 15. Help a child find a supportive peer group. Children sharing with children works wonders.

_____ 16. Become part of a caring team by communicating with school, family, religious group, and community.

_____ 17. If the child's or family's religious beliefs are strong, use their teachings and faith. Faith may be very valuable in giving the child hope and reinvigorating inner resources.

_____ 18. Grieving children need to establish their roles and current identity. Help them in their search.

_____ 19. Remember that children and young people will continue to deal with their loss as they mature. The loss will be revisited as they gain new understandings, life experiences, and insights. Continue to be available long after you think they "should be over it."

_____ 20. Recognize that no one lives forever. Nothing lasts or stays the same. Acknowledge this and provide support and guidance.

_____ 21. Be open and honest. Create an atmosphere of acceptance that invites questions and fosters confidence and trust.

_____ 22. Be available for continued support. Have some fun.

Study Guide

184 ⚬— Chapter 10   The Last Dance: Encountering Death and Dying, 6th ed.

🖳 *Internet Sites for Kids*

Directions   *Here, you will search the Internet to identify five web sites for kids in the area of death, dying, or bereavement. Please rank each listing from 1 (very good) to 5 (useless) and give a summary of the information to be found on the site.*

Some places to begin are:

National Cancer Institute kids page:
<http://cancernet.nci.nih.gov/occdocs/KidsHome.html>

Health and Human Services kids page:
<http://www.hhs.gov/kids/>

Taryn's World: About Switches
http://mcrcr2.med.nyu.edu/murphp01/taryn/switches.htm>

1. URL_____ Rating_____

_____

_____

_____

_____

_____

_____

_____

_____

2. URL_____ Rating_____

_____

_____

_____

_____

_____

_____

_____

3. URL_____ Rating_____

_____

_____

_____

_____

_____

_____

4. URL_____ Rating_____

_____

_____

_____

_____

_____

_____

5. URL_____ Rating_____

_____

_____

_____

_____

_____

_____

C H A P T E R   *11*

Death in the Lives of Adults

Chapter Summary

Chapter 11 continues the lifespan perspective of the previous chapter by focusing on loss experiences during adulthood. As with the years of childhood, particular psychosocial concerns—or developmental crises—are emphasized during the various stages of adulthood. Young adulthood is characterized by concerns involving intimacy versus isolation, middle adulthood by concerns involving generativity versus stagnation, and maturity by concerns involving integrity versus despair. The meaning given to a loss event—that is, how it is interpreted—depends in significant measure, therefore, on the nature of the developmental issues being dealt with by the individual experiencing the loss.

In the normal course of events, the incidence of loss increases as we grow older. Besides confronting the prospect of our own mortality as a result of aging, growing older increases the chances that we will experience the death of our parents, and, conversely, that, as parents, we may experience the death of a child. For most parents, a child's death is devastating. It represents not only a loss of the potential and unique future envisioned for the child, but also the loss of a kind of genetic and social immortality for the parent.

In coping with the death of a child, the individuals within a couple relationship may well have different styles of grieving the loss, and both may be overwhelmed by a sense of general chaos, confusion, and uncertainty. Each partner may feel isolated and unsupported by the only other person in the world who shares the magnitude of the loss. Behavior that is meant to be supportive may be interpreted by one's mate as being quite otherwise. Conflict is reduced and positive interaction promoted when couples engage in open and honest communication, share emotional responses as well as information, and validate one another's perception of the loss.

Miscarriage, induced abortion, stillbirth, and neonatal death are examples of childbearing losses that sometimes go unrecognized, unsupported, and unresolved. Yet the grief experienced by parents following such losses may be just as devastating as that resulting from the death of an older child. This is true also of individuals who give up a child for adoption or who find themselves unable to have children because of sterility or infertility. In mourning *unlived lives*, grief is felt not only for the physical loss, but also for the symbolic loss. When a person's identity as a nurturing parent is thwarted, healing the grief requires honoring the archetypal bonds between parent and child. It also requires that the wider community acknowledge the loss so that the necessary solace and social support can be offered to the bereaved person.

Adult survivors of a parent's death often encounter not only the loss of security represented by a parent's love and support, but also a thought-provoking reminder of their own mortality. Studies indicate that, for most midlife adults, the death of a parent is an important symbolic event, one that triggers a period of self-examination accompanied by a transition to a maturer stance toward life.

Spousal bereavement has been termed the most disruptive of all the transitions in the life cycle. The aftermath of a mate's death requires a multitude of adjustments. What were once shared pleasures become occasions for individual pain. Age, gender, and the nature of the relationship are among important factors that influence the experience of spousal bereavement. Research indicates that individuals who have lived out traditional sex roles find the transition especially difficult, as new skills must be learned to manage the needs of daily life. The availability of a stable social network appears to be crucial in determining how bereaved spouses adjust to their changed status. Besides maintaining the continuity of relationships with friends, neighbors, and family, one of the most valuable resources for the recently widowed is contact with other bereaved persons who have lost a mate, and who can serve as role models during the period of adjustment.

For the older adult, the experience of aging typically involves losses related to a variety of physical and mental declines. Although the debilitating effects of aging are being steadily pushed toward the end of the human lifespan, thus "compressing" morbidity and extending "active" life expectancy, the processes of senescence, or the aging of the human organism, eventually result in greater frailty and susceptibility to illness and injury. To receive adequate care, many frail elderly require institutional or community support, such as that provided by personal care homes, skilled nursing facilities, and home health care agencies. Yet, growing old is not essentially a medical problem. The latter part of life has its own distinct challenges, most notably the question of human mortality. Facing death has been characterized as the final developmental task of old age.

Objectives

- To list and describe Erik Erikson's psychosocial stages of adult development.
- To identify the kinds of losses adults experience.
- To distinguish the particular characteristics of parental bereavement and to identify the types of support available.
- To compare and contrast the emotional responses to miscarriage, abortion, stillbirth, neonatal death, SIDS (sudden infant death syndrome), and the loss of the "perfect" child.
- To describe disenfranchised grief, with examples of its occurrence, and to identify how grief resulting from such losses can be facilitated.
- To explain family interaction patterns that may be observed when a child is terminally ill.
- To compare and contrast ways of caring for the dying child.
- To identify the factors influencing grief in response to the death of an adult child.

- To describe the factors influencing spousal bereavement and to summarize the types of social support available.
- To distinguish the factors influencing the response to the death of a parent.
- To identify the factors influencing grief in response to the death of a friend.
- To summarize the physiological and psychological changes that typically occur with aging.

Key Terms and Concepts

abortion
adoption
childbearing losses
death of a parent
generativity vs. stagnation
infertility
integrity vs. despair
intimacy vs. isolation
meaning of death
miscarriage
mizuko
neonatal death

parental bereavement
peer support groups
perinatal death
postmortem photography
reframing behavior
senescence
SIDS (sudden infant death syndrome)
social support network
spousal bereavement
sterility
stillbirth
symbolic loss
widowhood

Questions for Guided Study and Review

1. How do the psychosocial stages of adulthood relate to coping with death?
2. What are some of the common features as well as unique features of the various types of parental bereavement?
3. What are the characteristics that tend to make the death of a child a high-grief death?
4. What factors influence conflict and cooperation in coping with parental bereavement as a couple?
5. What is a *reframe*, and why is it important?
6. What are the various childbearing losses?
7. What is the difference between *miscarriage* and *stillbirth*?
8. How is the birth of a severely disabled child a potential cause of grief over the "wished-for" child?
9. What are the dynamics of blame and anger in childbearing losses?
10. How does disenfranchised grief relate to childbearing losses?
11. What are some ways that hospitals can help parents cope with stillbirth?
12. What is SIDS?
13. What factors tend to complicate grief from a SIDS death?
14. How might different reasons for abortion lead to different loss reactions?
15. What are "water children"?
16. What are the major causes of death for school-age children?
17. What special factors in parental bereavement are likely to accompany the death of an adult child?

18. What kind of social support is available for bereaved parents?
19. How does the death of a parent affect the survivor?
20. What factors are important in affecting the outcome of spousal bereavement?
21. What kind of social support is available for widows and widowers?
22. When does aging begin?
23. What is *senescence*?
24. How does the National Council on Aging categorize older adults?
25. In what ways do stereotypes of old people differ from the reality?
26. What are the steps to be considered in choosing a nursing care facility?
27. What is the meaning of the statement, "Growing old is not essentially a medical problem"?

Practice Test Questions

MULTIPLE CHOICE

1. Among the Cree of North America, infants were given moccasins with holes in them so that ghosts would not take them away "because their moccasins need mending." This example is mentioned in the text to show that
   a. child rearing has a long history.
   b. if parents cannot protect children, they should resort to explanations involving ghosts.
   c. feelings about the parental role of safeguarding children are universal.
   d. the ancient magic worked.

2. Giving up a child for adoption is an example of
   a. emotional stress.
   b. philanthropy.
   c. reproductive loss.
   d. cruel parenting.

3. Cases of SIDS (sudden infant death syndrome) have sometimes been subjected to criminal investigation because the
   a. parents neglected the infant.
   b. law of child abuse requires such investigation.
   c. parents were responsible for the death.
   d. infant died of unexplained causes.

4. Which of the following is an example of psychic distancing in connection with a dying child?
   a. The child prefers to spend time playing with people his or her own age.
   b. Professional caregivers spend extra time with dying children.
   c. Parents visit the child less often and stay a shorter time.
   d. Relatives refrain from visiting the child because of fear about contracting the disease.

5. According to the text, the elderly tend to be more
   a. monotonous than other age groups.
   b. carefree than other age groups.
   c. individually distinct than other age groups.
   d. active than other age groups.

TRUE/FALSE

_____   1. An appropriate way to console a couple suffering from a childbearing loss is to remind them that they are still young and have plenty of time to have another baby.

_____   2. Parents who experience a miscarriage generally find minimizing or denying the loss very helpful in their recovery.

_____   3. After initial adjustments, both widowers and widows appear to have a happier life than their married counterparts.

_____   4. The availability of a stable social support network is crucial in the adjustment of bereaved spouses.

_____   5. Younger adults generally have accurate expectations about the process of aging and being old.

MATCHING

Match each of the following phrases to the appropriate topic.

_____   1. accidents are the major cause of death   a. death of a parent

_____   2. has comparatively few social support resources available   b. childbearing loss

_____   3. typically represents the loss of a long-term relationship   c. death of an older child

_____   4. usually includes actual and symbolic loss   d. death of a spouse

_____   5. often new skills must be learned to manage the needs of daily life e. death of an adult child

❧ Answers to practice questions can be found in Part IV ❧

Related Readings

📖 Indicates selection from *The Path Ahead: Readings in Death and Dying*, eds. Lynne Ann DeSpelder and Albert Lee Strickland (Mountain View, Calif.: Mayfield, 1995).

GENERAL READINGS

📖 Thomas Attig, "Coping with Mortality: An Essay on Self-Mourning," pp. 337–341.

📖 Sandra L. Bertman, "Bearing the Unbearable: From Loss, the Gain," pp. 348–354.

📖 John D. Kelly, "Grief: Re-forming Life's Story," pp. 242–245.

📖 Alfred G. Killilea, "The Politics of Being Mortal," pp. 342–347.

PARENTAL BEREAVEMENT

📖 Kenneth J. Doka, "Disenfranchised Grief," pp. 271–275.

📖 Stephen J. Fleming and Leslie Balmer, "Bereaved Families of Ontario: A Mutual-Help Model for Families Experiencing Death," pp. 281–288.

Kathleen R. Gilbert and Laura S. Smart. *Coping with Infant or Fetal Loss: The Couple's Healing Process.* New York: Brunner/Mazel, 1992.

Henya Kagan-Klein. *Gili's Book: A Journey into Bereavement for Parents and Counselors.* New York: Teachers College Press, 1998.

📖 Dennis Klass, "Solace and Immortality: Bereaved Parents' Continuing Bond with Their Children," pp. 246–259.

Dennis Klass. *Parental Grief: Solace and Resolution.* New York: Springer, 1988.

Ronald J. Knapp. *Beyond Endurance: When a Child Dies.* New York: Schocken, 1986.

Hannah Lothrop. *Help, Comfort, and Hope After Losing Your Baby in Pregnancy or the First Year.* Tucson, Ariz.: Fisher Books, 1997.

Therese A. Rando, ed. *Parental Loss of a Child.* Champaign, Ill.: Research Press, 1986.

DEATH OF A PARENT

📖 Janmarie Silvera, "Crossing the Border," pp. 301–302.

SPOUSAL BEREAVEMENT

Robert C. DiGiulio. *Beyond Widowhood: From Bereavement to Emergence and Hope.* New York: Free Press, 1989.

Susan Heinlein, Grace Brumett, and Jane Tibbals, eds. *When a Lifemate Dies: Stories of Love, Loss, and Healing.* Minneapolis: Fairview Press, 1997.

Helena Znaniecka Lopata. *Current Widowhood: Myths and Realities.* Thousand Oaks, Calif.: Sage Publications, 1996.

📖 Margaret Stroebe, Mary M. Gergen, Kenneth J. Gergen, and Wolfgang Stroebe, "Broken Hearts or Broken Bonds: Love and Death in Historical Perspective," pp. 231–241.

AGING

📖 Allan B. Chinen, "The Mortal King," pp. 335–336.

Sharon R. Kaufman. *The Ageless Self: Sources of Meaning in Later Life*. Madison: University of Wisconsin Press, 1995.

Jay Sokolovsky, ed. *The Cultural Context of Aging: Worldwide Perspectives*. New York: Bergin & Garvey, 1990.

Major Points in This Chapter

- The meaning of death is interpreted differently as a person grows older. Erikson's model of psychosocial development identifies three stages of adulthood: young adulthood, adulthood, and maturity.

- Many issues of parental bereavement span the adult life cycle. They are present for twenty-year-old parents, forty-year-old parents, and eighty-year-old parents. To understand the nature of a particular parent's grief and the specific losses involved, both the parent's age and the child's age must be taken into account.

- The death of a child places considerable stress on the marital relationship; thus, it is important to be aware of ways to minimize potential conflict between grieving parents and to promote positive interactions that aid in coping with the tragedy of a child's death.

- Childbearing losses typically involve the additional stress of the parent's not having an opportunity to get to know the child as a person. This sense of "mourning an unlived life" is rarely recognized in the bereaved parent's social milieu, reinforcing the mourner's perception that his or her loss is neither understood nor acknowledged.

- Perinatal bereavement support can be very helpful to parents who experience such childbearing loss. Support programs of this kind typically offer a variety of mechanisms for recognizing and affirming the loss, thereby facilitating healthy coping by the bereaved parent.

- The main causes of death among children between the ages of five and fourteen are accidents (with a death rate of 8.3 per 100,000), cancer (3.5), homicide (2.6), congenital anomalies (0.9), suicide (0.8), heart disease (0.8), chronic obstructive pulmonary disease (0.4), and pneumonia and influenza (0.3). Of the deaths resulting from accidents in this age group, over half involve motor vehicles.

- When a young person's life is threatened by serious illness, it affects the whole fabric of family life. In families that deal openly with such a crisis, the parents tend not to derive their personal identity solely from the role of "being a parent."

- A parent's death can have a lasting impact as the bereaved adult child mourns the loss of the special bond that had been shared with the deceased parent. The death of a parent can also evoke a "developmental push" as parentally bereaved adults no longer think of themselves as children.

- Spousal bereavement often follows years of shared experience and mutual commitment; the death of a mate can disrupt the very meaning of the surviving partner's existence. The transition from being a couple to being single can be especially difficult when the surviving spouse is also a parent, because it involves the added burden of making a transition to single parenthood.

- The death of a close friend is a significant loss that can evoke grief similar to that experienced following the death of a relative. For older adults, friendships are sometimes more important than family relationships. Yet there are few socially sanctioned opportunities to openly mourn the death of a friend.
- In the later years of life, the processes of aging can result in a variety of debilitating conditions that are experienced as losses of various kinds. The older person may require assistance with many activities of daily life. The need for appropriate and economical care is a matter of concern not only to older people and their relatives, but to society as a whole.

Observations and Reflections

It is likely that as an adult you have had some experience in dealing with the loss issues presented in this chapter, such as the death of a mate or intended mate, miscarriage, abortion, perinatal death, death of a child, or death of a parent.

If this is the case, think about your experience and the issues involved. What information presented in this chapter allows you to understand your grief in a different way?

Consider also the issue of social support. Did you make use of a survivor support group of some kind? What other forms of social support have been useful to you in coping with loss and grief?

Use the space below to make notes about the topics covered in this chapter and your own experiences.

⟶ *For an Adult Who Had a Parent Die
in Childhood or Adolescence: An Assessment*

Directions: As a quick exercise to see how your experience compares to that of others who had a parent die in childhood or adolescence, check off any of the following statements which are true for you. (Adapted from Never the Same: How Your Parent's Death in Childhood Impacts you Now . . . And What to Do About It, *by Donna Schuurman.)*

❑ When my parent died, no one really included me or explained everything that had happened or what was happening.

❑ For a long time after my parent's death, I felt alone, isolated, and different.

❑ My family and other adults didn't talk together much about my deceased parent in the months following his or her death.

❑ My family members still don't talk about it much.

❑ Since the time my parent died, I've always felt different.

❑ No one gave me all the facts and information or answered all my questions. In fact, I still have unanswered questions, and there are many things I don't know that I'd like to know about what happened.

❑ I wasn't given a choice about attending the memorial service, funeral home, or cemetery.

❑ No one explained what decisions were being made about what we'd call the "disposition of the body." I had no opportunity to say how I felt about burial versus cremation, where my parent would be buried, the type of service, or participation in the service.

❑ Everyone in my family handled my parent's death in a different way and still does.

❑ It was hard going back to school.

❑ I had many difficult times around holidays and the anniversary of my parent's death.

❑ I still have difficulties with holidays and the anniversary time of my parent's death.

❑ I didn't talk about it much to anyone back then.

❑ I haven't really talked all that much to others as an adult about the impact of my parent's death on me.

❑ I wanted to "protect" my surviving parent, so I didn't talk about it much with him or her.

❑ I felt different from other kids after my parent died.

❑ I didn't really know many, if any, other kids who'd had a parent die.

❑ There are parts of what happened when my parent died that I remember like they happened yesterday.

❑ I remember having some experiences or feelings that made me wonder if I was going crazy, or if something was wrong with me.

❏ There are parts of what happened when my parent died that remain a blur.

❏ For a long time I put it out of my mind and didn't think about it.

❏ We didn't do much as a family around the anniversary date of my parent's death.

❏ I sometimes wonder how things would have been different if my parent hadn't died.

❏ At some point in my adult life I realized my parent's death had a great impact on me.

❏ I suspect in some ways that my adult relationships have been affected by how I responded to my parent's death.

Scoring:

Now, count how many boxes you have checked. _____

Here's what your responses indicate.

If you checked 0–5 boxes:
If few of the 25 statements above are true for you, your experience is extremely rare. The adults around you apparently handled the aftermath of your parent's death in a supportive way and you have completed some significant work in your adult psychological life. Or you're in major denial!

If you checked 6–10 boxes:
Sounds like there was a great deal of support for you when your parent died and that you feel fairly resolved about how its impact on you. You're in the minority here, but there still may be some avenues left for you to explore.

If you checked 11–15 boxes:
You're on the fence as far as your awareness of the impact of your parent's death on you as a child, and what work you have left to do. There are still some important roads you have not walked along. Your sense of self and your relationships can be strengthened by applying the ideas and information in the book by Donna Schuurman, *Never the Same: How Your Parent's Death in Childhood Impacts You Now . . . And What to Do About It* (New York: St. Martin's, in press).

If you checked 16–20 boxes:
You will benefit tremendously from reading *Never the Same*, hearing about the experiences of others, and exploring what your parent's death means for you now. You've likely had difficulty with intimacy in your relationships and have felt like something is disconnected inside you.

If you checked 21–25 boxes:
Stop whatever you have planned for the next several days, carve out some time alone, and read *Never the Same*. It could help you make significant positive changes in your life. The quality of all of your relationships is related to your relationship with yourself, and there are parts—important parts—you have not explored.

However many of these statements are true for you, take heart in the belief that you're exploring these issues at this time in your life because you're ready to do so. Experiencing your parent's death changed the course of your life in some good ways, and in some ways that have not served you well. Your parent's death forced a premature maturity on you compared to your peers. As a result, you have a deeper inner knowing about what matters in life and how quickly people who matter can be taken away from us.

After completing this activity from Donna Schuurman's book, use the space below and on the following page to reflect on your experience.

_____

_____

_____

_____

_____

_____

_____

_____

_____

_____

_____

_____

_____

_____

_____

_____

_____

⌨ *Children and Life-threatening Illness: Internet Support*

Directions   *There is Internet support and information for adults dealing with the life-threatening illness of a child. In this activity, you will search and report on five web sites. Rate each of the five sites from 1 (excellent) to 5 (very poor).*

Some places to start are:

Pediatric Pain: Professional and Research Resources
<http://is.dal.ca/%7Epedpain/prohp.html>

Candlelighters Childhood Cancer Foundation
<http://www.candlelighters.org/>

HealthWeb: Pediatrics
<http://www.galter.nwu.edu/hw/ped/>

1. URL_____ Rating_____

_____

_____

_____

_____

_____

_____

_____

2. URL_____ Rating_____

_____

_____

_____

_____

_____

_____

_____

3. URL_____ Rating_____

_____

_____

_____

_____

_____

_____

4. URL_____ Rating_____

_____

_____

_____

_____

_____

_____

5. URL_____ Rating_____

_____

_____

_____

_____

_____

_____

_____

🖥 *Death of a Child: Internet Support*

Directions: *There are many internet sites devoted to information and support for adults grieving the death of a child. In this activity you will search and report on five sites. Rate each of the five sites from 1 (excellent) to 5 (very poor).*

Some places to start are:

Bereaved Families Online
\<http://www.inforamp.net/~bfo/index.html\>

Compassionate Friends
\<http://www.compassionatefriends.org/\>

SIDS Network
\<http://sids-network.org/\>

1. URL_____ Rating_____

_____

_____

_____

_____

_____

_____

_____

2. URL_____ Rating_____

_____

_____

_____

_____

_____

_____

_____

3. URL_____ Rating_____

_____

_____

_____

_____

_____

_____

_____

3. URL_____ Rating_____

_____

_____

_____

_____

_____

_____

_____

3. URL_____ Rating_____

_____

_____

_____

_____

_____

_____

_____

Suicide

Chapter Summary

Chapter 12 examines suicidal behavior by focusing on theoretical explanations of suicide, types of suicide, risk factors influencing suicide, patterns of suicidal behavior during different stages of the lifespan, methods used in attempting or committing suicide, suicide notes, and efforts related to suicide prevention, intervention, and postvention. Until the late 1960s, suicide rates generally increased directly with age, with the lowest rates among the young and the highest among the aged. More recently, this pattern has shifted, with a decrease in the suicide rate among older persons being offset by an increase among adolescents and young adults. Both of these trends are due largely to changes in the behavior of white males, a group that accounts for the majority of suicides in the United States.

Generally speaking, suicide is listed as the cause of death only when circumstances are unequivocal. Hesitancy about classifying a death as suicide is due largely to the social stigma of suicide, which is commonly viewed as a failure on the part of the person who commits suicide, his or her family and friends, and society as a whole. Some automobile fatalities, for example, are believed to be suicides in disguise, as are some victim-precipitated homicides. Thus, the actual extent of suicide is likely to be greater than official statistics suggest.

One of the methods devised to improve the accuracy of suicide statistics is the *psychological autopsy*, which involves gathering information that sheds light on the life style of the victim, any stresses that he or she may have been experiencing, and whether any suicidal communications were made prior to the death. In addition to being an investigative tool for correctly classifying deaths, the psychological autopsy is also a valuable research tool that can help to identify risk factors for suicide.

Efforts to explain suicidal behavior have generally looked either to the social context in which it occurs or to the mental and emotional dynamics within the life of the individual victim. Whereas the sociological model focuses on the relationship between the individual and society, the psychological model focuses on the individual's conscious and unconscious motivations. Both of these approaches contribute to our understanding of suicide. Recent efforts to provide a theoretical perspective on suicide usually draw from both approaches and conclude that suicide is best understood as behavior influenced by both culture and personality, as well as by the unique circumstances of an individual's situation.

Our understanding of suicide is also broadened by examining it from various perspectives, such as types of suicide, the nature of risk factors influencing it, and patterns of suicidal behavior throughout the lifespan. For example, when we examine the characteristics of suicidal behavior, we can distinguish at least four types. First, suicide can be an escape, as with terminally ill persons who see no other exit from unremitting suffering; second, suicide can result from psychotic illness or depression; third, suicide can be subintentional and chronic, when the victim plays a partial or subliminal role in his or her own demise, perhaps over a period of time due to an unhealthy life style; and fourth, suicide can be a "cry for help," a form of communication intended to elicit some change, but which has lethal consequences.

Examining risk factors for suicide, we find that they generally comprise four broad areas—culture, personality, the individual situation, and biological factors—some or all of which may overlap when we consider an individual instance of suicidal behavior. Our understanding of risk factors is broadened by looking at suicide from a lifespan perspective. Different motives and influences are found to be relatively more or less important during the different stages of life of childhood, adolescence and young adulthood, middle adulthood, and late adulthood.

To gain a comprehensive understanding of suicide, it is also useful to consider how a suicidal person progresses from thought to action, from contemplating the possibility of killing oneself to obtaining the means to do so, thereby setting into motion the logistics that make suicide a real possibility. Although the steps toward lethality can be presented in an orderly sequence, a suicidal person is likely to experience them very differently. Suicide typically involves an array of conflicting thoughts and emotions. The particular method chosen to carry out a suicidal intention may be based on personality factors, as well as ease of access. It is important to recognize that there is an "order of lethality" in the various methods; some have a greater risk of lethality than others.

Suicide notes, which have been called "cryptic maps of ill-advised journeys," have been studied with the aim of better understanding the factors and circumstances that lead to suicide. Such notes usually display a variety of messages and intentions. Often, they express confused logic and an intense love-hate ambivalence that points up the dyadic nature of many suicidal acts. Suicide notes can provide clues about a person's intentions and emotional state, but they rarely tell the whole story. Their effect on survivors, however, can be significant. Whether the final message is one of affection or blame, survivors have no opportunity to respond.

Over the past several decades, as suicide has increasingly become a matter of public concern, various activities related to suicide prevention, intervention, and postvention have become widespread. Much can be done to reduce suicide risk, and education is an essential element in any program of suicide prevention. Such education generally emphasizes two key points. Firstly, since life is complex, all of us will inevitably experience disappointment, failure, and loss in our lives and, secondly, we can learn to deal with such experiences by developing appropriate coping techniques, including a healthy sense of humor. Whereas the goal of suicide prevention is primarily to eliminate or minimize suicide risk, the goal of suicide intervention is to reduce the lethality of a particular suicidal crisis. The emphasis of intervention is on short-term care and treatment of persons in crisis. The cardinal rule is to do something, such as take the threat seriously, answer cries for help by offering support and compassion, and provide constructive alternatives to suicide. Suicide postvention refers to the assistance given to survivors, including those who survive suicide attempts as well as the families, friends, and associates of those who kill themselves by suicide.

Objectives

- To identify potential suicide populations.
- To construct a comprehensive definition of suicide.
- To describe the sociological and psychological models of suicide.
- To list and describe four types of suicide and to give examples of each.
- To explain the risk factors influencing suicide through the lifespan.
- To describe the various methods of suicide and to analyze them for information regarding the suicidal person's intent.
- To differentiate between myths and facts about suicide.
- To create a model of suicide intervention.
- To plan a suicide postvention strategy.

Key Terms and Concepts

acute suicidal crisis
altruistic suicide
ambivalence
anomic suicide
assisted suicide
attempted suicide
chronic suicide
cluster suicides
crisis suicide
cry for help
depression
dyadic nature of suicide
egoistic suicide
fatalistic suicide
gender differences in suicide
mass suicide
neurobiologic markers
order of lethality
psychache
psychological autopsy
psychological model of suicide

psychotic suicide
rational suicide
referred suicide
risk factors in suicide
romantic suicide
seppuku
sociological model of suicide
subintentioned suicide
suggestibility
"suicidal success syndrome"
suicide as escape
suicide intervention
suicide notes
suicide pacts
suicide postvention
suicide prevention
suicide rates
suttee
telephone hotlines
unintentioned death
victim-precipitated homicide

Questions for Guided Study and Review

1. What is the definition of suicide?
2. What do statistics tell us about suicide?
3. Why is discussion of suicide sometimes considered taboo?
4. What are two examples of the possible underreporting of suicide?
5. What is victim-precipitated homicide?

6. What is a *psychological autopsy*?
7. When and why is a *psychological autopsy* done?
8. What are two major theoretical models for explaining suicide?
9. How does Durkheim's model of the social context of suicide add to our understanding?
10. What are the differences between anomic suicide, fatalistic suicide, egoistic suicide, and altruistic suicide?
11. What are *seppuka* and *suttee*, and what category of suicide do they fit into?
12. What are the key features of the psychodynamic model of suicide?
13. What are the roles of aggression and ambivalence in the psychological model of suicide?
14. How long does the acute suicidal crisis generally last?
15. In what way can suicidal events be described as *dyadic*?
16. What is *psychache*, and why is it important in understanding suicide?
17. What are the types of suicide discussed in the text, and how do they differ?
18. List and describe at least three cultural and three individual meanings of suicide.
19. What is the relationship between depression and suicide?
20. Why is some suicidal behavior described as a "cry for help"?
21. What gender differences have been noted between attempted and completed suicides?
22. Differentiate between intentioned, unintentioned, and subintentioned deaths, and identify at least two specific patterns in each category.
23. How do culture, personality, individual situation and biologic factors influence suicide risk?
24. How does Brian Barry's model of "pro-life" and "pro-death" forces relate to cultural factors that may increase suicide risk?
25. How might reducing the fear of death facilitate suicidal behavior?
26. How are stress and suicide correlated?
27. How does a lifespan perspective add to our understanding of suicide?
28. What is the effect of the different developmental periods on suicide?
29. Why is labeling a young child's death as suicide problematic?
30. How serious a problem is suicide during the teen and early adult years?
31. What are some of the risk factors for suicide during adolescence and young adulthood?
32. What are *cluster suicides*?
33. What are *suicide pacts*, and at what ages do they occur?
34. Which age group has the highest risk for suicide?
35. What are the three most commonly used methods for suicide?
36. How does the *order of lethality* relate to suicide?
37. What do suicide notes tell us about suicide?
38. What are the goals of suicide prevention, intervention, and postvention?
39. What are the four main ways people express suicidal intent?
40. What are some warning signs of suicide?
41. List and refute the myths about suicide.
42. What are some ways to help a person who is suicidal?

Practice Test Questions

MULTIPLE CHOICE

1. Suicide among Japanese samurai following disgrace in battle is an example of
   a. anomic suicide.
   b. egoistic suicide.
   c. altruistic suicide.
   d. fatalistic suicide.

2. Most people who engage in suicidal behavior
   a. want to change the nature of society.
   b. actually care about their preservation.
   c. want to psychologically damage their loved ones.
   d. actually are ambivalent about living or dying.

3. A suicide attempt that is purposely intended to fail
   a. always fails.
   b. usually will fail.
   c. may be lethal.
   d. usually is lethal.

4. Which of the following forms the MOST deadly link with suicide?
   a. media coverage of suicide
   b. literature about suicide
   c. heavy metal music
   d. substance abuse

5. When a suicidal person shows signs of improvement, it is important to be aware that
   a. family history is important at this stage.
   b. the person is now prepared to face life.
   c. the upward trend will continue.
   d. such behavior can indicate a time of danger.

TRUE/FALSE

_____ 1. Victim-precipitated homicides are included in suicide statistics.

_____ 2. Psychotic suicide is associated with a surprisingly complex logical perspective.

_____ 3. Subintentioned death is defined as one in which the person plays some partial, covert, subliminal, or unconscious role in hastening his or her own demise.

_____ 4. Males attempt suicide more often than do females, but females actually kill themselves more often than do males.

_____ 5. The emphasis of suicide intervention is to provide short-term care to individuals who are actively in crisis.

MATCHING

Match each of the suicide risk factors on the right with the appropriate age group on the left.

____ 1. Young adulthood

____ 2. Middle adulthood

____ 3. Childhood

____ 4. Late adulthood

a. may not be fully aware of the consequences

b. desire to avoid being a burden to others

c. family dissolution, economic hardship, and increased mobility

d. accumulation of negative life events

❧ Answers to practice questions can be found in Part IV ❧

Related Readings

📖 Indicates selection from *The Path Ahead: Readings in Death and Dying*, eds. Lynne Ann DeSpelder and Albert Lee Strickland (Mountain View, Calif.: Mayfield, 1995).

GENERAL STUDIES

Antoon A. Leenaars, ed. *Suicidology: Essays in Honor of Edwin Shneidman*. Northvale, N.J.: Jason Aronson, 1993.

Edwin S. Shneidman. *The Suicidal Mind*. New York: Oxford University Press, 1996.

📖 Judith M. Stillion, "Premature Exits: Understanding Suicide," pp. 182–197.

Judith Stillion, Eugene McDowell, and Jacque May. *Suicide Across the Life Span: Premature Exits*, 2d ed. Washington, D.C.: Taylor & Francis, 1996.

LIFESPAN AND CULTURAL PERSPECTIVES

Fred Cutter. *Art and the Wish to Die*. Chicago: Nelson-Hall, 1983.

📖 Kevin E. Early and Ronald L. Akers, "It's a White Thing—An Exploration of Beliefs About Suicide in the African-American Community," pp. 198–210.

Kevin E. Early. *Religion and Suicide in the African-American Community*. Westport, Conn.: Greenwood, 1992.

📖 Kathleen Erwin, "Interpreting the Evidence: Competing Paradigms and the Emergence of Lesbian and Gay Suicide as a 'Social Fact,'" pp. 211–220.

Norman L. Farberow, ed. *Suicide in Different Cultures*. Baltimore: University Park Press, 1975.

Carolyn S. Henry, Andy L. Stephenson, Michelle Fryer Hanson, and William Hargett. "Adolescent Suicide and Families: An Ecological Approach," *Adolescence* 28 (Summer 1993): 291–308.

Israel Orbach. *Children Who Don't Want to Live: Understanding and Treating the Suicidal Child*. San Francisco: Jossey-Bass, 1988.

Major Points in This Chapter

- It is generally agreed that official suicide statistics understate the actual number of suicides, perhaps by as much as fifty percent. Such underrepresentation is due to social stigma against suicide, the need for unequivocal proof before classifying a death as suicide, suicides that masquerade as accidents or victim-precipitated homicides, and sensitivity to survivors' concerns, as well as to differences in the manner in which coroner's and medical examiner's investigations of possible suicides are conducted in different jurisdictions.

- The psychological autopsy is a potent investigative tool for improving suicide statistics as well as enhancing knowledge about the factors that influence suicidal behavior.

- Theoretical approaches to explaining suicide are based mainly on a sociological model, which focuses on the relationship between the individual and society, and a psychological model, which focuses on the dynamics of an individual's mental and emotional life. A comprehensive understanding of suicide makes use of both models.

- Typologically, suicidal behavior can be classified as an escape from some mental or physical pain, as due to impaired logic caused by clinical depression or psychosis, as the unconscious result of chronic or subintentional factors hastening death, or as a "cry for help" in alleviating some problem.

- There may be two fairly distinct populations of people engaging in suicidal behaviors: attempters and completers. It must be recognized, however, that any suicide attempt can end in death.

- Culture, personality, and the unique combination of circumstances affecting a particular individual's life each play a role in determining the degree to which a person may be at risk of suicide; neurobiological correlates may also be important as a risk factor in suicide.

- The varying risk of suicide also corresponds to changes in outlook and circumstance that occur throughout the lifespan. Suicide among adolescents and young adults is viewed as a major public health problem.

- The likelihood of a fatal outcome increases as a suicidal person plans his or her demise and acquires the means to carry out the plan; as the potential lethality of the method increases, the more likely the outcome will be death. There is an "order of lethality" among the various methods people employ when engaging in suicidal behavior.

- Suicide notes reflect a range of concerns of the people who kill themselves, from simple reminders directed to survivors about carrying out ordinary tasks to complex explanations about why the person chose to end his or her life. A sense of ambivalence is a hallmark of many suicide notes.

- Suicide prevention, intervention, and postvention are important avenues for reducing the incidence of suicidal behavior and easing the pain of loss for people who are bereaved as a result of a loved one's suicide.

- Distinguishing fact from fallacy is a crucial step toward recognizing the warning signs of suicide and helping the person in a suicidal crisis.

Observations and Reflections

Your responses to suicide—for instance, whether a particular suicide evokes feelings of anger or forgiveness—will depend partly on your cultural, religious, and psychological background. Can you distinguish between these components of understanding? Take time to identify from which part of your belief system and background your response to suicide arises.

Use the space below to record your notes and responses to the topics covered in this chapter.

⟫ *Suicidal Behavior*

Directions: *Indicate your beliefs about the suicidal intent of the following persons in the situations described. Rank each item on a scale from 1 to 5 (with 1 indicating no suicidal intent whatsoever, 2 probably not suicidal, 3 could be either, 4 likely suicidal, 5 definitely suicidal).*

A person who . . .

_____ 1. Drives 10 miles over the speed limit on a winding mountain road.

_____ 2. Assassinates a world leader.

_____ 3. Sacrifices his or her life to protest a political cause.

_____ 4. Suffers from a terminal illness and refuses medical treatment.

_____ 5. Points a loaded gun at his or her head and pulls the trigger.

_____ 6. Knowingly drinks poison when directed to by an authority figure.

_____ 7. Takes a drug overdose.

_____ 8. Refuses to change his or her lifestyle despite two previous heart attacks.

_____ 9. Consumes alcohol to the point of intoxication and then drives a car.

_____ 10. Goes on an extended hunger strike in order to force a particular issue.

_____ 11. Uses a motorcycle to jump long distances (over cars, over canyons, etc.)

_____ 12. Gains a large amount of weight.

_____ 13. Talks constantly about what a drag life is and frequently says, "I feel like ending it all."

_____ 14. Pours gasoline upon himself or herself and lights a match.

_____ 15. Walks into a post office, randomly firing a gun, killing many people.

⟾ *Suicidal Tendencies*

Directions: *Respond to the following statements, indicating true or false, and explain the reason for your answer.*

_____ 1. People who talk about suicide do not commit suicide.

_____

_____

_____ 2. Improvement in a suicidal person means the danger has passed.

_____

_____

_____ 3. Once a suicide risk, always a suicide risk.

_____

_____

_____ 4. Suicide is inherited.

_____

_____

_____ 5. Suicide affects only a specific group or class of people.

_____

_____

_____ 6. Suicidal behavior is insane.

_____

_____

_____ 7. Suicidal people are fully intent on dying.

_____

_____

_____ 8. The motive for suicide is always clearly evident.

_____

_____

Risks of Death in the Modern World

Chapter Summary

Chapter 13 examines a broad range of environmental encounters with death, including risk taking, accidents, disasters, violence, war, the nuclear threat, and emerging diseases such as AIDS. Some of these encounters seem remote from our own lives; others are pervasive, though we may give little conscious attention to them. News reports are filled with accounts of disasters, natural and human-caused. But until we ourselves confront such a threat to well-being, we may not comprehend all the dimensions of loss such events represent. Yet, consciously or not, we risk subtle, and sometimes dramatic, encounters with death as we engage in our life's pursuits.

Indeed, all life involves risk, although the degree of risk we are willing to assume is often subject to personal choice. Individuals can exercise control over risks related to smoking, driving habits, and the kinds of recreational activities they pursue. In many areas of life, steps can be taken to minimize our exposure to risk. Simply ignoring or denying the risk inherent in an activity does not make the danger disappear, but it may result in our failure to take adequate steps to counteract the risk.

As a leading cause of death, especially among young people, accidents deserve our attention, both as individuals and as a society. Although accidents are commonly viewed as events that "just happen," deeper analysis reveals that many accidents are preventable. Instead of being unavoidable, accidents frequently result from carelessness, lack of awareness, or ignorance. Thus, accidents are often events over which individuals do have varying degrees of control. For example, about half the drivers involved in fatality accidents are under the influence of alcohol. Such accidents represent tragedies that could have been avoided.

Accidents are influenced both by intrinsic factors, or a person's own physical and mental qualities, and by extrinsic factors, such as conditions in the environment. Unsafe conditions in the environment are sometimes called "accidents waiting to happen." In many instances, these conditions are due to negligence. If we view accidents as due solely to chance or fate, then we ignore the significant role of carelessness and neglect. Attention to such factors might well lead to constructive actions toward prevention. Although life can never be completely free of risk, steps usually can be taken to minimize it.

Disasters, which can be defined as life-threatening events that affect many people within a relatively brief period of time, bringing sudden and great misfortune, result from both natural phenomena and human activities. Floods and earthquakes are examples of natural disasters; airplane crashes and chemical spills are examples of disasters resulting from human activities. Population growth, urbanization, and industrialization have increased exposure to disasters related to human activities. Despite the fact that communities can decrease the risk of injury and death by taking measures to lessen the impact of a potential disaster, the effects of a disaster are difficult to fully anticipate. Adequate warnings of an impending disaster can save lives. Yet necessary information may be withheld because of greed or political expediency, or simply because of uncertainty about the nature and extent of the threat, or because of concern about causing panic. Even with an adequate warning system, however, people do not always respond to the threat prudently. Just as some people ignore the risks associated with smoking or place themselves in situations more prone to accidents, individuals frequently believe themselves immune to the effects of a disastrous situation.

In the aftermath of disaster, meeting the immediate needs of survivors, such as food and shelter, medical care, vital services, is essential. Important, too, is attending to survivors' emotional needs. Although efforts directed toward coping with disaster tend to focus on the initial period of emergency, the return to financial and emotional stability may take years. The needs of caregivers who offer supportive services to survivors also need to be acknowledged as part of a comprehensive program of disaster postvention.

Violence, one of the most potent and frightening encounters with death, can affect our thoughts and actions even though we ourselves have not been victimized. Special emphasis has been placed on the prevalence of interpersonal violence. In a recent year, nearly twice as many murders were related to arguments of one kind or another than were related to the commission of a felony. Besides the violence related to interpersonal conflict and criminal activities, many people are concerned about terrorism, which may involve either planned or indiscriminate killing. Occurring outside the boundaries of the social sanctions that are intended to regulate conduct between individuals and between groups, terrorism is an affront to civilization.

Within the framework of the U.S. judicial system, the circumstances of a particular killing, the relationship between killer and victim, and the killer's motivation and intent are all considered in assessing a homicidal act. Research shows that the legal outcome for a person who kills a close relative is usually quite different from the outcome for a person who combines killing with theft, robbery, or other such criminal or antisocial acts. The most severe penalty is usually reserved as punishment for killing a stranger. The killer who chooses a stranger as his or her victim overtly threatens the preservation of the social order. In this respect, killings carried out by terrorists can be likened to other homicidal acts involving strangers.

Within the context of ordinary human interaction, our moral as well as legal codes stand in strict opposition to killing. In war, however, killing is not only acceptable and necessary, but possibly heroic. Yet, despite society's efforts to convert civilians into warriors, those who face the prospect of

Study Guide
The Last Dance: Encountering Death and Dying, 6th ed.

214　　Chapter 13

kill-or-be-killed in war often pay a high emotional and psychological price as a result of the trauma of war. In addition to the burden it places on combatants, war also creates a "phantom army" composed of the spouses, children, parents, and friends who serve invisibly at home. The mourning of losses accompanies even the most joyous of victory celebrations.

Whether or not war is an inescapable part of the human condition, it is easy to discern a wide variety of needs and motives relating to its onset. To prepare the way for war, we engage in a psychological process of creating the enemy. Dividing the world into "us" and "them" devalues and dehumanizes the members of the outgroup, thus paving the way for hostile acts. In searching for ways to civilize hostilities, therefore, we must investigate the processes that promote or deter war in both the individual psyche and social institutions.

Technological alienation has been called the central feature of modern warfare. It is exemplified by the mass deaths in Dresden, Hiroshima, and Nagasaki. Exposed to such destruction and death, our self-protective psychological response is to become insensitive, unfeeling, and numb. Although we can be grateful for lessened hostility between the keepers of the world's major nuclear arsenals, the nuclear threat has not entirely disappeared. The proliferation of such weapons and the possibility of nuclear accident remain cause for concern.

Although the conquest of infectious diseases over the past century has led to a sense of complacency, AIDS has been a wake-up call about emerging diseases that present a new threat to health worldwide. Despite great advances in its treatment, AIDS continues to have a devastating impact on individuals and societies. Many survivors—the friends, neighbors, mates, and relatives of people with AIDS—have experienced multiple losses. The greatest impact of AIDS at present is in the developing world, particularly in sub-Saharan Africa. According to a United Nations report, more than 30 million people are currently living with the AIDS virus and about 16,000 are newly infected every day. In the United States, as the options for treating AIDS produce more positive outcomes, the focus is changing from "dying with AIDS" to "living with AIDS." Although improvements in treatment and extended survival are certainly welcome news, they have presented a new set of challenges to individuals and societies. Some believe that AIDS may be the first of a series of emerging diseases that will threaten people on a global scale. In recent years, there have been localized epidemics of hermorrhagic fever viruses such as the Marburg, Ebola, Lassa, and Hanta viruses, as well as yellow fever, swine flu, Legionnaires' disease, and cholera. Expansion of human population, forest clearing, and other human-initiated activities disturb previously stable ecosystems, thereby facilitating contact with pathogenic viruses that threaten life and health.

Risks of various kinds, such as accidents, disasters, violence, war, and epidemic diseases, affect us to varying degrees as we go about our daily lives. Sometimes the encounter is subtle; at other times it is overt, requiring concerted action to counter the threat. Understanding the nature of such risks is a first step toward successfully coping with the range of encounters with death that can threaten both societies and individuals.

Objectives

- To assess one's level of risk-taking activities.
- To describe the incidence and extent of accidents and to compare the factors influencing accidents in specific populations.
- To identify helping strategies for survivors of disaster.
- To define homicide and distinguish various categories and types.
- To identify and explain the cultural standards by which homicidal acts are judged.
- To evaluate the effects of capital punishment.
- To develop an alternative model for punishment.
- To name and give examples of the factors increasing the likelihood of violence.
- To differentiate between the moral standards of war and peacetime relative to the taking of life.
- To assess the effects of war and its aftermath on both combatants and noncombatants.
- To identify the needs and motives that give rise to war and evaluate strategies for reducing conflict.
- To identify and explain the impact of AIDS and other emerging diseases.
- To describe a healthy response in coping with risks of death in the modern world.

Key Terms and Concepts

accident proneness
accidents
AIDS (acquired immunodeficiency syndrome)
capital punishment
children and violence
conversion of the warrior
coping with disaster
disaster preparedness
emerging diseases
environmental disaster
gang warfare
genocide
hemorrhagic fevers
HIV (human immunodeficiency virus)
Holocaust

horrendous death
homicide
karoshi
natural disasters
"normal accidents"
nuclear threat
nuclearism
occupational hazards
psychic maneuvers
psychic numbing
PTSD (posttraumatic stress disorder)
risk taking
technological alienation
terrorism
urban desertification
violence

Questions for Guided Study and Review

1. What are some of the different kinds of risks of death?
2. In what ways is the degree of risk a person faces subject to his or her own choices?
3. What is *karoshi* and what causes it?

4. How do accidents sometimes occur as a result of something besides chance?
5. What factors influence "accident proneness"?
6. How might gender affect risk-taking and accidents?
7. What is the definition of *disaster*?
8. What accounts for the increased risk of disaster in the United States in recent years?
9. How can the impact of disasters be reduced?
10. What role do warning systems play in managing the threat of disasters?
11. What needs must be addressed in disaster relief, and what are some shortcomings in most relief efforts?
12. How is "survivor guilt" a factor in grief reactions following disasters?
13. Why is violence now considered a public health problem?
14. What are the circumstances that led one commentor to say that "Being a child in America can be deadly"?
15. What factors are correlated with violence?
16. What are the two main categories of criminal homicide?
17. How do the legal system and community standards affect the way an act of homicide is judged?
18. What are the three components of a medical-legal investigation of homicide?
19. Assess the differences between homicidal acts directed toward strangers, and homicidal acts that occur within the family unit or between individuals known to one another.
20. In considering the impact of violence on children, who are the "silent victims"?
21. What are the arguments for and against capital punishment?
22. What are the *psychic maneuvers* that lead to violence?
23. Evaluate the argument that violence is endemic in American society.
24. How are conventional sanctions against killing altered in war?
25. What is *genocide*?
26. What is the relationship between "technological alienation" and "psychic numbing"?
27. What is *posttraumatic stress disorder*, and how is it related to warfare?
28. How does war create a "phantom army"?
29. Review the steps toward civilizing hostilities.
30. What is "nuclearism"?
31. Why are newly emerging diseases a cause for concern?
32. In what ways is AIDS a challenge socially, politically, culturally, and individually?
33. How is AIDS transmitted, and how does it affect the body's immune system?
34. What is the typical progression of infection with human immunodeficiency virus (HIV)?
35. Assess the current status of AIDS in both developed and developing countries.
36. What are three of the important lessons from AIDS with respect to similarly threatening diseases?
37. Why are hemorrhagic fever viruses such as Ebola and Lassa becoming of increasing concern?
38. What infectious disease episode occurred in 1918, and what were its effects?
39. What are some typical examples of "horrendous death"?

Practice Test Questions

MULTIPLE CHOICE

1. When someone involved in a high-risk sport suffers an accident and dies, others in that sport often talk of how the deceased failed to take adequate precautions. Why?
    a. This explanation allows others to rethink the sport and consider ways to improve upon its safety.
    b. This explanation allows others to continue with the sport, while realizing that an accident could also happen to them.
    c. This explanation enables others to continue in the sport, while not focusing on the inherent dangers of the activity.
    d. This explanation prevents others from thinking about the individual, so they can continue to focus on the activity and its dangers.

2. What is a common shortcoming of disaster relief efforts?
    a. They provide for physical needs, but are indifferent to the emotional needs of survivors.
    b. They lack adequate financial support.
    c. They fail to understand the affected communities and thus tend to make mistakes that complicate recovery.
    d. They provide short-term support during the emergency, but neglect the long-term consequences of a disaster.

3. Research indicates that capital punishment is
    a. not an effective deterrent to murder.
    b. an effective deterrent for criminal behavior.
    c. the strong penalty needed to make the criminal justice system work.
    d. an exception to the notion that killing solves problems.

4. Genocide involves the effort to
    a. modify genetic factors that cause violence.
    b. determine the biological roots of violence.
    c. destroy an entire nation or human group.
    d. eradicate social practices that favor violence.

5. Which one of the following is NOT one of the three primary routes of AIDS transmission?
    a. birth by an infected mother
    b. exposure to infected blood or blood products
    c. drinking from the cup of an infected person
    d. sexual intercourse with an infected person

TRUE/FALSE

_____ 1. A person who murders his or her spouse is likely to receive a much harsher punishment than a person who murders a stranger.

_____ 2. Parents who wish to lessen their children's potential for violence must foster human resources that promote sharing and reduce impulsivity.

_____ 3. Before nations can begin to handle hostilities in a more civil manner, citizens must become aware of the role of political propaganda.

_____ 4. In some parts of the world, the AIDS virus is transmitted mainly through heterosexual contact.

_____ 5. In 1918, more than 20 million people died from the flu.

MATCHING

Match each of the terms on the left with the appropriate definition on the right. Each definition may be used only once.

_____ 1. Psychic numbing

_____ 2. Karoshi

_____ 3. Posttraumatic stress disorder

_____ 4. Psychic manuever

a. stress reaction also known as "shell shock" or "battle fatigue"

b. for people who are victims of violence

c. negative byproduct of the work ethic

d. factor that facilitates murder or homicide

e. method of coping with the consequences of modern technological warfare

✧ Answers to practice questions can be found in Part IV ✧

Related Readings

📖 Indicates selection from *The Path Ahead: Readings in Death and Dying,* eds. Lynne Ann DeSpelder and Albert Lee Strickland (Mountain View, Calif.: Mayfield, 1995).

ENCOUNTERS WITH DEATH

📖 Thomas Attig, "Coping with Mortality: An Essay on Self-Mourning," pp. 337–341.

📖 Robert Kastenbaum, "Reconstructing Death in Postmodern Society," pp. 7–18.

📖 Alfred G. Killilea, "The Politics of Being Mortal," pp. 342–347.

Robert M. Sapolsky. *Why Zebras Don't Get Ulcers: A Guide to Stress, Stress-Related Diseases, and Coping.* New York: W. H. Freeman, 1994.

ACCIDENTS AND DISASTERS

Kai Erikson. *A New Species of Trouble: Explorations in Disaster, Trauma, and Community*. New York: W. W. Norton, 1994.

Graham A. Tobin, and Burrell E. Montz. *Natural Hazards: Explanation and Integration*. New York: Guilford Press, 1997.

VIOLENCE AND WARFARE

Zlata Filipovic, "Zlata's Diary: A Child's Life in Sarajevo," pp. 175–178.

James Garbarino, "Challenges We Face in Understanding Children and War: A Personal Essay," pp. 169–174.

Dave Grossman. *On Killing: The Psychological Cost of Learning to Kill in War and Society*. Boston: Little, Brown, 1995.

Ice T, "The Killing Fields," pp. 178–181.

Daniel Leviton, "Horrendous Death: Improving the Quality of Global Health," pp. 165–168.

Jack Lule, "News Strategies and the Death of Huey Newton," pp. 33–40.

Albert J. Reiss, Jr., and Jeffrey A. Roth, eds. *Understanding and Preventing Violence*. Washington, D.C.: National Academy Press, 1993.

Nancy Scheper-Hughes, "Death Without Weeping: The Violence of Everyday Life in Brazil," pp. 41–58.

Jonathan Shay. *Achilles in Vietnam: Combat Trauma and the Undoing of Character*. New York: Atheneum, 1994.

Herbert S. Strean and Lucy Freeman. *Our Wish to Kill: The Murder in All Our Hearts*. New York: St. Martin's Press, 1991.

AIDS AND EMERGING DISEASES

Harold Brodkey, "To My Readers," pp. 295–300.

Kenneth J. Doka. *AIDS, Fear, and Society: Challenging the Dreaded Disease*. Washington, D.C.: Taylor & Francis, 1997.

Laurie Garrett. *The Coming Plague: Newly Emerging Diseases in a World Out of Balance*. New York: Farrar, Straus and Giroux, 1994.

Albert R. Jonsen and Jeff Stryker, eds. *The Social Impact of AIDS*. Washington, D.C.: National Academy Press, 1993.

Charles E. Rosenberg, "What Is an Epidemic? AIDS in Historical Perspective," pp. 29–32.

Major Points in This Chapter

- The likelihood of an encounter with death is increased by excessive risk taking, occupational stress, avoidable accidents, violence, war, environmental pollution, and AIDS and other emerging diseases.

- Life unavoidably involves risk, but personal choices and social conditions can increase our exposure to potentially lethal risks.

- Stress is a natural part of human existence, but its nature has changed markedly in modern times because of more complex life styles, rising expectations, and inner discontent. In Japan, occupational stress has been named as a cause of death from <u>karoshi</u>, or sudden death from overwork.

- Accidents involve events over which individuals have varying degrees of control; thus, the choices we make affect the probabilities of most accidents. A consideration of such factors as carelessness, lack of awareness, and neglect can lead to a better understanding of how and why accidents occur. When accidents of all types are considered, young males are at greatest risk of death.

- Whether natural or caused by human activities, disasters can be defined as life-threatening events that affect a large number of people within a relatively brief period of time, bringing sudden and great misfortune. The risk of death from disasters can be minimized when communities take precautionary measures to lessen their impact.

- The aftermath of a disaster entails both meeting the immediate needs of survivors and providing adequate postvention support to emergency workers who are exposed to the tragedy of human suffering.

- Interpersonal violence is officially recognized as a public health problem. A powerful encounter with death, violence in its various forms can affect our well-being even though we ourselves have not been directly victimized.

- Gang warfare is comparable to other forms of war; the members of gangs have been likened to combat veterans, and their thousands of casualties to soldiers who have died on a bloody battlefield. According to a nationwide survey of schoolyard violence, more than one in ten high school students said they had carried a weapon on school property.

- Terrorism, another manifestation of violence, seeks to cause political, social, and economic disruption; in doing so, terrorists engage in both planned and indiscriminate acts of murder.

- Community standards of morality and justice play major roles in determining how an act of killing is assessed by a society and its judicial system. The killer's motivation and intent, along with the relationship between killer and victim, are among the factors considered in assessing whether a homicide is lawful or unlawful and, if unlawful, whether it constitutes murder.

- Capital punishment has a twofold purpose, which is to punish the offender and deter potential offenders. Whether the death penalty serves this purpose is a matter of debate; many people believe that it is inconsistent for a society to try to prevent murder by itself engaging in killing.

- To reduce the level of violence in society, it is useful to consider how violent behaviors might be prevented. Avoiding the use of derogatory labels, eliminating conditions that underlie dehumanizing perceptions of oneself and others, and promoting communication between potential adversaries are among the methods that can lessen the potential for violence.

- War abrogates the conventional social sanctions against killing by substituting a different set of conventions and rules concerning moral conduct.

- Modern warfare is characterized by technological alienation and psychic numbing; moreover, the traditional distinction between combatants and noncombatants has become increasingly blurred, if not erased. Genocide was practiced with dire results during the course of the twentieth century.

- Posttraumatic stress disorder (PTSD), a term used to describe a variety of protracted reactions to war, can also be considered as a kind of "delayed grief syndrome" that results from contact with the horror of killing and death and the absence of any formal rituals for grieving that might allow warriors to find solace.

- AIDS is viewed in some quarters as the harbinger of an unknown number of emerging deadly diseases that will increasingly threaten the health of human beings worldwide. The threat of such emerging diseases is even more potent because of the political abandonment of urban areas in many countries, a situation that is intensifying conditions that cause rapid spread of infectious and virulent diseases. Such "urban desertification" is thought to be at least partially responsible for the reemergence of diseases believed to be under control, such as tuberculosis, as well as the emergence of new diseases such as the hemorrhagic fevers associated with Ebola virus, Marburg virus, and Lassa virus.

Observations and Reflections

Because of the wide range of topics included in this chapter, you may wish to focus particularly on one of the topics mentioned. You can take this opportunity to explore your interest in greater depth. One way to do additional research is to consult the directory of organizations in the appendix to this Study Guide. There you will find contact information for such organizations as Mothers Against Drunk Drivers (MADD), Parents of Murdered Children (POMC), and AIDS education and support organizations, as well as many other organizations of interest. Many organizations have web sites that can be visited for further information.

List several topics that you would like to explore further.

_____

_____

_____

_____

_____

_____

_____

_____

_____

⟶ Movies and War

Directions   *Watch a movie that depicts war, such as* Platoon, Full Metal Jacket, Hamburger Hill, Born on the Fourth of July, Gone with the Wind, Saving Private Ryan, *or* Schindler's List. *After viewing the film, answer the following questions.*

1. How accurately do you believe the film depicted reality? _____
    _____

2. What did the film tell the viewer about war? _____
    _____
    _____

3. How were the dead treated? _____
    _____
    _____

4. Was grief depicted? _____
    _____
    _____

5. Were funerals or other mourning rituals shown? _____
    _____
    _____

6. Were the deceased ever mentioned again? _____
    _____
    _____

7. What does the film communicate about the long-term effects of war? _____
    _____
    _____

8. What suggestions could you make for improving the filmmaker's depiction of war? _____

_____

_____

_____

_____

_____

_____

_____

_____

_____

9. Could you serve in combat and kill an enemy? Why or why not? _____

_____

_____

_____

_____

_____

_____

_____

_____

_____

▥➡ *Violence and Your Environment*

Directions   *Imagine that you visit a store within walking distance of your home. As you start to open the door, you notice the sign below posted on the glass at eye level. Read it carefully, paying attention to your reactions. Remember, this is in your neighborhood.*

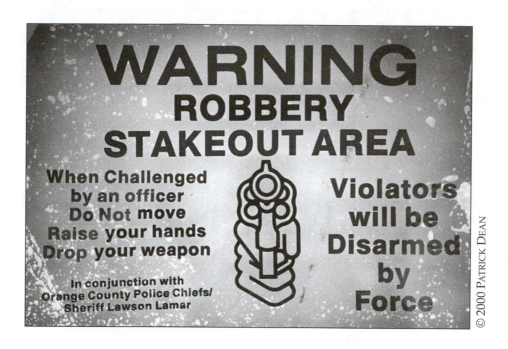

1.   Use the space below and on the following page to describe your thoughts and reactions to this sign being posted in your neighborhood.

   _____

   _____

   _____

   _____

   _____

   _____

   _____

   _____

   _____

   _____

_____

_____

_____

_____

_____

2. Now imagine that this poster is on the door of a store that is NOT in your neighborhood. What are your reactions? Do you think twice about going into the store?

_____

_____

_____

_____

_____

_____

_____

_____

_____

_____

_____

_____

_____

➤ *Violent Death and Children's Attitudes*

Directions: *Here is a child's list of the ways people die. Count the number of violent deaths. Compare it to the number of natural deaths.*

```
1. Heart Attack
2. Smoke / Cancer
3. Drugs
4. Choke on food
5. Shot to death
6. Car Accident
7. Stabbed
8. Stroke
9. Killed by a bomb
10. Fire in house
11. Cut your head off
12. Drinking too much
13. Drown
```

Note the incidence of sudden death due to accidents. What proportion of the list are they?

_____

_____

List the kinds of deaths that are violent to you.

_____

_____

_____

_____

_____

_____

_____

_____

_____

_____

Review the statistics for your community. How many people were murdered last year? Did any of these involve decapitation?

_____

_____

_____

_____

_____

_____

_____

_____

_____

CHAPTER *14*

Beyond Death/After Life

Chapter Summary

Chapter 14 explores the major philosophical, religious, and parapsychological views concerning immortality. The notion that earthly existence continues on in some form following death is one of the oldest concepts held by human beings, as attested to by discoveries made in the earliest known graves. In traditional societies, death usually represents a change of status for the deceased, and some kind of transition from the land of the living to the land of the dead.

In the West, our views about immortality have been influenced by the Judaic, Hellenistic, and Christian traditions, as well as by secular ideas of the modern era. At the risk of oversimplifying, a capsule statement of the conventional Western view is that human beings live a single life, that the individual soul survives the death of the body, and that conduct during earthly life determines the ultimate fate of the soul. For the most part, the emphasis on survival of the individual soul is a later development, having been preceded by an emphasis on some type of corporate survival involving the continued existence of the community as a whole. Even so, the emphasis on one's conduct in the present life as a determinant of some future state is ancient. The concept of immortality in the Islamic tradition shares many features with the other Abrahamic traditions, Judaism and Christianity. Although neither the Bible nor the Qur'an provides a systematic treatment of death, the subject is not ignored. Rather, the emphasis is on living righteously and on moral accountability.

Whereas Western thought is noted for its tendency to make distinctions, point up contrasts, and establish differences, Eastern philosophies and religions typically seek to discover the unity that lies behind apparent opposites. Distinctions are subsumed within a holistic "both/and" perspective. The Eastern view is that life and death are complementary aspects of an essentially undivided reality. This viewpoint informs both Hinduism and Buddhism, and it is reflected throughout the holy books of the East, although individual sects exhibit a diversity of opinion with respect to how these insights should be applied in daily life. The doctrine of reincarnation, for example, can be understood as referring to physical transmigration (the passing of the soul from one body to another at death) as well as to continuous transmigration, which is the insubstantial and ineffable process of psychophysical events that constitute moment-to-moment experience. Either way, the aim is to know the unconditioned state beyond both birth and death.

For many people, death has been divorced from its mythic and religious connotations. The underpinnings for traditional beliefs no longer carry the same weight in a culture that emphasizes scientific method and empirical verification. The present milieu is one in which secular alternatives to religion are pervasive. It is not unusual for a person to hold several competing worldviews at the same time, combining a vague religious faith (perhaps carried over from childhood) with a more secular faith in scientific modes of knowledge and humanitarian ideals of conduct. Despite the option of unbelief, most people still affirm belief in God and, to a somewhat lesser degree, belief in more or less conventional notions of heaven and hell. It may be that, for persons steeped in the materialist culture of the modern West, religious beliefs about the afterlife represent a comforting backdrop to more concrete forms of immortality found in the biological continuity represented by one's children, or the social continuity represented by creative work or heroic deeds.

Stories of travel to another realm beyond the earthly existence can be found in virtually all cultures. Near-death experiences (NDEs) represent a modern variation of such otherworld journeys. These accounts by persons who have reportedly glimpsed the afterworld, or the path that leads to it following death, have been interpreted variously. Some believe these journeys are proof of personality survival after death. Others view them as nothing more than a psychological or neurophysiological response to the stress of life-threatening danger. An individual's own model of reality is likely to favor one or the other of these differing interpretations. Each requires a form of faith. In the fragmented religious situation that characterizes modern society, the accounts that derive from near-death experiences (and experiences resulting from the ingestion of LSD and other psychedelic substances) remind us of the universal human need to make meaning of life and death.

Whether we view death as a wall or as a door, our beliefs about the nature of the cosmos and our place in it exert a powerful influence on how we choose to live and on how we care for and relate to persons who are dying or bereaved.

Objectives

- To compare and contrast the views of immortality in the Judaic, Hellenistic, Christian, Islamic, and secular traditions.
- To compare and contrast Western and Eastern religious views of life after death.
- To describe the main features of near-death experiences.
- To analyze the alternative interpretations of near-death experiences.
- To summarize death-related experiences associated with dreams and the use of psychedelic substances.
- To demonstrate how beliefs about what follows death influence a person's understanding of death, and how they evidence themselves in choices regarding care of the dying as well as in daily life.

Key Terms and Concepts

after-death states	*nirvana*
afterlife	otherworld journeys
bardo	panoramic life review
Buddhism	paradise

Christianity

psychedelic experiences

death dreams

rebirth

heaven

reincarnation

Hebrew/Judaic tradition

resurrection

hell

samsara

Hellenistic concepts

secularism

Hinduism

soul

immortality of the soul

spiritual care

Islam

symbolic immortality

Judgment Day

Tao

karma

transcendence

NDE (near-death experience)

transmigration of the soul

Questions for Guided Study and Review

1. How does the question of life after death relate to the meaning of life?
2. What are some key features of traditional concepts about life after death, such as those associated with Hawaiian beliefs?
3. How is the idea of "judgment" related to beliefs about the afterlife?
4. How did Jewish beliefs about death and resurrection change over time?
5. What is the Hebrew concept of *She'ol*, and how was this concept refined?
6. How do the customary mourning rituals of Judaism relate to reaffirmation of life?
7. What are the main views of death and immortality associated with Hellenistic (Greek) traditions?
8. In ancient Greece, how did heroism relate to immortality?
9. What is the relationship among Hebrew, Hellenistic, and Christian concepts of the soul?
10. Contrast the idea of resurrection of the body with the concept of an immortal soul.
11. What are the characteristics of afterlife beliefs in the Islamic tradition?
12. What role do Munkar and Nakir play in visiting the grave?
13. How does the *Book of Deeds* relate to Islamic concepts of the Last Judgment and a person's eternal state?
14. What are the key features of a traditional Islamic funeral, and why are they important?
15. How do Eastern and Western thought differ regarding life and death?
16. How are *samsara* and *karma* related?
17. With respect to the afterlife, what is the view of self and selfhood in Hinduism and Buddhism?
18. What is the Zen Buddhist understanding of *transmigration*?
19. How is *nirvana* related to birth and death?
20. In Tibetan Buddhism, what is the meaning of the term *bardo*?
21. Why is the period immediately following death of special importance to Buddhists?
22. What is the effect of secularization on traditional beliefs about the meaning of death?
23. How do *positivism* and *humanitarism* relate to the secularization of death?
24. How does the concept of personal immortality persist in secular, or nonreligious, responses to death?
25. What are near-death experiences (NDEs)?
26. How do NDEs relate to other forms of *otherworldly journeys*?
27. What are the core elements of NDE?

28. What is *panoramic life review*?
29. What are the three main theories for interpreting or explaining near-death experiences?
30. In the typical near-death experience, what are the three stages distinguished by Russell Noyes and Roy Kletti?
31. What cautions should be kept in mind regarding NDEs?
32. How do "death dreams" relate to near-death experiences?
33. In pioneering studies of the therapeutic effects of LSD (lysergic acid diethylamide) with patients suffering intense pain, what were the results?
34. How does the "wall and door" metaphor help to summarize various beliefs after the afterlife?

Practice Test Questions

MULTIPLE CHOICE

1. The notion that life continues after death
   a. originated in Egypt.
   b. originated in early Greece.
   c. is one of the oldest human concepts.
   d. is a relatively recent idea.

2. The Hebrew word *She'ol* refers to
   a. hell.
   b. heaven.
   c. everlasting life.
   d. the underworld of the dead.

3. Christian beliefs about the afterlife emphasize the
   a. need to be concerned with the present, not the future.
   b. uncertain nature of afterlife states.
   c. destiny of the soul.
   d. non-existence of an afterlife.

4. Islamic teachings about death emphasize that
   a. hellish states are only temporary.
   b. hell does not exist.
   c. God has no power over an individual's fate.
   d. God determines a person's lifespan.

5. In terms of the "wall/door" metaphor discussed in the text, Hindus would most likely view death as
   a. a wall.
   b. a door.
   c. both a wall and a door.
   d. neither a wall nor a door.

TRUE/FALSE

_____ 1. The idea of the resurrection of the body is NOT evident in Judaic thought.

_____ 2. The early Greek philosophers generally believed that the soul is a vital principle that exists in some fashion after death.

_____ 3. Death holds a central place in the teachings of Buddhism.

_____ 4. Studies indicate that the typical near-death experiencer has achieved a sense of what is important in life and strives to live in accordance with that understanding.

_____ 5. The majority of adult Americans respond in the negative when asked whether they believe in life after death.

MATCHING

Match each religious or cultural belief system with the most appropriate description. Not all descriptions are used.

_____ 1. Buddhism

_____ 2. Secularism

_____ 3. Judaism

_____ 4. Islam

a. Life represents affirmation and death represents negation.

b. Death and life are seen as complementary facets of an underlying process.

c. _Gehinom_ and _Pardes_ are part of the afterlife beliefs in this tradition.

d. Life review precedes actual death and provides a final chance to make ultimate choices.

e. For the believer, death is a release from the sorrows and troubles of life.

❖ Answers to practice questions can be found in Part IV ❖

Related Readings

📖 Indicates selection from _The Path Ahead: Readings in Death and Dying_, eds. Lynne Ann DeSpelder and Albert Lee Strickland (Mountain View, Calif.: Mayfield, 1995).

GENERAL STUDIES

📖 Thomas Attig, "Coping with Mortality: An Essay on Self-Mourning," pp. 337–341.

John Bowker. _The Meanings of Death_. New York: Cambridge University Press, 1991.

📖 Robert Kastenbaum, "Reconstructing Death in Postmodern Society," pp. 7–18.

Allan Kellehear. _Experiences Near Death: Beyond Medicine and Religion_. New York: Oxford University Press, 1996.

CULTURAL AND RELIGIOUS PERSPECTIVES

Carl B. Becker. *Breaking the Circle: Death and the Afterlife in Buddhism*. Carbondale: Southern Illinois University Press, 1993.

Caroline Walker Bynum. *The Resurrection of the Body in Western Christianity, 200–1336*. New York: Columbia University Press, 1995.

John J. Collins and Michael Fishbane. *Death, Ecstasy, and Otherworldly Journeys*. Albany: State University of New York Press, 1996.

Neil Gillman. *The Death of Death: Resurrection and Immortality in Jewish Thought*. Woodstock, Vt.: Jewish Lights, 1997.

Murray J. Harris. *Raised Immortal: Resurrection and Immortality in the New Testament*. Grand Rapids, Mich.: Eerdmans, 1985.

Kenneth Kramer. *The Sacred Art of Dying: How World Religions Understand Death*. Mahwah, N.J.: Paulist Press, 1988.

Geddes MacGregor. *Images of Afterlife: Beliefs from Antiquity to Modern Times*. New York: Paragon House, 1992.

Jack Riemer, ed. *Wrestling with an Angel: Jewish Insights on Death and Mourning*. New York: Schocken, 1995.

J. I. Smith and Y. Haddad. *The Islamic Understanding of Death and Resurrection*. Albany: State University of New York Press, 1981.

SYMBOLIC IMMORTALITY AND CONTINUING BONDS

Christine Longaker. *Facing Death and Finding Hope: A Guide to the Emotional and Spiritual Care of the Dying*. New York: Doubleday, 1997.

📖 Dennis Klass, "Solace and Immortality: Bereaved Parents' Continuing Bond with Their Children," pp. 246–259.

📖 Nancy Scheper-Hughes, "Death Without Weeping: The Violence of Everyday Life in Brazil," pp. 41–58.

📖 Phyllis R. Silverman, Steven Nickman, and J. William Worden, "Detachment Revisited: The Child's Reconstruction of a Dead Parent," pp. 260–270.

Major Points in This Chapter

- The belief that human personality continues in some form after death is among the oldest concepts held by human beings. In traditional societies, death is usually viewed as a change of status, a transition from the land of the living to the land of the dead.
- Traditional Hawaiian beliefs about death and the afterlife emphasize the clan and punishment for wrongdoing.
- Western views of immortality have been influenced by Judaic, Hellenistic, and Christian traditions, as well as by secular ideas of the modern era.
- Hebrew tradition views the human person as an undivided psychophysical entity; it is not as if the soul inhabits a body, but rather that the body has life.
- Plato refined the Hellenistic concept of the soul and advanced a number of "proofs" that the soul is eternal and is released from the body at death.

- Christian beliefs about the afterlife emphasize the resurrection of the body and the destiny of the individual soul.

- Islamic teachings embody a vision of the afterlife that is both spiritual and physical; Allah (God) determines the span of each life, and each person's deeds, good or evil, determine whether the nature of the after-death existence will be eternal bliss or everlasting torment.

- A distinguishing feature of Hinduism is belief in the transmigration of the soul; at death, the soul passes from one body or "being" into an incarnation in another form, animal or human.

- Buddhism emphasizes the impermanence of the self, and the after-death state is conceived of as involving successive reincarnations toward the ultimate goal of nirvana, literally implying extinction, as when the flame of a candle, deprived of fuel, goes out.

- Otherworld journeys, stories of travel to other realms beyond the earthly, are found in virtually all cultures.

- Near-death experiences (NDEs) are accounts by people who have seemingly returned from the edge of death. These accounts are interpreted variously, with some people taking them as an indication that the human personality survives death while others believe that the phenomena associated with NDEs reflect a psychological or a neurophysiological reaction to the stress of a life-threatening experience.

- Suggestive hints about the afterlife are also associated with "death dreams" and experiences related to the ingestion of psychedelic, or mind-altering, substances.

- The spiritual component of care for dying patients should be acknowledged by caregivers so that the appropriate resources can be made available to individuals who desire them.

Observations and Reflections

This chapter explores different beliefs about whether there is life after death and, if so, what form it may take. Which beliefs discussed in the text are similar to those you hold? What do you notice about beliefs that bring you comfort or resolution in coping with or thinking about death?

You may discover differences between what you actually believe and what you would like to believe. Such differences may be important information for you. Beliefs can provide a basis for appropriate change and may reflect the recognition that what served us well at one point in our lives does not necessarily serve us equally well later on.

Use the space below and on the next page to record your notes and responses to the topics covered in this chapter.

Name _____ Section_____ Date_____

⟶ *Beliefs and How They Serve*

Directions   *People generally hold beliefs about death and afterlife that serve a purpose. Here is a chance to examine your beliefs and the purpose they serve. Pay attention to distinctions between what you actually believe and what you would like to believe. Answer the following questions.*

1. In the space below, write in detail what you believe happens at and shortly after the moment of death.

_____

_____

_____

_____

_____

_____

_____

_____

_____

_____

_____

_____

_____

_____

_____

_____

_____

_____

_____

2. As you think about the purpose of your beliefs, use this space to answer the question, How does this belief serve or comfort you?

_____

_____

_____

_____

_____

_____

_____

_____

_____

_____

_____

_____

_____

_____

_____

_____

_____

➠ 💻 *Near-Death Experiences*

Directions *Begin your Internet search with the information provided by the International Association for Near-Death Studies located at <http:www.iands.org/>. From there, locate five web sites that have interesting information about NDEs. List each site's address, include a summary of the content, and rate it from 1 (very useful) to 5 (useless).*

1. URL_____ Rating_____

_____

_____

_____

_____

_____

_____

_____

2. URL_____ Rating_____

_____

_____

_____

_____

_____

_____

_____

3. URL_____ Rating_____

_____

_____

_____

_____

_____

_____

_____

4. URL_____ Rating_____

_____

_____

_____

_____

_____

_____

_____

5. URL_____ Rating_____

_____

_____

_____

_____

_____

_____

_____

🖳 *Religious Traditions*

Directions *Begin your Internet search using the links from about.com [http://dying.about.com/health /dying/]. Pick a particular religion (Protestant, Catholic, Islam, or another you are interested in). Enter it into the search box. For example, Religion-Protestant in "this search site." Review the information from various links, reporting on the five that you find most useful and interesting. For each one, note the URL and give a summary of the source.*

1. URL_____

   Summary _____

   _____

   _____

   _____

   _____

   _____

   _____

2. URL_____

   Summary _____

   _____

   _____

   _____

   _____

   _____

   _____

   _____

3. URL_____

   Summary _____

   _____

   _____

   _____

_____

_____

_____

4. URL_____

Summary _____

_____

_____

_____

_____

_____

5. URL_____

Summary _____

_____

_____

_____

_____

_____

_____

💻 *Internet Beliefnet*

Directions   One of the most interesting sites on the Internet for information about religious traditions and spiritual support is Beliefnet [http://beliefnet.com]. Access this site and select religious issues or traditions. Explore the issues by topic or by religion and summarize the information found on the web site. Also rate the usefulness of the information from 1 (extremely useful) to 5 (useless). Include the URL of the pages you visit.

1. URL_____ Rating_____

_____

_____

_____

_____

_____

_____

_____

2. URL_____ Rating_____

_____

_____

_____

_____

_____

_____

_____

3. URL_____ Rating_____

_____

_____

_____

_____

_____

_____

_____

4. URL_____ Rating_____

_____

_____

_____

_____

_____

_____

_____

5. URL_____ Rating_____

_____

_____

_____

_____

_____

_____

_____

The Path Ahead:
Personal and Social Choices

Chapter Summary

Chapter 15 brings our survey of death and dying to a close with opportunities for reflection on the topics discussed throughout the text. Acknowledging the impact of death in our lives can awaken us to just how precious life is and lead us into a greater appreciation of relationships. One of the benefits gained through an exploration of death and dying lies in the new choices such study offers. Death is exposed to discussion and scrutinized from a variety of perspectives. The close examination of death often brings insights that help to dissipate or resolve feelings of guilt or blame related to grief over a loved one's death. New and more comforting perspectives may shed light on experiences that were previously unsettling.

Many people discover that their study of death and dying has application not only to personal or professional concerns, but also to issues facing society at large. Questions concerning such issues as the allocation of scarce health care resources, care for dying patients and the elderly, and the use of life-sustaining medical technologies require an informed public, consisting of individuals who can participate knowledgeably in the shaping of public policy. Confronting the meaning of death in social as well as personal contexts may alter our political consciousness and offer a deeper dimension of reality to issues involving public safety, disarmament, environmental pollution, and violent crime.

Death education is a young discipline, one in which curricula and standards for measuring outcome are still being defined. The tag line of virtually every journal article, regardless of discipline, states, "More research is needed." This is perhaps especially so in the field of thanatology. Students who undertake further work in the discipline will find innumerable opportunities to make significant contributions. Because thanatology deals with both scientific and humanitarian concerns, the qualities of objectivity and caring are both necessary. Needed, too, is a dedication to maintaining communication among theorists, researchers, and practitioners.

The field of thanatology—and, by extension, death education and the death awareness movement—has already made important contributions to the quality of our communal life with respect to humanizing medical relationships, advancing appropriate care for the dying, and calling attention to the essential human values that sustain us through experiences of loss and grief. The compassionate acts of service that have been encouraged and promoted thus far are founded on a recognition of the identity and worth of each human being.

As we look to the future, and as the field of death education continues to mature, new questions and issues will demand our attention. Will care of the dying become big business? Or will dying be brought back into the personal realm of the individuals and families who are closest to a particular death? Individuals who have become sensitive to issues of terminal care as a result of studying death and dying will be equipped to make meaningful choices and to share information with others as they move toward the goal of ensuring compassionate care. The pace of social change is such that most people devote little time to the rituals of celebration and gathering together that were so important in traditional communities. If we believe that funerals are a time-honored means for facilitating the expression of grief and coping with loss, how can the essential features of such ritual be maintained or altered in such a way that the therapeutic importance of the ritual remains intact? Again, individuals who have gained some understanding of the meaning of funeral ritual and the process of grief will be in a position to make personally meaningful choices as well as to share their insights with others.

Death is an intensely human experience. In beginning to make room for loss and change in our lives, we may find it useful to balance our fears with openness, our anxieties with trust. But in gaining more familiarity with death, we ought to be wary about becoming overly casual about it, or it might turn out that we have confronted only our image of death, not death itself. In facing death, perhaps we should let go of our desire for a "good" death and attend rather to the possibility of an appropriate death. In the context of such a death, the social and emotional needs of the dying person are met to the fullest extent possible, and suffering is kept to a minimum. There is no place for dehumanizing or demeaning procedures. An appropriate death is the death that someone would choose for himself or herself if there were a choice.

Objectives

- To identify and evaluate the social and personal consequences of studying death and dying.
- To assess the current state of death education and to suggest concerns that should be addressed.
- To analyze speculation about attitudes and practices related to death in the future and to assess the potential effects of these changes on individuals and society.
- To identify and appraise for oneself the qualities associated with an appropriate death.

Key Terms and Concepts

appropriate death
death anxiety research
death awareness movement
death education

death in the future
death studies
horrendous death
humanizing death

Questions for Guided Study and Review

1. What lesson is learned in the story of the "mortal king"?
2. What are some benefits of studying death and dying?
3. What are some of the challeges and areas of concern facing death education?
4. What do studies of death anxiety tell us?
5. What are some of the problems and difficulties with research into death anxiety?
6. What are some of the significant contributions of death education and the death-awareness movement to our collective well-being?
7. How have spiritual values been important in the evolution of palliative and hospice care?
8. How might death education help to alleviate instances of "horrendous death"?
9. Projecting from current trends in modern societies, what are some possible future concerns related to death and dying?
10. What is the personal value of exploring issues related to dying and death?
11. How can we "humanize" death and dying?
12. What are the characteristics of a "good" death?
13. What is an "appropriate" death?
14. How was the death of Charles Lindbergh an example of an appropriate death?
15. What have you learned through taking this course?

Practice Test Questions

MULTIPLE CHOICE

1. The message communicated in the Chinese folk tale, "The Mortal King," is that
   a. life is too short.
   b. the desire for immortality is a worthy, but not attainable, goal.
   c. life is too long.
   d. the desire for immortality has pitfalls.

2. The curricula of death education and standards for measuring outcome are
   a. well-defined, but difficult to measure.
   b. impossible to define adequately.
   c. well-defined and easy to measure.
   d. still being defined.

3. Research about death anxiety indicates that it is
   a. higher among females than males.
   b. higher among whites than blacks.
   c. higher among the elderly than adolescents.
   d. higher among middle-aged adults than adolescents.

4. Dan Leviton and William Wendt characterize large-scale, premature, human-caused, and unnecessary death as
   a. tragic.
   b. heroic.
   c. horrendous.
   d. gripping.

5. An extremely casual attitude toward death may
   a. show a deeper acceptance.
   b. result from investigation and study.
   c. mask a more subtle denial.
   d. result from an NDE.

TRUE/FALSE

_____ 1. Awareness of death and dying leads naturally to the arena of political decisions and ultimately involves choices of an emphatically personal nature.

_____ 2. Death education can result in insights that help dissipate or resolve long-held feelings of guilt.

_____ 3. Religious people appear to experience less death anxiety than their non-religious counterparts.

_____ 4. In the United States, during the next two decades, the population of persons age 65 and older is expected to decrease substantially.

_____ 5. The concept of a good death is essentially the same in all cultures.

MATCHING

Match each of the following individuals with the brief description that most appropriately applies to him or her. Each statement may be used only once.

_____ 1. Avery Weisman   a. awareness of death can improve quality of life

_____ 2. Charles Lindbergh   b. funeral ceremonies in South Pacific societies

_____ 3. Daniel Leviton   c. conditions for an appropriate death

_____ 4. Ron Crocombe   d. death viewed as another event in life, as natural as birth

❧ Answers to practice questions can be found in Part IV ❧

Related Readings

📖 Indicates selection from *The Path Ahead: Readings in Death and Dying*, eds. Lynne Ann DeSpelder and Albert Lee Strickland (Mountain View, Calif.: Mayfield, 1995).

DEATH EDUCATION

📖 Patrick Vernon Dean, "Is Death Education a Nasty Little Secret? A Call to Break the Alleged Silence," pp. 323–326.

Robert Kastenbaum and Beatrice Kastenbaum, eds. *Encyclopedia of Death*. Phoenix: Oryx Press, 1989.

Robert A. Neimeyer, ed. *Death Anxiety Handbook: Research, Instrumentation, and Application*. Washington, D.C.: Taylor & Francis, 1993.

Maura Spiegel, and Richard Tristman, eds. *The Grim Reader: Writings on Death, Dying, and Living On*. New York: Anchor-Doubleday, 1997.

Robert G. Stevenson, ed. *Curing Death Ignorance: Teaching Children About Death in Schools*. Philadelphia: Charles Press, 1994.

Tony Walter. *The Revival of Death*. London: Routledge, 1994.

📖 Hannelore Wass, "Visions in Death Education," pp. 327–334.

LIVING WITH AWARENESS OF MORTALITY

📖 Thomas Attig, "Coping with Mortality: An Essay on Self-Mourning," pp. 337–341.

📖 Sandra L. Bertman, "Bearing the Unbearable: From Loss, the Gain," pp. 348–354.

Daniel Callahan. *The Troubled Dream of Life: Living with Mortality*. New York: Simon & Schuster, 1993.

📖 Allan B. Chinen, "The Mortal King," pp. 335–336.

📖 Herman Feifel, "Psychology and Death: Meaningful Rediscovery," pp. 19–28.

F. Gonzalez-Crussi. *The Day of the Dead and Other Mortal Reflections*. New York: Harcourt, Brace, 1993.

📖 Robert Kastenbaum, "Reconstructing Death in Postmodern Society," pp. 7–18.

📖 Alfred G. Killilea, "The Politics of Being Mortal," pp. 342–347.

J. Krishnamurti. *On Living and Dying*. San Francisco: HarperCollins, 1992.

📖 Daniel Leviton, "Horrendous Death: Improving the Quality of Global Health," pp. 165–168.

Stephen Strack, ed. *Death and the Quest for Meaning: Essays in Honor of Herman Feifel*. Northvale, N.J.: Jeffrey Aronson, 1997.

Major Points in This Chapter

- Death may be viewed as a threat or as a catalyst toward greater awareness and creativity in life.
- Death is inseparable from the whole of human experience; the study of death touches on the past, present, and future.

Study Guide
The Last Dance: Encountering Death and Dying, 6th ed.

Chapter 15 ⌒ **249**

- The study of death takes into account the actions of individuals as well as the customs of entire societies; it leads naturally to the arena of political decisions and ultimately brings us to choices of an emphatically personal nature.

- Coming to terms with personal mortality can be understood as a process of mourning, and as a lifelong experience in coping with uncertainty, impermanence, and vulnerability, which are all qualities inherent in being human.

- Thanatological studies create movement both individually and as a society toward knowledge and actions that allow us to deal with death intelligently and with compassion.

- Research on death anxiety and its related concepts of fear, threat, and concern with the prospect of one's own death should be applied to practical issues that human beings experience in their encounters with dying, death, and bereavement.

- The interrelated disciplines of death education, counseling, and care of the dying continue to evolve; one of the most pressing needs involves a deeper recognition of the diversity of experiences present in modern, pluralistic societies.

- The conceptualizing of death in the future raises intriguing questions relating to technology, ethics, law, and the whole range of customs and practices that have been part of the way humans traditionally have dealt with death. For example, given an ever-growing population and increasing demand for land, will ground burials continue to be a reasonable option for future generations?

- Achieving an appropriate death, which is defined as the death a person would choose for himself or herself should such a choice be possible, requires that we first rid ourselves of the notion that death is never appropriate.

Observations and Reflections

Do you envision the future as one wherein technology dominates our decisions about death, dying, and bereavement? Or are you confident about the evolution of a more humane approach to dealing with death?

Use the space below to record your thoughts and reflections about dying, death, and bereavement in the future.

⇒ *Death in the Future*

Directions *Imagine yourself as an anthropologist arriving on Earth from another planet in the year 2050. Your job is to look at the behaviors related to death, dying, and bereavement. Be imaginative in your responses to the following.*

1. What do you envision? Recall each of the chapters in *The Last Dance* and write about the changes you imagine will come.

   _____

   _____

   _____

   _____

   _____

2. What kinds of life-threatening illnesses prevail? Is AIDS still a threat?

   _____

   _____

   _____

   _____

   _____

3. How are the dying treated?

   _____

   _____

   _____

   _____

   _____

4. How is death defined?

_____

_____

_____

_____

_____

5. Does the imagined future include "neomorts," bodies in suspended animation from which parts are taken when needed?

_____

_____

_____

_____

_____

6. What kinds of death rituals are observed?

_____

_____

_____

_____

_____

7. What beliefs would be present in such a future society?

_____

_____

_____

_____

_____

252   Chapter 15

Study Guide
The Last Dance: Encountering Death and Dying, 6th ed.

🖳 Death Predictions

Directions   *Will medical scientists develop techniques to accurately predict the time of a person's death? Access each of the two sites listed below. Notice the similiarities and differences between the predictions of your death date. Describe your reactions to the information contained on each site.*

1.   <http://www.deathclock.com/>

_____

_____

_____

_____

_____

_____

_____

_____

_____

_____

_____

_____

_____

_____

_____

_____

_____

_____

_____

_____

_____

2. <http://www.msnbc.com/modules/quizzes/lifex.asp>

_____

_____

_____

_____

_____

_____

_____

_____

_____

_____

_____

_____

_____

_____

_____

_____

_____

_____

_____

_____

_____

_____

⇒ *Influence of the Pioneers*

Directions   *Review your readings about the beginnings of death education. Below is a recent photograph of Elisabeth Kübler-Ross. Remembering what you know about her contributions, write several paragraphs summarizing what you believe to be her impact.*

© 2000 PATRICK DEAN

Now, imagine that you are in a conversation with Dr. Elisabeth Kübler-Ross. She is ailing from a series of strokes that have left her immobile. You ask, "How are you?" In the next section, you will construct her imagined response based on the stages of her model of coping with illness.

1. Stage one response: _____

    _____

    _____

    _____

    _____

    _____

2. Stage two response: _____

_____

_____

_____

_____

_____

3. Stage three response: _____

_____

_____

_____

_____

_____

4. Stage four response: _____

_____

_____

_____

_____

_____

5. Stage five response: _____

_____

_____

_____

_____

_____

⫸ *Create Your Own Activities*

Directions *The activities in this Study Guide are designed to give you added experiences with the material in* The Last Dance. *Here is an opportunity for you to give us some ideas for activities to include in the next edition of this Study Guide. Some of these activities might use the Internet. Following the format for the activities you've completed in this Study Guide, include a title, directions and content.*

➠ *Postscript and Farewell*

We hope you have enjoyed using this Study Guide for *The Last Dance: Encountering Death and Dying*. We would like to have your suggestions and submissions for the next edition. If you have developed activities that might be included, please send them to us.

It will also be helpful for us to know which parts of the Study Guide were most beneficial in your course of study.

Please consider using the following response form. When you fill it out, you can send it to Pacific Publishing Services, Post Office Box 1150, Capitola-by-the-Sea, California 95010-1150.

We appreciate all of your comments.

1. Which parts of the Study Guide did you use?

	Always	*Usually*	*Some of the time*	*1–2 times*	*Never*
Chapter Summary					
Objectives					
Key Terms and Concepts					
Questions for Guided Study and Review					
Practice Test Questions					
Related Readings					
Major Points in This Chapter					
Observations and Reflections					
Learning Activities					

2. What particular parts of the Study Guide were most helpful?

_____

_____

_____

_____

3. What comments can you make about improvements?

_____

_____

_____

_____

4. What other activities or materials would you like to see included?

_____

_____

_____

_____

5. Did you share the activities with classmates or with others? If so, what kind of responses did you get?

_____

_____

_____

_____

Thanks for your help! We'd appreciate hearing from you.

Reading a Journal Article

Academic journals are among the most reliable sources for information about death studies. The articles in such journals are scholarly and well-researched. Furthermore, the articles are generally reviewed by academic peers to ensure their scholarliness and accuracy. They should nevertheless be read critically. In evaluating studies, the sample size and composition of the sample are important.

If a journal or article is unavailable at your school's library, most libraries are now able to take advantage of services to fax or send articles from elsewhere. You may wish to check with your librarian early in the semester to see if this service is available to you. Many opportunities also exist to gather information through the Internet. Many journals have web sites that contain the table of contents from the journals, while others have abstracts or complete articles available. Check with your librarian and academic computing personnel to see which resources you can access. A commercial service such as America Online or CompuServe is another, more expensive source of information.

The Structure of Scholarly Articles

Scholarly articles generally have six sections: Abstract, Introduction, Methods, Results, Discussion, and References. These sections may be briefly described as follows:

Abstract   Summarizes the article. It briefly gives you the hypothesis, theories, methodology, results, and interpretation of the findings.

Introduction   Discusses the topic, reviews previous research, and states the study's hypothesis and predictions.

Methods   Describes how the research was conducted. It is usually broken up into three subsections: (1) Subjects, describing the people studied; (2) Materials, describing materials used in the study; and (3) Procedure, describing how the study was done.

Results   Gives the results of the research. It provides the statistics and quantitative results.

Discussion   Refers to ideas, hypotheses, and studies examined in the Introduction; it also suggests future research or argues for or against a theory.

References   Provides a bibliography of the article's sources.

Useful Reading Tips

1. *Read the abstract first.* The abstract gives you a general idea of what to expect.

2. *Scan the article.* This will give you a feel for what is being covered.

3. *Skip around.* You don't have to read the article in any particular order. Reading the Introduction and Discussion sections first often makes it easier to understand the article.

4. *Read the article at least twice.* Don't think that something is wrong with you if you don't understand everything after the first reading. Scholarly articles can be difficult to comprehend.

5. *Read the Methods and Results sections for general information.* Usually all you need to know from these sections is how the research was conducted and what its results were. You usually don't need to know every detail.

6. *Think critically.* Just because an article is scholarly doesn't mean it is without errors or biases. Its research, for example, may not support its conclusions.

Evaluating the Article

In evaluating a journal article, keep in mind the following considerations about research samples and methodological limitations.

Sampling Issues   The choice of a sample is critical. To be useful, a sample should be representative, meaning that this small group represents a larger group in terms of age, sex, ethnicity, social class, orientation, and so on. Samples that are not representative of the larger group are known as biased samples. Most samples in death studies research are limited because they depend on volunteers and ethnic groups are generally underrepresented.

Clinical Research   A major limitation of clinical research is its focus on unhealthy behavior. Ask yourself how a condition was defined as healthy or unhealthy, whether inferences gathered from the behavior of patients can be applied to others, and whether the individuals are representative of the group.

Survey Research   Limitations of survey research include people inaccurately reporting their behaviosr; interviewers allowing preconceptions to influence the way they frame their questions, thereby biasing their interpretations; the discomfort some respondents feel about revealing information; the interviewer's gender, which may influence respondents' comfort level; and the reluctance of some ethnic groups to reveal personal information.

Observational Research   Limitations of observational research include volunteer bias, whether awareness of being observed affects behaviors, whether participant observation affects objectivity, and ethical responsibilities regarding informing those being studied.

Differences in sampling and methodological techniques help explain why scientific studies of the same phenomenon may arrive at different conclusions. Sometimes conclusions differ because of errors concerning different assumptions about death studies.

Journals

If we were to choose only five journals with which to stay current with the field, they would be the ones listed below in alphabetical order. They should be part of your library's basic journal collection. (If not, see if the library can acquire the missing titles.)

Death Studies

Journal of Palliative Care

Mortality

Omega: Journal of Death and Dying

Suicide and Life-Threatening Behavior

Other useful journals are listed below. Although most of these are not solely devoted to death studies, they all frequently publish relevant articles.

AIDS Care: Psychological and Socio-Medical Aspects of AIDS/HIV

AIDS Patient Care and Standards

American Journal of Nursing

American Journal of Orthopsychiatry

American Journal of Psychiatry

American Journal of Public Health

American Psychologist

American Sociological Review

Archives of Suicide Research

Australian Psychologist

Cambridge Quarterly of Healthcare Ethics

Cancer Nursing

Cancer Practice

Gerontologist

Hastings Center Report

Health Communication

Illness, Crisis, and Loss

JAMA: Journal of the American Medical Association

Journal for the Scientific Study of Religion

Journal of Advanced Nursing

Journal of Applied Social Psychology

Journal of Clinical Ethics

Journal of Consulting and Clinical Psychology

Journal of Gerontological Social Work

Journal of Law, Medicine & Ethics

Journal of Loss and Trauma

Journal of Medical Ethics

Journal of Medicine and Philosophy

Journal of Personality

Journal of Personality and Social Psychology

Journal of Psychosocial Oncology

Journal of the American Academy of Child and Adolescent Psychiatry

Journal of the American Geriatrics Society

Journal of Traumatic Stress

Kennedy Institute of Ethics Journal

Medical Care

Millbank Quarterly

New England Journal of Medicine

Nursing Clinics of North America

Patient Education and Counseling

Psycho-Oncology

Social Science and Medicine

Social Work

Sociology of Religion

Theoretical Medicine and Bioethics

Writing a Research Paper

There are nine basic steps to writing a research paper. The following will help guide you through the decisions you will need to make and tasks you will need to accomplish in writing a research paper. Notice that actually writing the paper doesn't occur until step eight.

Step One   Start with an idea that interests you. Begin with a subject, idea, or question that you find interesting. Because you may be spending considerable time working on it, make sure it's not boring. This initial idea may evolve into something entirely different, but you need to find a starting point.

Step Two   Make sure your idea is specific. Once you've found an idea that interests you, do some background reading and researching to get a feel for the topic. See what research has been done. Talk with your instructor or teaching assistant to make sure that your topic is specific and that there are available resources.

Step Three   Create a bibliography. Once you know your idea is workable, create a bibliography on your topic. Use general bibliographies of scholarly articles, such as Sociological Abstracts or Psychological Abstracts, or do a search on computer bibliographic databases, such as PsycLit and Sociofile. Your reference librarian can assist you.

Step Four   Read relevant articles and books. Read other works on your topic to find whether your idea has already been researched, other research changes what you want to do, and you can incorporate earlier research into your paper.

Step Five   Decide on your methodology. Decide which methodology you will use, such as survey, observational, or clinical methods.

Step Six   Write an outline. Writing an outline will help you organize your ideas and clarify the steps you will need to do in your research. Remember, however, that writing a research paper is an evolving process. You will probably change your outline as you go along.

Step Seven   Conduct your research. At this point you need to conduct your actual research. This involves constructing the materials for the survey or experiment; planning how to conduct the survey, interviews, or observation; and collecting the data.

Step Eight Write your paper. Use your outline to write a first draft. If you use the American Psychological Association style, your paper will be divided into six parts. See the discussion on the structure of scholarly articles in the previous resource section, "Reading a Journal Article."

Step Nine Rewrite. Rewriting is the key to good writing. After you've written your paper, put it aside for a few days, then come back to it fresh and reread it, pencil in hand. (If you've typed the paper on a computer, read the hard copy.)

An excellent technique for refining your paper is to read it aloud. Reading it aloud will help you "hear" awkward sentences, bad grammar, and incomplete sentences. It will also help you "see" typos and misspellings.

Show your paper to a friend and ask for his or her reactions. Is the paper well organized? Is it complete? Does it read smoothly?

Finally, retype your paper. Be sure that you have corrected all typographical and spelling errors. A carefully typed or printed paper reflects the care you put into your project.

Adapted by permission from Bobbi Mitzenmacher and Barbara Werner Sayad, *Study Guide to Accompany Human Sexuality*, 3rd ed., Strong, DeVault & Sayad. Copyright © 1999 Mayfield Publishing Company, Mountain View, Calif.

Organizations and Internet Resources

This listing includes a broad spectrum of organizations and Internet resources related to death and dying. When the purpose of an organization or web site is not immediately obvious by its title, a brief description follows. Because organizations move, merge, and disband, we have listed telephone and FAX numbers when known, as well as e-mail addresses. In accessing web sites, the prefix *http://* generally forms part of the internet address.

AARP Grief and Loss Programs: <www.aarp.org/griefandloss/organizations.html>. 601 E Street NW, Washington, DC 20049. (202) 434-2260. Fax: (202) 434-6474. Links to peer-support programs sponsored by the American Association of Retired Persons, including the AARP Widowed Persons Service and AARP Bereavement Outreach Service.

AIDS Action: <www.aidsaction.org>. 1906 Sunderland Place NW, Washington, DC 20036. (202) 530-8030. Fax: (202) 530-8031. Advocates responsible federal policy for improved HIV-AIDS care and services, medical research, and prevention.

AIDS Hotline: (800) 342-AIDS.

AIDS Resource Foundation for Children: <community.nj.com/cc/aidsresource>. 182 Roseville Avenue, Newark, NJ 07107. (973) 483-4250. Fax: (973) 483-1998. E-mail: <info@aids resource.org>. Operates homes for children with HIV, AIDS, or AIDS-related complex.

Alliance for Cannabis Therapeutics: <marijuana-as-medicine.org/alliance.htm>. P.O. Box 21210, Kalorama Station, Washington, DC 20009.

Alzheimer's Disease and Related Disorders Association: <www.alz.org>. Suite 1000, 919 Michigan Avenue, Chicago, IL 60611. (312) 335-8700 or (800) 272-3900. Fax: (312) 335-1110. E-mail: <info@alz.org>.

AMEND (Aiding Mothers and Fathers Experiencing Newborn Death): <www.amendinc. com>. P.O. Box 20260, Wichita, KS 67208. (316) 268-8441. E-mail: <info@amendinc.com>.

American Association of Suicidology: <www.suicidology.org>. Suite 408, 4201 Connecticut Avenue NW, Washington, DC 20008. (202) 237-2280. Fax: (202) 237-2282. Nonprofit organization dedicated to understanding and preventing suicide.

American Cancer Society: <www.cancer.org/>. 1599 Clifton Road NE, Atlanta, GA 30329. (404) 320-3333 or (800) ACS-2345. Supports education and research programs related to cancer prevention and care.

American Cryonics Society: <www.jps.net/cryonics/>. P.O. Box 1509, Cupertino, CA 95015. (650) 254-2001 or (800) 523-2001.

American Ex-Prisoners of War: <www.ax-pow.com/>. National Headquarters, #40, 3201 East Pioneer Parkway, Arlington, TX 76010. (817) 649-3398. Fax: (817) 649-0109. E-mail: <pow@flash.net>.

American Foundation for AIDS Research: <www.amfar.org>. Suite 3025, 5900 Wilshire Blvd., Los Angeles, CA 90036. (323) 857-5900 or (800) 39AMFAR. Fax: (323) 857-5920. Fund-raising organization for AIDS research.

American Foundation for Suicide Prevention: <www.afsp.org/index-1.htm>. 120 Wall Street, 22nd Floor, New York, NY 10005. (212) 363-3500 or (888) 333-AFSP. Fax: (212) 363-6237. Research, education, and information about suicide.

American Geriatrics Society: <www.americangeriatrics.org>. Suite 801, 350 Fifth Avenue, New York, NY 10118. (212) 308-1414. Fax: (212) 832-8646. Focuses on concerns and issues related to aging and the aged.

American Heart Association: <www.americanheart.org/>. 7272 Greenville Avenue, Dallas, TX 75231. (214) 373-6300 or (800) AHA-USA1. Fax: (214) 706-1341. Supports programs intended to reduce morbidity and mortality due to cardiovascular diseases and stroke.

American Hospital Association: <www.aha.org/index.asp>. Suite 2700, One North Franklin, Chicago, IL 60606. (312) 422-3000 or (800) 424-4301. Fax: (312) 422-4796.

American Life Lobby: <www.all.org/>. P.O. Box 1350, Stafford, VA 22555. (540) 659-4171. Advocates "Human Life Amendment" to U.S. Constitution to legally recognize personhood of the unborn.

American Medical Association: <www.ama-assn.org/>. 515 North State Street, Chicago, IL 60610. (312) 464-5000. Fax: (312) 464-5600.

American Sudden Infant Death Syndrome Institute: <www.sids.org/contents.html>. Suite 380, 2480 Windy Hill Road, Marietta, GA 30067. (770) 612-1030 or (800) 232-SIDS. Fax: (770) 612-8277. E-mail: <prevent@sids.org>.

American Trauma Society: <www.amtrauma.org/>. Suite 512, 8903 Presidential Parkway, Upper Marboro, MD 20772. (301) 420-0617 or (800) 556-7890. Nonprofit organization devoted to injury prevention and safety issues.

Americans for Better Care of the Dying: <www.abcd-caring.org/mainpage.htm>. Suite 210, 4125 Albemarle Street, N.W., Washington, DC 20016. (202) 895-9485. Fax: (202) 895-9484.

Association for Death Education and Counseling (ADEC): <www.adec.org/>. 342 Main Street, Hartford, CT 06117. (860) 586-7503. Fax: (860) 586-7550. E-mail: <info@adec.org>. Multidisciplinary professional organization dedicated to promoting excellence in death education, bereavement counseling, and care of the dying.

Barr-Harris Center for the Study of Separation and Loss During Childhood: <www.parenting-qa.com/cgi-bin/detail/familytransitions/deathloss/2775.core.organization>. 180 North Michigan Avenue, Chicago, IL 60603. (312) 922-7474.

Batesville Casket Company: <www.batesville.com>. One Batesville Blvd., Batesville, IN 47116. (812) 934-7500 or (800) 622-8373. Literature for the bereaved.

Befrienders International: <www.befrienders.org>. 26/27 Market Place, Kingston-upon-Thames, Surrey, U.K. KT1 1JH. (20) 8541-4949. Fax: (20) 8549-1544. Composed of volunteers from forty-one countries who befriend suicidal and other lonely, anxious, or depressed people, and who distribute information about suicide.

Bereaved Families of Ontario: <www.bereavedfamilies.org>. Suite 204, 6700 Century Avenue, Mississauga, Ontario L5N 2V8, Canada. (905) 831-4337 or toll-free (877) 826-3566. Fax: (905) 831-4339. An association of families who have lost a child by death.

Bereavement and Hospice Support Netline: <www.ubalt.edu/www/bereavement/>. An online directory of bereavement support groups and services and hospice bereavement programs from across the United States; provides information to assist people with finding appropriate help and support in coping with issues of loss and grief. Due to funding cuts in 1997, minimal updates and maintenance have been done to this site; however, it is still a good source of information.

Big Brothers/Big Sisters of America: <www.bbbsa.org/>. 230 North 13th Street, Philadelphia, PA 19107. (215) 567-7000. Fax: (215) 567-0394. E-mail: <national@bbbsa.org>. Help for children who are without a parent because of divorce, death, or other losses.

Hospice of Boulder County: <www.boulderhospice.com/>. 2495 Trailridge Drive East, Suite A, Lafayette, CO 80026. (303 479-7740.

Cancer Information Service: <cis.nci.hih.gov/>. National Cancer Institute, Building 31, Room 10A24, 9000 Rockville Pike, Bethesda, MD 20892. (800) 4-CANCER; (800) 524-1234 (within Hawaii); (800) 638-6070 (within Alaska).

Candlelighters Childhood Cancer Foundation: <www.candlelighters.org/>. 3910 Warner Street, Kensington, MD 20895. (800) 366-2223. Fax: (301) 718-2686. E-mail: info@candlelighters.org>. International support and educational group for parents of children with cancer.

Caregiver Network: <www.caregiver.on.ca:80/index.html>. Canadian organization designed as a resource to make life as a caregiver easier.

Caregiver Survival Resources: <www.caregiver911.com/>. Designed to help people cope with the demands of caregiving.

Casket Manufacturers Association of America: 708 Church Street, Evanston, IL 60201. (708) 866-8383.

Center for Attitudinal Healing: <www.health.gov/nhic/NHICScrips/Entry.cfm?HRCode-HR1757>. 33 Buchanan Drive, Sausalito, CA 94965. (415) 331-6161. Fax: (415) 331-4545. Help for adults and children with life-threatening illnesses.

Center for Loss and Life Transition: <www.centerforloss.com/>. Alan Wolfelt, Ph.D., 3735 Broken Bow Road, Fort Collins, CO 80526. (970) 226-6050. Fax: (970) 226-6051. E-mail: <wolfelt@centerforloss.com>.

Center for Thanatology Research and Education: <www.thanatology.org/>. 391 Atlantic Avenue, Brooklyn, NY 11217. (718) 858-3026. Fax: (718) 852-1846. Email: <rhalporn@pipeline.com>

Center to Improve Care of the Dying: <www.gwis.circ.gwu.edu/~cicd>. Suite 820, 2175 K Street NW, Washington, DC 20037. (202) 467-2222. Interdisciplinary organization focusing on research, education, and advocacy to improve care of dying patients.

Centers for Disease Control (CDC): <www.cdc.gov/>. 1600 Clifton Road, Atlanta, GA 30333. (404) 639-3311 or (800) 232-1311. Through the CDC's site, you can link to other sources of statistics, reports, and health care data.

Centers for Disease Control, National AIDS Clearinghouse: <www.employerhealth.com /EHR_Sample_page/Sp2840.htm>. P.O. Box 6003, Rockville, MD 20849. (800) 458-5231. Fax: (301) 738-6616. Collects, analyzes, and disseminates information on HIV/AIDS.

The Centre for Living with Dying: <www.thecentre.org>. 554 Mansion Park Drive, Santa Clara, CA 95054. (408) 980-9801. Volunteer organization for those facing life-threatening illness and their families.

Children's Bereavement Center: <www.childbereavement.org/>. 1501 Venera Avenue, Suite 225, Coral Gables, FL 33146. (305) 668-4902. Fax: (305) 662-2765.

Children's Hospice International: <www.chionline.org/>. 2202 Mount Vernon Avenue, Suite 3C, Alexandria, VA 22301. (703) 684-0330 or (800) 242-4453. Fax: (703) 684-0226. Email: <chiorg@aol.com>. Supports hospice care for children.

Children with AIDS Project: <www.aidskids.org/>. Information and education about children with AIDS along with a variety of services for children affected by AIDS, including those who need foster or adoptive care. Links to the Apple-sponsored online community where sick kids can communicate with each other.

Choice in Dying: <www.choices.org/>. Program Office, 475 Riverside Drive, Room 1852, New York, NY 10115. (212) 870-2003. Fax: (212) 870-2040. Nonprofit group promoting access to information about advance directives.

Compassion Books: <www.compassionbooks.com/>. 477 Hannah Branch Road, Burnsville, NC 28714. (828) 675-5909. Fax: (828) 675-9687. Books, audios, videos, and other resources about illness, loss, death, and grief for children and adults.

The Compassionate Friends: <www.compassionatefriends.org/>. P.O. Box 3696, Oak Brook, IL 60522. (630) 990-0010. Fax: (630) 990-0246. International support organization for bereaved parents.

Concerns of Police Survivors (COPS): <www.nationalcops.org/>. P.O. Box 3199, South Highway 5, Camdenton, MO 65020. (573) 346-4911 or (800) 784-COPS (2677). Fax: (573) 346-1414. E-mail: <cops@nationalcops.org>. Provides support to families of officers who have died in the line of duty.

Cremation Association of North America: <www.cremationassociation.org/>. 401 North Michigan Avenue, Chicago, IL 60611. (312) 644-6610. Fax: (312) 321-4098. E-mail: <CANA@sba.com>.

Day of the Dead: <www.azcentral.com/rep/dead>. Educational site devoted to information about El Día de los Muertos, including history, events, food, photographs, and altars.

DeathNET: <www.rights.org/deathnet/>. Provides resources about "choice in dying" issues, including physician-assisted suicide and euthanasia.

Department of Health and Human Services (U.S.): <www.organdonor.gov/>. Information and resources about organ donation, including donor cards.

The Dougy Center: <www.dougy.org/>. P.O. Box 86582, Portland, OR 97286. (503) 775-5683. Support groups for bereaved children.

Dream Foundation: <www.dreamfoundation.com/v2/index.html>. Suite D, 621 Chapala Street, Santa Barbara, CA 93101. (805) 564-2131. Fax: (805) 564-7002. National organization granting wishes to terminally ill adults.

Dying Well: <www.dyingwell.com/>. Hospice physician Ira Byock's Misoula Demonstration Project, defining wellness through the end of life. Includes resources for patients and families facing life-limiting illness.

FinalThoughts: <www.finalthoughts.com/>. Combines end-of-life issues with estate planning in a creative way.

Five Wishes: <www.agingwithdignity.org/>. Source for forms for an advanced directive that is currently valid in 33 states.

Foundation of Thanatology: <www.lifethreat.org/japanese/founcation.htm>. 630 West 168th Street, New York, NY 10032. (212) 928-2066. Publications and seminars focusing on death education.

Fred Hutchinson Cancer Research Center: <www.fhcrc.org/>. 1124 Columbia Street, Seattle, WA 98104. (800) 4-CANCER.

Funeral and Memorialization Information Council: <www.famic.org/>. Suite 301, 30 Eden Alley, Columbus, OH 43215. (614) 461-5852. Fax: (614) 461-1497. Promotes education and information exchange between funeral and memorial service organizations; web site provides links to member death-care organizations.

Gerontological Society of America: <www.geron.org/>. Suite 250, 1030 15th Street NW, Washington, DC 20005. (202) 842-1275. Fax: (202) 842-1150.

Gilda's Club® Worldwide: <www.gildasclub.org/>. 95 Madison Avenue, Suite 609, New York, NY 10016. (212) 686-9898. Fax: (212) 686-9290. Provides programs for people with cancer and their families and friends to join together to build social and emotional support.

GriefNet: <griefnet.org/>. A site where participants can communicate with others via e-mail support groups in the areas of death, grief, and major loss, including life-threatening and chronic illness.

Growth House: <www.growthhouse.org/>. With the goal of improving the quality of care for the dying, this site offers an extensive directory of Internet resources relating to life-threatening illness and end-of-life care; also offers a monthly e-mail newsletter.

HAND (Helping After Neonatal Death) of the Peninsula: <www.handsupport.org/>. P.O. Box 3693, Redwood City, CA 94064. (650) 367-6993. Volunteer group of parents who have experienced the death of a baby. Other chapters of HAND located in San Mateo, Santa Clara, Santa Cruz, and Alameda counties, as well as a new chapter in the Central Valley of California.

The Hastings Center: <www.thehastingscenter.org/>. Garrison, NY 10524. (914) 424-4040. Fax: (914) 424-4545. Programs and publications concerning issues of medical ethics.

HealthWeb: <http://healthweb.org>. HealthWeb provides evaluated, annotated links to health-related Internet resources, including professional associations, academic departments, and government agencies.

Helping Children Deal with Grief: <http://users.erols.com/lgold>. Information to assist grieving children.

Hemlock Society: <www.hemlock.org>. P.O. Box 101810, Denver, CO 80250. (303) 639-1202 or (800) 247-7421. Fax: (303) 639-1224. Information and advocacy for physician-assisted suicide and euthanasia.

Hospice Association of America: 228 Seventh Street, NE, Washington, DC 20003. (202) 546-4759. Fax: (202) 547-3540.

Hospice Education Institute: 190 Westbrook Road, Essex, CT 06426. (860) 767-1620 or (800) 331-1620. Fax: (203) 767-2746.

Hospice Foundation of America: <www.hospicefoundation.org>. Suite 300, 2001 S Street NW, Washington, DC 20009. (202) 638-5419 or (800) 854-3402. Fax: (202) 638-5312. E-mail: <hfa@hospice-foundation.org>. Nonprofit organization promoting hospice concept of care through education and leadership.

Hospice Hands: <http://hospice-cares.com>. This web site promotes the hospice philosophy by providing an online source of hospice-related information, including original articles and book reviews. The focus is global and multicultural.

HospitalWeb: <http://neuro-www.mgh.harvard.edu/hospitalweb.shtm>. Looking for information about hospitals? The Department of Neurology at Massachusetts General Hospital has created a small but growing list of hospitals to provide a simple and globally accessible way for patients, medical researchers, and physicians to get information on any hospital in the world. Listings of interesting medical sites (for example, *Convomania* <www.mania.apple.com>, a community of teens with serious illnesses) and links to medical resources on the Internet make this a worthwhile resource.

HUGS (Help, Understanding, and Group Support for Hawaii's Seriously Ill Children and Their Families): <www.hugslove.org>. 3636 Kilauea Avenue, Honolulu, HI 96816. (808) 732-4846.

Huntington's Disease Society of America: Seventh Floor, 58 West 29th Street, New York, NY 10011. (212) 242-1968 or (800) 345-4372. Fax: (212) 243-3430.

Illinois Coalition Against the Death Penalty: Suite 1405, 203 North LaSalle, Chicago, IL 60601. (312) 849-2279. Fax: (312) 201-9760. Promotes abolition of the death penalty.

Indian Health Service: <www.ihs.gov>. Room 5A-43, 5600 Fishers Lane, Rockville, MD 20857. (301) 443-2546. Fax: (301) 594-3146. Concerns include high rate of suicide among some Native American populations.

International Association for Near-Death Studies: P.O. Box 502, East Windsor Hill, CT 06028. (860) 644-5216. Fax: (860) 644-5159.

International Anti-Euthanasia Task Force: <www.iaetf.org>. P.O. Box 760, Steubenville, OH 43952. (740) 282-3810. Fax: (740) 282-0769. Opposes assisted suicide and voluntary euthanasia.

International Association of Pet Cemeteries: 5055 Route 11, Ellenburg Depot, NY 12935. (518) 594-3000. Fax: (518) 594-8801.

International Association for Suicide Prevention: <www.who.int/ina-ngo/ngo/ngo027.htm>. Rush Center for Suicide Research and Prevention, Suite 955, 1725 West Harrison Street, Chicago, IL 60612. (312) 942-7208. Fax: (312) 942-2177.

International Cemetery and Funeral Association: <www.icfa.org>. Suite 220, 1895 Preston White Drive, Reston, VA 20191. (703) 391-8400 or (800) 645-7700. Fax: (703) 391-8416.

International Council of AIDS Service Organizations (ICASO): <www.icaso.org>. Fourth Floor, 399 Church Street, Toronto, Ontario N5B 2J6, Canada. (416) 340-2437. Fax: (416) 340-8224. Network of community-based AIDS organizations; coordinates and works in partnership with key international agencies.

International Federation of Telephonic Emergency Services: Pannenwag 4, Siebengewald, Netherlands NL-5853. 31-885-21448. Facilitates exchange of information among providers of telephone help-lines in twenty countries.

International Order of the Golden Rule: <www.ogr.org>. 13523 Lakefront Drive, St. Louis, MO 63045. (314) 209-7142 or (800) 637-8030. Fax: (314) 209-1289. Association of independently owned and operated funeral homes, founded in 1928; provides publications and films.

International Work Group on Death, Dying, and Bereavement (IWG): <http://users. imag.net/~lon.death/iwg/iwg.html>. C/O Robert Bendiksen, Department of Sociology/ Archaeology, University of Wisconsin, La Crosse, WI 54601. (608) 785-6781. E-mail: <iwg@uwlax.edu>. Composed of clinicians, researchers, and educators, IWG is dedicated to the development of knowledge, research, and practice dealing with death, dying, and bereavement, and with education about death, dying, and bereavement.

Internet Cremation Society: <www.cremation.org>. A web site that screens local cremation societies to provide information on the least expensive alternative for body disposition in a particular location in the United States and Canada.

Jewish Funeral Directors of America: <www.jfda.org>. Suite 506, 150 Lynnway, Seaport Landing, Lynn, MA 01902. (781) 477-9300. Fax: (781) 477-9393. Information about customs and traditions of Jewish funerals.

KARA: <www.kara-grief.org>. 457 Kingsley Avenue, Palo Alto, CA 94301. (650) 321-5272. Fax: (650) 473-1828. Emotional support services for people with life-threatening illness, limited life expectancy, or grief.

The Kids' Place: <www.kidsplace.org>. P.O. Box 258, Edmond, OK 73083. (405) 844-5437. Fax: (405) 348-6777. Community-based nonprofit dedicated to providing a supportive environment to grieving children and their adult family members.

King's College: <www.wwdc.com/death/>. 266 Epworth Avenue, London, Ontario, Canada N6A 2M3. (519) 432-7946. Fax: (519) 432-0200. Sponsors annual conferences on topics of interest to death educators, counselors, and caregivers and offers graduate program in thanatology.

Leukemia and Lymphoma Society of America: Twenty-first Floor, 475 Park Avenue South, New York, NY 10016. (212) 448-9206. Fax: (212) 448-9216. Raises funds to fight leukemia by means of research, health care, and education.

Library of Congress: <http://lcweb.loc.gov>. Provides access to the catalogs of the Library of Congress, other libraries, databases on special topics, and other Library of Congress Internet resources, including government resources, Internet search tools, and resources for learning more about the Internet and the World Wide Web.

Living Bank: <www.livingbank.org>. P.O. Box 6725, Houston, TX 77265. (800) 528-2971. E-mail: <info@livingbank.org>. Information regarding organ donation.

Living/Dying Project: P.O. Box 357, Fairfax, CA 94978. Provides education, counseling, and direct care, offered within an Eastern spiritual framework to individuals and families living with life-threatening illness.

Longwood College Library/Doctor Assisted Suicide—A Guide to Web Sites and the Literature: <http://web.lwc.edu/administrative/library/suic.htm>. Selections cover print and electronic sources of information on physician-assisted suicide.

Make-A-Wish Foundation of America: <www.wish.org>. Suite 300, 3550 North Central Avenue, Phoenix, AZ 88012. (602) 279-9474 or (800) 722-9474. Fax: (602) 279-0855. E-mail: <mawfa@wish.org>. Grants wishes of terminally ill children.

Medic Alert Foundation: <www.medicalert.org>. P.O. Box 819008, Turlock, CA 95381. (209) 668-3333 or (888) 633-4298. Provides information about members' medical conditions; sells bracelets, necklaces, emblems to signify medical alert status.

Medicine in the Public Interest: Suite 500, 192 South Street, Boston, MA 02111. (617) 728-7977. Fax: (617) 728-9135. Nonprofit corporation concerned with public health and welfare, including concerns with bioethics.

MedNet Interactive: <www.mednet-i.com>. The online companion to COR Healthcare Resources' monthly print publication, *Medicine on the Net*, MedNet offers healthcare-related links grouped by topic.

The Melissa Institute for Violence Prevention and Treatment: <www.melissainstitute.org>. 6200 Southwest 73rd Street, Miami, FL 33143. (305) 668-5210. Fax: (305) 668-5211. Consultation, education, and direct sponsorship of various projects relating to youth violence and firearms injury.

Monument Builders of North America: <www.monumentbuilders.com>. Suite 224, 3158 South River Road, Des Plaines, IL 60018. (847) 803-8800. Fax: (847) 803-8823.

Mothers Against Drunk Driving (MADD): <www.madd.org>. Suite 700, 511 East John Carpenter Freeway, Irving, TX 75062. (214) 744-6233 or (800) 438-MADD. Support and educational group related to deaths caused by drunk drivers.

Names Project Foundation AIDS Memorial Quilt: <www.aidsquilt.org>. Suite 310, 310 Townsend Street, San Francisco, CA 94107. (415) 882-5500 or (800) USA-NAMES. Fax: (415) 882-6200. E-mail: <info@aidsquilt.org>. Provides information, bookings, and resources related to the AIDS Quilt, including panel construction information and mail-order services for Quilt-related items.

NARAL (National Abortion and Reproductive Rights Action League): <www.naral.org>. Suite 700, 1156 15th Street NW, Washington, DC 20005. (202) 973-3000. Fax: (202) 973-3096.

National Abortion Federation: <www.prochoice.org>. Suite 600, 1755 Massachusetts Avenue NW, Washington, DC 20036. (202) 667-5881. Hotline: (800) 772-9100. Fax: (202) 667-5890. Pro-choice organization.

National Association for Home Care: <www.nahc.org>. 228 7th Street SE, Washington, DC 20003. (202) 547-7424. Fax: (202) 547-3540. Information about patient home care.

National Association of Atomic Veterans: <www.naav.com>. P.O. Box 1691, Los Lunas, NM 87031. (505) 866-5332 or (800) 784-6228.

National Association of People with AIDS: <www.napwa.org>. 1413 K Street NW, Washington, DC 20005. (202) 898-0414. Fax: (202) 898-0435. Provides support for people diagnosed with AIDS, AIDS-related complex, or HIV; advocates community awareness of AIDS; and promotes participation of local organizations in AIDS-related health care and social services.

National Catholic Cemetery Conference: 710 North River Road, Des Plaines, IL 60016. (708) 824-8131. Fax: (708) 824-9608.

National Center for Death Education: Mount Ida College, 777 Dedham Street, Newton, MA 02159. (617) 928-4649. Offerings include resource library and summer institute.

National Center for Victims of Crime: <www.nvc.org>. Suite 300, 2111 Wilson Blvd., Arlington, VA 22201. (703) 276-2880. Fax: (703) 276-2889.

National Citizens' Coalition for Nursing Home Reform: <www.nccnhr>. Suite 202, 1424 16th Street NW, Washington, DC 20036. (202) 332-2275. Fax: (202) 332-2949.

National Coalition for Cancer Survivorship: <www.cansearch.org>. Suite 770, 1010 Wayne Avenue, Silver Spring, MD 20910. (301) 650-9127 or (877) 622-7937. Fax: (301) 565-9670.

National Coalition to Stop Handgun Violence: 100 Maryland Avenue NE, Washington, DC 20002. (202) 544-7190. Fax: (202) 544-7213.

National Council on Aging: <www.ncoa.org>. 409 Third Street SW, Washington, DC 20024. (202) 479-1200.

National Funeral Directors Association (NFDA): <www.nfda.org>. 13625 Bishops Drive, Brookfield, WI 53005. (262) 789-1880 or (800) 228-6332. Provides resources related to funerals and funeral costs, body disposition, and bereavement support.

National Hospice and Palliative Care Organization (NHPCO): <www.nhpco.org>. Suite 300, 1700 Diagonal Road, Alexandria, VA 22314. (703) 243-5900 or (800) 658-8898. Formerly the National Hospice Organization (NHO), NHPCO provides information about hospice care and supplies an online national directory of hospices listed by state and city.

National Institute for Jewish Hospice: Suite 652, 8723 Alden Drive, Los Angeles, CA 90048. (213) 467-7423 or (800) 446-4448. Association of individuals, businesses, and organizations interested in helping terminally ill Jewish persons and their families.

National Institute for Nursing Research: National Institutes of Health, Building 31, Room 5B03, 9000 Rockville Pike, Bethesda, MD 20882. (301) 496-8230.

National Institute on Aging: <www.nih.gov/nia>. Building 31, Room 5C27, 31 Center Drive, MSC 2292, Bethesda, MD 20892. (301) 496-1752. Research and information.

National Kidney Foundation: <www.kidney.org>. 30 East 33rd Street, New York, NY 10016. (212) 889-2210 or (800) 662-9010. Fax: (212) 689-9261. Sponsors Gift of Life organ donation program.

National Library of Medicine: <www.nlm.nih.gov>. 8600 Rockville Pike, Bethesda, MD 20894. (301) 496-6308. Fax: (301) 496-4450.

National Library of Medicine PubMed Project: <www.ncbi.nlm.nih.gov/PubMed>. PubMed is a project developed by the National Center for Biotechnology Information (NCBI) at the National Library of Medicine (NLM), located at the National Institutes of Health (NIH). It has been developed in conjunction with publishers of biomedical literature as a search tool for accessing literature citations and linking to full-text journals at web sites of participating publishers.

National Native American AIDS Prevention Center: <www.nnapc.org>. Suite 1020, 436 Fourteenth Street, Oakland, CA 94612. (510) 444-2051. Fax: (510) 444-1593. Email: <info@nnapc.org>. Research, prevention, care, public policy, and resources.

National Organization for Victim Assistance (NOVA): <www.try-nova.org>. 1757 Park Road NW, Washington, DC 20010. (202) 232-6682. Fax: (202) 462-2255.

National Public Radio: The End of Life—Exploring Death in America: <www.npr.org/programs/death>. Beginning in November 1998, National Public Radio broadcast regular programs in a series, "The End of Life: Exploring Death in America." At this site you can access transcripts of the original broadcasts, as well as resources, a bibliography, and readings. There is also a place to tell your own story and give feedback to the programmers. Among the topics covered in this series are palliative medicine at life's end, grief and bereavement, doctors and death, reincarnation and Tibetan Buddhism, and the biology of suicide.

National Reference Center for Bioethics Literature: <www.georgetown.edu/research/nrcbl/>. Kennedy Institute of Ethics, Georgetown University, Washington, DC 20057. (202) 687-3885 or (800) MED-ETHX. Fax: (202) 687-6770.

National Right to Life Committee: <www.nrlc.org>. Suite 500, 419 Seventh Street NW, Washington, DC 20004. (202) 626-8800.

National Self-Help Clearinghouse: <www.selfhelpweb.org>. Suite 330, 365 Fifth Avenue, New York, NY 10036. (212) 817-1822. Maintains current information on self-help groups.

National SIDS Resource Center: <www.circsol.com/SIDS/>. Suite 450, 2070 Chain Bridge Road, Vienna, VA 22182. (703) 821-8955. Fax: (703) 821-2098.

Neptune Society: <www.neptunesociety.com>. 4922 Arlington Avenue, Riverside, CA 92504. (909) 359-2021. Fax: (909) 359-8607. Memorial society.

New England Center for Loss & Transition: <www.neclt.org>. P.O. Box 292, Guilford, CT 06437. (203) 458-1734. Provides training and education for mental health professionals in the area of death, dying, and bereavement.

New Orleans Jazz Club: Suite 265, 828 Royal Street, New Orleans, LA 70116. (504) 455-6847. Devoted to historical preservation and performance of jazz developed from the music accompanying African American funeral processions.

Nolo Press—Wills and Estate Planning: <www.nolo.com>. Provides answers to questions about planning for death, from writing a basic will to organ donation. There is also information about probate, methods for eliminating or reducing death taxes, funeral planning, and choosing someone to handle your affairs if you become incapacitated.

On Our Own Terms—Public Broadcasting System: <www.pbs.org/wnet/onourownterms>. Reporting on the movement to improve care at the end of life, this web site is a companion to the Bill Moyers' series of television programs aired on PBS in September 2000. It includes information about the series, video clips, articles on the major themes of the series, descriptions of local initiatives, personal stories, and an extensive resources section.

OncoLink: University of Pennsylvania Cancer Center: <www.oncolink.upenn.edu>. This site contains an extensive resource directory about cancer. From specific information about particular types of cancer to psychosocial support and personal experiences, the global resources include institutions, organizations, associations, support groups, online journals, book reviews, and other resources for cancer patients and physicians.

Oncology Nursing Society: <www.ons.org>. 501 Holiday Drive, Pittsburgh, PA 15220. (412) 921-7373. Fax: (412) 921-6565.

Open Doors ... Where Cultures Meet: <www.opendoors@bigstep.com>. 2017 Castro Way, Sacramento, CA 95818. (916) 455-1537. Fax: (916) 451-5740. Specializes in foreign tours (especially India, Thailand, China, and Bali) with emphasis on participating in spiritual practices, including death rituals and ceremonies. Contact: Robin Van Doren or Fran Rothman.

Oregon Health Division, Center for Health Statistics and Vital Records: <www.ohd.hr. state.or.us/chs/pas/pas.htm>. Provides information about Oregon's Death with Dignity Act, which allows physician-assisted suicide in certain cases.

Pain Consultation Center: <www.um-cprc.com>. Mount Sinai Medical Center, 4300 Alton Road, Miami, FL 33140. (305) 674-2070. Fax: (305) 674-2357. Help for the control of pain.

Parents of Murdered Children, Inc. (POMC): <www.pomc.com>. National POMC, Suite B-41, 100 East Eighth Street, Cincinnati, OH 45202. (513) 721-5683 or (888) 818-POMC. Fax: (513) 345-4489. National support group for families and friends of persons who died by violence; local chapters in some areas.

Park Ridge Center for the Study of Health, Faith, and Ethics: <www.prchfe.com>. Suite 800, 211 East Ontario, Chicago, IL 60611. (312) 266-2222. Fax: (312) 266-6086. Programs and publications concerning issues of medical ethics.

Partnership for Caring: <www.partnershipforcaring.org>. 1035 30th Street NW, Washington, DC 20007. (800) 989-9455. Provides information about right-to-die issues and supplies advance directives that meet specific state requirements.

People Animals Love (PAL): <www.tidalwave.net/~pal>. Suite N, 14101 Parke Long Court, Chantilly, VA 20151. (703) 968-5744 or (888) 400-WAVE. Fax: (703) 803-0377. Provides pets (including veterinary care and food) to elderly, widowed, and institutionalized persons.

Philadelphia Geriatric Center: <www.pgc.org>. The Pavilion, Suite 427, 261 Old York Road, Jenkintown, PA 19046. (215) 780-1000. Fax: (215) 780-1009. Researches issues in aging and loss.

Planned Parenthood Federation of America: <www.plannedparenthood.org>. 810 Seventh Avenue, New York, NY 10019. (212) 541-7800. Fax: (212) 245-1845. Pro-choice organization.

Plays for Living: Family Service of America, 49 West 27th Street, New York, NY 10010. (212) 689-1616. Offers theatrical performances on issues of aging, death, and dying; distributes production kits.

Project Inform: <www.projectinform.org>. Suite 2001, 205 Thirteenth Street, San Francisco, CA 94103. (415) 558-8669. Treatment hotline: (800) 822-7422. Fax: (415) 558-0684. Information clearinghouse on experimental drug treatments for persons with HIV or AIDS.

Reincarnation International: <www.dircon.co.uk/reincarn>. Updated weekly, this site provides a platform for opinions about reincarnation and its implications. Leaning heavily towards belief in reincarnation, the site includes criticism and skepticism. Features Buddhist, Hindu, and other religious beliefs that embrace reincarnation.

The Robert Wood Johnson Foundation—Last Acts: <www.lastacts.org>. The goals of this foundation (<www.rwjf.org>) include the funding of projects that improve the way services are organized and provided to people with chronic health conditions and the search for better ways to care for the dying, thus bringing end-of-life issues into the public arena and helping individuals and organizations do health-services research and public education.

Saint Mary's Grief Support Center: 407 East Third Street, Duluth, MN 55805. (218) 726-4402. Fax: (218) 726-4067. Support services for bereaved adults and children.

The Samaritans: <www.samaritans.org>. 10 The Grove, Slough, Berkshire SL1 1QP, England. (01) 753-216500. Fax: (01) 753-775787. Volunteers who befriend the suicidal, the despairing, and the lonely around the world.

SA\VE: Suicide Awareness\Voices of Education: <www.save.org>. Provides education and information about suicide and suicide prevention, as well as outreach and grief support for those who have lost loved ones to suicide. Includes the CDC's most recent statistics on death by suicide, frequently asked questions about suicide, book reviews, and other resources about suicide.

Service Corporation International: <www.sci-corp.com>. 1929 Allen Parkway, Houston, TX 77019. (713) 522-5141. SCI is the world's largest provider of funeral and cemetery services; site provides information on arranging a funeral and grief support services.

Shanti Project: 730 Polk Street, San Francisco, CA 94109. (415) 674-4700. Fax: (415) 674-0370. Counseling support service for persons with AIDS and their families and loved ones.

SIDS Alliance: <www.sidsalliance.org>. Suite 210, 1314 Bedford Avenue, Baltimore, MD 21208. (410) 653-8226 or (800) 221-7437. Fax: (410) 653-8709.

Society of Military Widows: <www.militarywidows.org>. 5535 Hempstead Way, Springfield, VA 22151. (800) 842-3451, extension 3009.

Soros Foundation—Project on Death in America: <www.soros.org/death.htm>. Through this project, the Soros Foundation provides funding for programs and individuals who are doing research and creating models of care that address the obstacles modern society and high-tech medicine place in the way of achieving a good death. This site is multidisciplinary, focusing on different approaches to the subject of dying—from the technical to the spiritual.

Starbright Foundation: <www.starbright.org>. Suite 500, 11835 West Olympic Blvd., Los Angeles, CA 90064. (310) 479-1212. Fax: (310) 479-1235. Supports projects that empower seriously ill children and teens to deal with the challenges that accompany prolonged illness.

Starlight Children's Foundation: <www.starlight.org>. International Headquarters, Suite 2530, 5900 Wilshire Blvd., Los Angeles, CA 90036. (323) 634-0080. Fax: (323) 634-0090. Organization to help meet the wishes of terminally and chronically ill children; administers programs in 50 states and internationally through various chapters.

Suicide Information and Education Centre: <www.siec.ca/>. Suite 201, 1615 Tenth Avenue SW, Calgary, Alberta, Canada T3C 0J7. (403) 245-3900. Fax: (403) 245-0299.

Sunshine Foundation: <www.sunshinefoundation.org>. 1041 Mill Creek Drive, Feasterville, PA 19053. (215) 396-4770 or (800) 767-1976. Fax: (215) 396-4774. Volunteer organization dedicated to fulfilling the wishes of dying children.

Sunshine Foundation of Canada: <www.sunshine.wwdc.com>. 1710-148 Fullarton Street, London, Ontario, Canada N6A 5P3. (519) 642-0990 or (800) 461-7935. With over 30 chapters across Canada, "Sunshine Dreams for Kids" fulfills wishes for children living with severe physical disabilities or life-threatening illnesses.

Tamanawit Unlimited: <www.tamanawit.com>. Suite 575, 1122 East Pike Street, Seattle, WA 98122. (206) 632-8124. Fax: (509) 463-4983. Dr. Terry Tafoya's site for consulting and education about Native American perspectives on death, dying, and bereavement.

THEOS Foundation: Suite 105, 322 Boulevard of the Allies, Pittsburgh, PA 15222. (412) 471-7779. Fax: (412) 471-7782. THEOS is an acronym for "They Help Each Other Spiritually." National self-help organization for widowed men and women and those who work with them.

TIHAN (Tucson Interfaith HIV/AIDS Network): <www.tihan.org>. 4625 East River Road, Tucson, AZ 85718. (520) 299-6647. Support and advocacy for people living with HIV/AIDS and their loved ones.

Today's Caregiver Magazine: <www.caregiver.com>. Suite 3006, 6365 Taft Street, Hollywood, FL 33024. (954) 893-0550. Fax: (954) 893-1779.

Tragedy Assistance Program for Survivors, Inc. (T.A.P.S.): <www.taps.org>. Suite 300, 2001 S Street NW, Washington, DC 20009. (800) 959-TAPS. National nonprofit organization serving families who have lost a loved one on active duty in the U. S. armed forces.

United Network for Organ Sharing (UNOS): <www.unos.org>. Suite 500, 1100 Boulders Parkway, Richmond, VA 23225. (804) 330-8500 or (800) 243-6667. Coordinates allocation and distribution of organs for transplantation.

University of Toronto Joint Centre for Bioethics: <www.utoronto.ca.jcb>. Designed to be a model of interdisciplinary collaboration creating new knowledge and improving practices with respect to bioethics, this site features information about clinical ethics and serves as a resource for the media, policymakers, and community groups.

Wings of Light: <www.wingsoflight.org>. Suite 1-448, 16845 North 29th Avenue, Phoenix, AZ 85023. (602) 516-1115. Support network for survivors, family members, and rescue personnel involved in aircraft accidents.

Wisconsin Grief Education Center: <www.griefwork.com>. 29205 Elm Island, Waterford, WI 53185. (262) 534-2904. Fax: (262) 534-6039. Education, counseling, and consulting to large and small groups in and out of state.

Zen Hospice Project: <www.zenhospice.org>. 273 Page Street, San Francisco, CA 94102. (415) 863-2910. Fax: (415) 863-1768. Volunteer services, residential care, and educational resources.

Answers to Practice Test Questions

Chapter 1 Attitudes Toward Death: A Climate of Change

Multiple Choice
1. c   (page 10)
2. c   (page 12)
3. a   (pages 16–17)
4. d   (page 21)
5. b   (page 33)

True/False
1. False   (page 6)
2. True   (page 18)
3. False   (page 24)
4. True   (page 31)
5. False   (page 33)

Matching
1. a
2. a
3. b
4. b
5. a
6. b
7. b
 (pages 6, 8, 11, 14)

Chapter 2 Perspectives on Death: Cross-Cultural and Historical

Multiple Choice
1. b   (page 44)
2. c   (page 49)
3. d   (page 55)
4. c   (page 65)
5. b   (page 68)

True/False
1. False   (page 41)
2. True   (page 49)
3. True   (page 50)
4. True   (page 58)
5. False   (page 75)

Matching
1. c
2. a
3. d
4. b
 (pages 58, 62, 68, 71)

Chapter 3 Learning About Death: The Influence of Sociocultural Forces

Multiple Choice
1. c   (page 78)
2. c   (pages 85–86, 87)
3. b   (page 88)
4. c   (page 93)
5. d   (page 96)

True/False
1. True   (page 87)
2. True   (page 93)
3. True   (page 101)
4. False   (page 105)
5. False   (page 103)

Matching
1. d
2. e
3. a
4. b
5. c
 (pages 78, 99–100, 101, 103–104)

Chapter 4 Health Care Systems: Patients, Staff, and Institutions

Multiple Choice
1. c   (page 118)
2. d   (page 126)
3. c   (page 132)
4. d   (page 124)
5. b   (page 128)

True/False
1. True   (pages 121–122)
2. False   (page 133)
3. False   (page 122)
4. False   (page 141)
5. False   (page 128)

Matching
1. b
2. e
3. c
4. d
5. a
(pages 117, 118, 142, 145)

Chapter 5 Facing Death: *Living with Life-Threatening Illness*

Multiple Choice
1. c   (page 151)
2. c   (pages 154–155)
3. b   (page 155)
4. d   (page 169)
5. d   (page 166)

True/False
1. False   (page 156)
2. False   (page 158)
3. True   (page 166)
4. True   (page 170)
5. False   (page 171)

Matching
1. a
2. c
3. b
4. d
(pages 167, 169, 174–175)

Chapter 6 Medical Ethics: *Dying in a Technological Age*

Multiple Choice
1. c   (page 190)
2. d   (page 195)
3. c   (page 196)
4. c   (page 209)
5. d   (page 207)

True/False
1. False   (page 192)
2. True   (page 196)
3. False   (page 198)
4. False   (pages 204–205)
5. False   (page 210)

Matching
1. e
2. d
3. b
4. a
5. c
(pages 190, 198, 201, 211)

Chapter 7 Survivors: *Understanding the Experience of Loss*

Multiple Choice
1. b   (page 237)
2. c   (page 229)
3. d   (pages 235–236)
4. c   (page 256)
5. d   (page 258)

True/False
1. False   (page 226)
2. False   (page 233)
3. False   (page 234)
4. True   (page 251)
5. False   (page 246)

Matching
1. b
2. e
3. c
4. a
5. d
(pages 224, 248, 250, 255, 258)

Chapter 8 Last Rites: *Funerals and Body Disposition*

Multiple Choice
1. b   (page 266)
2. c   (page 281)
3. d   (page 275)
4. d   (page 288)
5. c   (page 293)

True/False
1. True   (page 265)
2. False   (page 283)
3. False   (page 283)
4. True   (page 287)
5. True   (page 290)

Matching
1. d
2. c
3. a
4. b
(pages 266, 269, 272–273, 289)

Chapter 9 The Law and Death

Multiple Choice
1. d   (page 311)
2. b   (page 320)
3. d   (page 320)
4. c   (pages 323–324)
5. c   (page 332)

True/False
1. False   (page 311)
2. True   (page 311)
3. True   (page 328)
4. True   (page 328)
5. True   (page 332)

Matching
1. e
2. d
3. a
4. b
(pages 309, 331, 332, 335)

Chapter 10 Death in the Lives of Children and Adolescents

Multiple Choice
1. a   (page 342)
2. b   (pages 351–352)
3. d   (page 359)
4. c   (pages 371–372)
5. c   (page 375)

True/False
1. True   (page 341)
2. False   (page 348)
3. True   (page 358)
4. False   (page 366)
5. False   (page 371)

Matching
1. c
2. a
3. d
4. e
(pages 349, 350, 351, 352)

Chapter 11 Death in the Lives of Adults

Multiple Choice
1. c   (page 384)
2. c   (page 387)
3. d   (page 393)
4. c   (pages 395–396)
5. c   (page 409)

True/False
1. False   (page 389)
2. False   (page 390)
3. False   (pages 400–403)
4. True   (page 403)
5. False   (page 407)

Matching
1. c
2. e
3. a
4. b
5. d
(pages 388, 395, 396–397, 398, 402)

Chapter 12 Suicide

Multiple Choice
1. c   (page 421)
2. d   (page 424)
3. c   (page 430)
4. d   (pages 437–438)
5. d   (page 450)

True/False

1. False   (page 416)
2. False   (page 427)
3. True   (page 427)
4. False   (pages 427–428)
5. True   (page 448)

Matching

1. c
2. d
3. a
4. b
   (pages 436, 437, 440)

Chapter 13 Risks of Death in the Modern World

Multiple Choice

1. c   (pages 458–459)
2. d   (page 463)
3. a   (page 475)
4. c   (page 477)
5. c   (page 490)

True/False

1. False   (page 472)
2. True   (page 477)
3. True   (page 486)
4. True   (page 490)
5. True   (page 496)

Matching

1. e
2. c
3. a
4. d
   (pages 456, 475, 479, 483)

Chapter 14 Beyond Death/After Life

Multiple Choice

1. c   (page 500)
2. d   (page 503)
3. c   (pages 506–507)
4. c   (page 510)
5. b   (page 530)

True/False

1. False   (page 503)
2. True   (page 505)
3. True   (page 514)
4. True   (page 522)
5. False   (page 526)

Matching

1. b
2. a
3. c
4. e
   (pages 504, 510, 514, 517)

Chapter 15 The Path Ahead: Personal and Social Choices

Multiple Choice

1. d   (page 533)
2. d   (page 539)
3. a   (page 540)
4. c   (page 543)
5. c   (page 551)

True/False

1. True   (page 534)
2. True   (page 536)
3. True   (page 540)
4. False   (page 544)
5. False   (page 552)

Matching

1. c
2. d
3. a
4. b
   (pages 543, 544, 554)